Tithes and Parishes in Medieval Italy

THE HISTORICAL ROOTS OF A MODERN PROBLEM

Tithes and Parishes

in Medieval Italy †

The Historical Roots of a Modern Problem

Catherine E. Boyd,
Associate Professor of History, Carleton College

PUBLISHED FOR

The American Historical Association

Cornell University Press ITHACA, NEW YORK

CORNELL UNIVERSITY PRESS
LONDON: GEOFFREY CUMBERLEGE
OXFORD UNIVERSITY PRESS

THIS VOLUME IS PUBLISHED FROM A FUND CONTRIBUTED TO THE AMERICAN HISTORICAL ASSOCIATION BY THE CARNEGIE CORPORATION OF NEW YORK.

PRINTED IN THE UNITED STATES OF AMERICA BY THE
VAIL-BALLOU PRESS, INC., BINGHAMTON, NEW YORK

To my teachers, George La Piana and Gaetano Salvemini
To Italy, teacher of us all

Preface

† IN THE transitional centuries that formed the threshold of
the Middle Ages, the Church imposed upon all believers the
duty of giving a portion of their revenues for religious and charitable purposes. In the course of time, and with the collabora-
tion of the secular powers, this contribution evolved in the
West into the well-nigh universal income tax known as the
ecclesiastical tithe. During the Middle Ages the tithe existed
in every country under the effective jurisdiction of the Roman
Church and its canon law; it touched, directly or indirectly,
every individual in the Western world. It has been described
by one historian as the most important tax in the economic
evolution of the West. It was certainly the first attempt on a
large scale to tap all incomes at their source, at that time
mostly in agriculture, and to make this tax proportionate to the
prosperity or decline of the land.

The tithe was gathered for the most part in the rural
parishes of Europe and was originally intended to benefit the
parish churches. Tithes and parishes, therefore, are inseparably
linked in history, a connection which has been underlined in
the title of the present book. This means that to trace the history of the tithe we must forsake the main-traveled highways
of history to plunge into uncut forests and unharvested fields.
From the domain of high ecclesiastical policy, as contested by

popes, emperors, and kings, the path of our story leads downward to the grass roots of medieval culture.

This book is an attempt to close a gap in historical writing by narrating the history of tithes and parishes in Italy from their obscure beginnings in the fifth and sixth centuries to the end of the high Middle Ages. The focus of the narrative is on the tithe rather than the parish, because there are already several excellent books dealing with the Italian parish, while the tithe in Italy constitutes a problem acutely in need of clarification. At the same time four chapters (III, V, VI, and VIII) trace the development of parochial institutions, stressing those aspects of the development which affected the tithe or which have not been covered thoroughly elsewhere.

In carrying out the research which is condensed in this volume, it was necessary to adopt geographical and temporal limitations. The tithe during the first three centuries of its existence as a compulsory tax was limited to northern and central Italy and was introduced into the South only toward the end of the eleventh century. Most of the material in this book has therefore been drawn from the northern half of the peninsula. For the sake of completeness a chapter has been added on Sicily and the South, but the conclusions there advanced are not based on the same depth of research as those in the rest of the book and should be regarded as more tentative. Rome and its immediate district are omitted from the discussion save for a brief mention at the beginning. Generally speaking, the end of the thirteenth century was adopted as the terminal point of the detailed narrative, although some documents from later periods have been cited. To go beyond this date would have necessitated a second volume.

Even with these limitations, criticism may be directed at the scope of this book. It may be asked why it was not limited to a shorter period of time or to a more restricted area such as a province or bishopric. The chronological sweep of this volume—from the eighth century to the fourteenth in its central

narrative, from Roman antiquity to 1942 in its larger setting—
was to some extent dictated by the problem to which the historian of the tithe in Italy must necessarily address himself,
the nature of the tithes which have survived into modern times.
This problem cannot be solved by a study limited to a brief
period; the total development of the tithe during its formative
period must be known in its essential features. It may also be
said that for no Italian province or bishopric are the records
sufficiently numerous and continuous over a long period of time
to permit a full historical reconstruction. But the primary reason for the method chosen was the writer's preference for a
subject with sufficient range to satisfy the need for philosoph-
ical insight and to give full scope to the type of historical
scholarship which cannot rest satisfied when it has established
a body of scientifically ascertained facts but must see those
facts in their total context of relationships. Throughout this
book I have tried to relate the evolution of the tithe to the
broader currents of Italian history and to suggest some of the
ways in which the functioning of the tithe reflected the changing relations of the Italian people with the land and the
Church.

In reconstructing this aspect of the medieval past, it was
impossible to avoid discussing at some length a subject of contemporary implications. In 1887 the Italian Parliament passed
a law in abolition of the ecclesiastical tithe. At the same
time it legitimized the existence of a second kind of tithe, the
so-called dominical tithe, which was defined as a perpetual rent
from land, consisting of a fraction of the produce. The conclusion which has emerged inescapably from the present study
of the ecclesiastical tithe is that the distinctions drawn in 1887
and in subsequent judicial decisions are not justified by an analysis of medieval documents and that, therefore, many Italian landowners and tenants after 1887 continued to pay to the Church
and to some lay proprietors, in the guise of rents for their lands,
ecclesiastical tithes which had been legally abolished by the

law of 1887 and were preserved only by means of a legal fiction. This situation was maintained by the Lateran Accords, which were later included in the constitution of the Republic of Italy. It is probably not necessary to state that this book was not written with a polemical purpose or with any desire to take sides in the controversy. The historical and the contemporary aspects of the tithe proved to be so closely interwoven that they had to be treated in conjunction.

I wish to express my deepest gratitude to Dr. George La Piana, Professor Emeritus of Harvard University, and to Professor Gaetano Salvemini of the University of Florence. Professor La Piana permitted me to begin this study as part of a doctoral dissertation written under his direction and has continued through the years to guide and counsel me. Professor Salvemini's enthusiasm for my subject, his quick awareness of its significance, gave me confidence and have held me to my self-imposed task.

In the course of my work I have received much courteous assistance from librarians and archivists on the staffs of the following institutions: The Vatican Library and Archives; the Ambrosian and Brera Libraries at Milan; the Archivio di Stato at Milan; the Laurentian Library and the Archivio di Stato at Florence; the Marcian Library and the Archivio di Stato at Venice; the Antichi Archivi at Verona; the Italian Chamber of Deputies; the Widener Library, Harvard University; and the libraries of the Law Schools of Harvard and Columbia Universities.

Finally, I wish to express my gratitude to the American Council of Learned Societies, which in 1935–1936 honored me with a postdoctoral fellowship for the study of Roman and canon law. Every chapter in the present work bears the imprint of the studies which I pursued in Rome and other Italian cities under these distinguished auspices.

CATHERINE E. BOYD

Venice, May 21, 1952

Contents

I The Problem of the Tithes in Contemporary Italy   1
II Origins of the Ecclesiastical Tithe   26
III The Italian Parish in the Early Middle Ages   47
IV Tithe and Patrimony   75
V Subjection of the Parishes   87
VI The Gregorian Reform   103
VII Distribution of Tithes in the Twelfth Century   129
VIII The Italian Parochial System in the High Middle Ages   154
IX Transformation of the Lay Tithe   165
X The Communal Revolt   178
XI Gathering the Tithes   196
XII Tithes and Rents in Agrarian Contracts   208
XIII Sicily and the South   228
XIV Conclusion: The Nature of the Tithes   241
Epilogue   250

APPENDIXES

I The Literature of the Private Church   252
II Tenth-Century Leases of Parish Churches in Lucca   255
III Parochial Tithes in the Archbishopric of Genoa   260
IV Monasteries and Tithes   263
Abbreviated Titles   267
Index   273

CHAPTER I

The Problem of the Tithes
in Contemporary Italy

† IN 1887 the Liberal majority in the Italian Chamber of Deputies took up the task of unifying the existing laws in regard to the tithes. The measure enacted in that year by Parliament after prolonged and acrimonious debate precipitated a legal controversy, the echoes of which had not completely died down a generation later and which was revived in full vigor on the eve of the Second World War. A question discussed in Italian law courts and legal journals at the present time and intimately connected with the problem of Church and State in modern Italy might seem to lie outside the domain of medieval studies. This view, however, would be a superficial one. Anyone at all acquainted with the problem will readily recognize that it cannot be solved without the cooperation of the medievalist, for it hinges, at bottom, upon the terminology and interpretation of medieval documents and more especially upon the several possible meanings of a trisyllabic Latin word.

The word *decima*, or "tithe," occurs with ever-increasing frequency in Italian documents from the eighth century onward, but its denotation is far from uniform. The following six mean-

1

important to observe that in his comments on specific lawsuits, De Luca tended to regard all tithes held by bishops as temporal, since canon law defined the spiritual tithe as a parochial revenue, and by the same token he upheld the spiritual nature of tithes held by parish priests.[13]

The growing confusion in regard to the nature of the tithes already evident in De Luca's time did not then have serious consequences because the validity of the ecclesiastical tithe as a means of supporting the clergy was not yet questioned. During the sixteenth and seventeenth centuries a government so little addicted to proclerical policies as that of the Venetian Republic not only respected and enforced the established customs of its subject provinces in regard to the tithe, it declared such customs to be unalterable and proclaimed that the tithe itself belonged to the ecclesiastical benefices of the provinces by divine law.[14] The situation changed in the eighteenth century, when the Neapolitan government, adopting the anticlerical policies characteristic of the other Bourbon dynasties of the period, led the way among the Italian states in enacting suppressive legislation in regard to the spiritual tithe. A dispute which arose in 1743 between the commune of Santa Menna and the bishop of Caserta was occasioned by popular resistance to the payment of episcopal tithes. The commune refused to pay tithe to the bishop, who laid it under an interdict. The commune then appealed to the government of Naples, which rebuked the bishop for using spiritual weapons in a secular matter. There the affair rested. It will be noted that this dispute turned upon the question of tithes claimed by a bishop and that the government re-

---

cording to De Luca, predial tithes are those "which are due legally to the church within whose boundaries the lands are situated, regardless of whether the owner of the lands lives and receives the sacraments in another parish." Personal tithes, in his definition, are those "owed by individuals solely by reason of the sacraments." *Ibid.*, p. 27.

[13] *Ibid.*, pp. 33, 40.

[14] Bartolomeo Cecchetti, *La repubblica di Venezia e la corte di Roma, nei rapporti di religione* (Venice, 1874, 2 vols.), i, 148–150.

garded the dispute as secular in nature. In regard to parochial tithes the government took decisive action not long thereafter. A law of 1759 abolished parochial tithes in the diocese of Caserta and put in their place a minimum salary (*congrua*) for parish priests to be paid by the communes; and in 1772 this legislation was extended from Caserta to the entire Kingdom of Naples. Excepted from the suppression were tithes derived from property rights, denominated as *decime dominicali,* a term which here appears for the first time in the legislation of an Italian state. The tithes owed to the bishop of Caserta and other prelates were deemed to be "dominical tithes," that is, tithes derived from property rights, since according to canon law the spiritual or ecclesiastical tithe was expressly stated to be a parochial revenue. It is obvious that the Neapolitan legislators shared the same conception of episcopal tithes which we have already encountered in the writings of De Luca.[15]

The governments of some of the north Italian states, notably that of Tuscany, also abolished parochial tithes in favor of the *congrua.*[16] When the French invaded Italy towards the end of the eighteenth century, having already abolished the ecclesiastical tithe in France by a decree of August 11, 1789, they not only confirmed existing tendencies in northern Italy, they added an idea of their own which was destined to create confusion at a later date. The constitution of the Cisalpine Republic proclaimed that no citizen was obliged to contribute in any way to the support of a religious sect; [17] but in 1803 the government of the Republic beat a partial retreat by issuing an explanatory circular in which a distinction was drawn between tithes which had been the object of an agreement or which formed part of a prebend or of the endowment of a benefice and tithes which were truly optional and voluntary on the part of the believer.

[15] For the legislation described in the text, see Diego Gatta, *Collezione dei reali dispacci* (Naples, 1773–1777, 11 vols.), i, 21:3, 4, 7.

[16] *Repertorio del diritto patrio toscano* (2nd ed., Florence, 1836), "Decime," iii, 182 ff.

[17] Constitution of the Year V, art. 355.

The government announced its intention of enforcing the first class of tithes but repudiated any obligation in regard to the second.[18] These provisions were not of long duration, for after 1815 all tithes which had not been swept away prior to the French invasion were restored to the Church by the governments of the Italian states. But the idea enunciated in the circular was fertile in consequences at a later period, when the distinction between the two classes of tithes was revived by the Venetian courts.

By the middle of the nineteenth century anticlericalism was again in the ascendant. The Kingdom of Sardinia abolished tithes in 1853, and as the House of Savoy progressively occupied other Italian states in 1859–1860, the suppressive movement accompanied its march. When the Kingdom of United Italy was established in 1861, the ecclesiastical tithe had already been abolished over a large part of Italy by a series of laws enacted by the provisional governments of the ex-states.[19] Only the provinces of Venetia, the Marches, Ferrara, part of the province of Rome, and a few scattered places elsewhere continued to pay tithe on the old basis.[20]

To some Italian politicians of the time, in whose minds liberalism and anticlericalism tended to merge, the spiritual tithe seemed to be an odious survival from the Middle Ages, and agitation began for total suppression. In 1866 the Chamber of Deputies, then sitting in Florence, expressed dissatisfaction with the lack of uniformity in existing laws and requested the minis-

[18] *Bollettino delle leggi della repubblica italiana,* ii (1803), 119–121.

[19] These laws are assembled in *Raccolta delle disposizioni legislative in materia ecclesiastica del regno d'Italia* (Rome, 1883, 2 vols.), i, 16, 67–68, 101–102, 132, 143–144.

[20] The tithe seems never to have been levied in Rome and its immediate territory because of the large clerical population. But in 1887 thirty communes in the province of Rome still paid tithes. Carlo Bertagnolli, *Politica agraria e politica ecclesiastica nella questione della decima* (Rome, 1887), pp. 14–19, gives a summary of the state of the tithes at the time of the abolition.

try to submit a bill for the abolition of tithes throughout the kingdom. No measure was then enacted. After 1870 the question was brought up again, and between 1877 and 1883 several bills were laid before the Chamber. The Conforti bill, as amended in committee, provided for the total abolition of tithes of all kinds, even if they formed part of the patrimony of the Church. This measure proved too radical for the Chamber. In 1880 Minister of Justice Villa, in reintroducing it without the objectionable amendment, maintained that tithes should be distinguished as sacramental, i.e., paid for the administration of the sacraments, and nonsacramental, i.e., derived from property rights; he further suggested that tithes forming part of a benefice should be included in the second class. Although a parliamentary committee reported favorably on Villa's bill, this measure, too, was shipwrecked, and a similar proposal, the Zanardelli bill of 1883, met the same fate.[21] The reef on which all these bills were shattered was the opposition of local interests, especially in the Venetian provinces, where tithes formed the greater part of many parochial endowments and were also held extensively by laymen. Finally, the deadlock was ended by a parliamentary committee on which the Venetians had a majority. In April 1887, this committee, eleven of whose twenty members were Venetians, submitted the Fagiuoli bill to the Chamber.[22] Adopting the language of the Neapolitan law of 1772, this bill distinguished between two classes of tithes: (1) the sacramental tithe, which it defined as a tax levied by the Church in return for its spiritual services; and (2) the dominical tithe, a rent from land, due to the Church or to lay proprietors "by virtue of ownership." Fagiuoli and his colleagues proposed to abolish the first class of tithes and to require the commutation or redemption of the second. Although this was a

[21] *Atti del parlamento italiano,* Chamber of Deputies, Legislature XV, First Session, 1882–1883, no. 86.

[22] *Ibid.,* XVI, First Session, 1886–1887, no. 177. The debates on this bill were recorded in full. *Ibid.,* Chamber of Deputies, Discussions, pp. 3707–3720, 3793–3811, 4399–4420; Senate, Discussions, pp. 1741–1777.

more conservative measure than its predecessors, in that it protected all holders of dominical tithes, the bill met with strong
opposition; but it was favored by Minister of Justice Zanardelli,
who appointed a second committee, including Fagiuoli and
other members of the original group, to examine its provisions.[23]
After a series of compromises and amendments, the bill passed
the Chamber by a vote of 140 to 92. It was enacted into law on
July 14, 1887.[24]

The law of 1887 decreed the total suppression of "tithes and
other dues established under any name and paid in any way
for the administration of the sacraments or for other services
of a spiritual nature" to ecclesiastical institutions. It preserved
dominical tithes by requiring that "all other perpetual dues
from land, consisting of a quota of the produce and paid to
corporations or individuals under any name whatsoever," should
be commuted into fixed money rents or redeemed by the payment of a capital sum.[25] Included with the dominical tithes

[23] Religious matters were a function of the Ministry of Grace, Justice,
and Worship (*Culto*). As Minister of Justice, Zanardelli was responsible
for the Fondo per il Culto, a government agency for the administration of
revenues dedicated to religious purposes. There is ample evidence throughout the debates that the Ministry of Justice was much concerned with the
financial aspects of abolition.

[24] Niccolo Coviello, *Manuale di diritto ecclesiastico* (Rome, 1922, 2
vols.), i, 273–297, discusses this law in an admirable brief account of the
whole controversy. See also Celso Caterbini, *Il diritto ecclesiastico italiano
e la legislazione ecclesiastica nelle terre redente: il nuovo codice
di diritto canonico* (Vicenza, 1920), pp. 475–493, and Vincenzo Del
Giudice, *Corso di diritto ecclesiastico*, 1st ed. (Milan, 1933, 2 vols.), i,
236 ff., and 4th ed. (Milan, 1939, 2 vols.), i, 114–115, 316–322, 339–340.
The historical background of the law of 1887 is discussed by A. C. Jemolo,
Chiesa e stato in Italia negli ultimi cento anni (Turin, 1949), ch. iv. The
contemporary pamphlet literature on the subject, of very unequal value,
is enormous. The text of the law, which has been buried beneath a mass
of commentary, is published in *Raccolta ufficiale delle leggi e dei decreti
del regno d'Italia*, lxxxv (1887), 2205–2206.

[25] Commutation was compulsory, while redemption was optional. Both
were to be carried out according to procedures established by laws of 1873
and 1876 abolishing feudal tenures in the Neapolitan and Sicilian provinces.

as subject to commutation or redemption and therefore exempt from suppression were sacramental tithes which had come into the hands of laymen by episcopal concession.[26] The law in its final form was a victory for the moderate Liberals. Total abolition of tithes of all kinds would have resulted in a wholesale confiscation of church property which would have been offensive to public opinion. It would also have inflicted material loss upon laymen who had inherited or purchased lands from which tithes were customarily paid.

But the legislators soon discovered that instead of composing the storm they had unloosed a whirlwind. The legal outlines of the sacramental and dominical tithes were distinct enough when stated in the language of modern legislation, but the institutions themselves, rooted in the medieval past, did not

---

In the debates of 1887 the sponsors of the Fagiuoli bill applied the term "dominical tithes" not only to dues literally of one-tenth but to all perpetual rents consisting of a part of the harvest. This usage caused a kind of ambivalence in later thinking and writing about the dominical tithe, without affecting the juridical concept. Research now in progress on the abolition of feudalism in Italy inclines the writer to believe that this usage originated during the Napoleonic period in Naples, when the French government tried to reduce all seigniorial dues to a tenth. It appears in the speeches of northern agrarian reformers after 1880, but derives no support from agrarian contracts then in use in northern and central Italy. Surveys made contemporaneously by the Ministry of Agriculture clearly distinguish the *decima* from all other fractions of the produce. *I contratti agrari in Italia* (Ministry of Agriculture, Rome, 1891), pp. 234, 242, 742. The demand for the suppression or commutation of tithes was closely linked with the movement of agrarian reform then going on in Italy, but this important aspect of the law of 1887 belongs properly to the history of the nineteenth century and has therefore been excluded from the present book.

[26] G. Caselli, "Passaggio delle decime sacramentali in mani laiche," *DE*, i (1890–1891), 305–328. Judging from the results of the investigation conducted by the Ministry of Grace and Justice in 1877, the extent of these lay tithes was small. Genoa, Naples, Turin, Brescia, and Milan reported the existence of lay tithes. *Ibid.*, pp. 315–318. But surveys made at the same time by the Ministry of Agriculture showed that in Venetia many ecclesiastical tithes had come into the hands of laymen. Bertagnolli, *Politica agraria e politica ecclesiastica*, pp. 15–17.

bend to the formula. The clergy were reluctant to surrender part of their income; from their ranks sprang champions of the theory that most if not all existing tithes were dominical. Numerous lawsuits ensued; and the courts, unprepared for this influx of litigation on unfamiliar material, in desperation adopted various pragmatic rules for the guidance of their practitioners. A controversial literature flowered overnight, its writers divided into two schools, sacramentalists and dominicalists. Liberals and anticlericals tended to regard all tithes as sacramental, while conservatives were stubbornly convinced that the tithes were ultimately derived from property rights and were therefore dominical. Confusion was worse confounded by the fact that in specific cases it was impossible to prove the nature of the disputed tithes because in the great majority of instances the original documentary titles had perished.

From this conflict on a subject eminently historical, Italian historians remained aloof. From the highly objective account of the tithes in Pertile's *Storia del diritto italiano* (1893), the reader would never guess that in the author's day the topic had become charged with political dynamite.[27] An exception to this rule was Giuseppe Salvioli, who, in an article contributed to a legal encyclopedia in 1898,[28] assumed a dominicalist position, stated even more strongly in his general history of Italian law.[29] In Italy during the Middle Ages, he contended, the sacramental tithe had a temporary and sporadic character and a limited geographical extension; when the word *decima* appeared in medieval Italian documents it referred to the dominical tithe,

[27] Antonio Pertile, *Storia del diritto italiano dalla caduta dell' Impero romano alla codificazione* (2nd ed., Turin, 1892–1902, 6 vols.), iv, 439–447.

[28] *Digesto italiano*, ix, pt. 1, 500 ff.

[29] *Manuale di storia del diritto italiano, dalle invasioni germaniche ai nostri giorni* (Turin, 1890). For a strong statement of the dominicalist position, see the sixth edition (Turin, 1908), pp. 518–519. In the eighth edition (1921) and the ninth and posthumous edition (Turin, 1930), Salvioli retreated from the extreme position but still tended to favor the presumption of dominicality.

owed to the Church in recognition of her original ownership of the land on which the tithe rested.

The most celebrated lawsuit provoked by the law of 1887 was the Girgenti case. The cathedral chapter of Girgenti, in Sicily, had long claimed the right to collect tithes from the inhabitants of its province, on the basis of a diploma of 1093 by which Count Roger I had founded the bishopric of Girgenti and endowed it with tithes. As early as the seventeenth century this right had been contested by the tithe payers on the ground that the diploma was spurious, but the nature of the tithes was not questioned.[30] In 1887 the people of the province regarded the tithes as sacramental and therefore subject to abolition under the new law. But the Palermo Court of Cassation, to which the chapter appealed, declared in 1892 that the tithes were dominical and hence had to be redeemed or commuted. This decision was attacked by the Sicilian liberals in a vigorous campaign of polemics designed to prove the sacramental nature of the tithes. In the course of the debate, Salvioli's article of 1898 was quoted to an extent embarrassing to the author, who in 1901 published a special study on the tithes of Girgenti, in which he partially reversed his former conclusions by affirming that these tithes could not be other than sacramental, although he was careful to state that this opinion was not necessarily applicable to all the Sicilian bishoprics.[31] The matter was finally regulated by a law of 1912, whereby a government agency, the Fondo per il Culto,

---

[30] The original diploma was lost, and the text survived in several sixteenth-century copies. The version of the diploma published by Roccho Pirro, *Sicilia Sacra Disquisitionibus et Notitiis Illustrata* (3rd ed., Palermo, 1733, 2 vols.), i, col. 695, is based upon late copies and includes an insertion on the tithe which he found in one of them. Under the Bourbon government Pirro's text was officially recognized as authentic, but the existence of other versions which did not mention the tithe gave rise to lawsuits.

[31] *Le decime di Sicilia e specialmente quelle di Girgenti* (Palermo, 1901). There is a bibliography on the Girgenti case in Francesco Scaduto, "Decime regie, specie siciliane, dominicali o sacramentali?," *DE*, iv (1894), 513–516.

was made responsible for the collection of the commuted tithes, most of which it was to pay over to the cathedral chapter of Girgenti.[32]

Although the Girgenti case was the most notorious, greater economic interests were at stake in the North, particularly in provinces where the tithes constituted an important part of parochial incomes. The law of 1887 had foreseen the possibility that the incomes of some churches might be so diminished by the abolition of the tithes that they would fall below the minimum prescribed by law and had stated that in such cases the Fondo per il Culto should pay an annual supplement to the churches so affected.[33] It was obvious that if most of the tithes were held to be sacramental and therefore abolished, a heavy burden would be placed upon the Fondo per il Culto.

We know how the Fondo discharged its functions in at least one instance. In the province of Friuli, public opinion regarded the tithes as unquestionably sacramental and for some time no commutations took place. In 1894 the Fondo, evidently fearing the drain upon its treasury if the tithes in Friuli were abolished, brought pressure to bear upon the parish priests to demand commutation of their tithes, threatening them with the loss of their benefices if they refused. One hundred and four parish priests declared that they believed their tithes to be sacramental and professed their willingness to lose their benefices rather than prosecute the landowners who had ceased to pay tithes.[34]

Notwithstanding the interests supporting the doctrine of dominicality, Italian jurisprudence wavered. Between 1889 and 1892 the courts of Rome, Turin, Bologna, and Ferrara set up

[32] Coviello, p. 297. Caterbini, pp. 419–430, describes the functions of the Fondo per il Culto. For its relation to the Ministry of Justice, see above, p. 10, n. 23.

[33] Article 2 of the law of 1887 fixed the minimum salaries for bishops and parish priests, but both minima had to be raised in the twentieth century as the purchasing power of money declined. Del Giudice (7th ed., 1949), p. 240. See also *DE*, lxii (1951), 933–940.

[34] O. Biasuti, *Sulla questione delle decime in Friuli* (Udine, 1901).

presumptions in favor of the sacramental nature of the tithes.[35] Meanwhile a new current of thought, drawing its inspiration from the French circular of 1803, was forming in Venetia, where a group of lawyers maintained that the sacramental tithe, essentially voluntary and adventitious, should be sharply distinguished from the fixed income derived from an ecclesiastical benefice. Adopting this distinction, the Appellate Court of Venetia in 1895 handed down a decision that tithes which formed part of the endowment of an ecclesiastical benefice were *ipso facto* dominical.[36] Thus arose the Venetian or Lombardo-Venetian theory of the tithes, so called because it became the official doctrine of the courts in those provinces. This theory, it should be noted, was not accepted with the same unanimity by Italy's scholars as by the courts. In 1902 the famous jurist and legal historian, Francesco Ruffini, challenged it in a richly documented treatise, in which he demonstrated that ever since the thirteenth century the ecclesiastical tithe had been recognized by all canonists and by the highest church tribunals as part of the normal endowment of a parish.[37] But Ruffini's protest was ignored by the Venetian courts, which continued to enforce and develop a doctrine more favorable to the economic interests of the local churches.

During the half century that followed the legal abolition of the ecclesiastical tithe, several bills were introduced in Parliament with the aim of eliminating disputes arising from the law

[35] The court of Ferrara ruled that by the very fact of being the exclusive income of the parish priest the *quartese* could not be dominical. *DE,* i (1890–1891), 795–804.

[36] *The Parish Priest of Peravolo* vs. *Zuliani,* Appellate Court of Venetia, February 22, 1895. Reported in *DE,* v, 232. According to Mario Falco (*Temi Emiliane,* i [1936], 27), the credit for inventing the legal category thenceforth known as the *quartesi del Veneto* should go to Giuseppe Minella, author of several pamphlets and especially of *Le decime ed altre prestazioni congeneri dopo la legge 14 luglio, 1887, n. 4727* (Padua, 1888).

[37] "Decime contrattuali o costituenti la dote di un beneficio," *Giurisprudenza italiana,* liv (1902), pt. 4, cols. 177–231; reprinted in Ruffini's collected papers, *Scritti giuridici minori* (Milan, 1936, 2 vols.), i, 529–614.

of 1887. Of these the most comprehensive was a bill of 1909 which tried to establish a presumption in favor of sacramentality. It was approved by the Senate and submitted to the Chamber but was never even debated by that body. An opponent of the bill commented thus on its miscarriage:

It is evident that the presumption of sacramentality contained in Article I of the bill would be extremely detrimental to the ecclesiastical institutions that collect the tithes because of the difficulty and in some cases the impossibility of proving their dominical nature; this is the reason that the bill was not debated in the Chamber of Deputies. . . . The moment would seem to have come to establish the presumption of dominicality for the existing tithes, in whatever way and for whatever cause they are paid.[38]

Despite the failure of this and similar bills to become law, the practical effect of Italian jurisprudence after 1887 was quite unintentionally to establish the very presumption against which the dominicalists were fighting. Since the tithe owner was almost invariably the plaintiff, and since, according to the Italian civil code, the burden of proof rested upon him, the plaintiff, therefore, in a tithe case had to prove that the tithes at dispute were dominical. Because of the disappearance of the contracts upon which such claims were postulated, the dominical nature of the tithes was usually impossible to prove. From this impasse, which began to be evident soon after 1887, the Venetian courts rescued the tithe owners in their province by setting up a series of presumptions or indices of dominicality. The most important of these was laid down by the decision of 1895 mentioned above: namely, that the inclusion of a tithe in the endowment of a benefice was evidence of its dominical nature.[39] Other proofs of dominicality accepted by the Venetian courts were the payment of tithe to a government official (the Royal Sub-Economo) during the vacancy of a parish and the collection of tithes by a

[38] Caterbini, p. 490.

[39] For a list of cases in which this doctrine was upheld, see *FV* (1933), cols. 753–754, n. 9.

parish priest outside the boundaries of his parish. The courts also tended to uphold the dominicality of tithes paid to a bishop when he could show that in the Middle Ages he had been granted regalian rights by king or emperor, in which case the tithe was assumed to be a right to tax the landowners of the province. Where any of these conditions existed, the tithe in dispute was held by the courts to be dominical. These presumptions, not the law of 1887, provided the basis on which tithe cases were decided in Venetia; the text of the law of 1887 had certainly not authorized any such definition of the dominical tithe.

Neither the Code of Canon Law, promulgated in 1918, nor the Lateran Accords of 1929 made any new provisions in regard to tithes. The Code merely prescribed adherence to existing national and regional laws and customs.[40] The Lateran Accords implicitly recognized and maintained the law of 1887.[41] For a revelation of the attitudes of Church and State towards the law of 1887 it is necessary to consult recent textbooks of ecclesiastical law and the records of actual lawsuits. Then it becomes manifest that the issue was not a purely legal one but was closely interwoven with economic considerations.

The complex relations between Church and State in Italy after 1870 form the background for the whole problem. Despite the strained relations between the Italian government and the papacy in the post-unification period, the government recognized a definite responsibility towards the Catholic Church. Inheriting from the ex-states the principle and practice of the *congrua*, Parliament enacted legislation fixing minimum salaries for priests and bishops.[42] It was expected that a good part of

[40] *Codex Juris Canonici* (Rome, 1918), p. 437 (canon 1502).

[41] This is the interpretation generally given to the Concordat, Art. 30, c. 3. The maintenance of this law is certainly implied in royal decrees of 1929 and 1931 which implemented the Concordat. Most of the relevant documents are published in Raffaele Jacuzio, *Commento della nuova legislazione in materia ecclesiastica* (Turin, 1932). The Accords, however, do not specifically mention the tithes.

[42] For a comprehensive treatment of the *congrua*, see Saverio Fino, *La congrua beneficiaria nel diritto ecclesiastico italiano* (Rome, 1922). Del

the *congrua* would be derived from the endowments of ecclesiastical benefices as well as from the gifts and fees of the
faithful; but a series of laws provided that when the income of
a church fell short of the prescribed minimum, the difference
would be made up by the government, through the agency of
the Fondo per il Culto. The Fondo had originally been created
to administer the property of suppressed monasteries and in
theory it was supposed to meet its other obligations from the
income from this property. But the decline in monetary values
after World War I made it necessary to raise the amount of the
congrua and thus threw a heavier burden upon the Fondo, which
had to have recourse to the National Treasury in order to pay
the required supplements to clerical incomes. After 1918 the
contributions made by the Treasury mounted by leaps and
bounds. Thus in 1918–1919 the governmental contribution to
the Fondo for this purpose approximated eighteen million lire;
from 1920 to 1925 it climbed to thirty-eight million lire; and
from 1926 onward it reached the sum of 71,500,000 lire annually.[43] In addition to these supplements to the *congrua*, the
Treasury also had to help the Fondo pay to some former tithe
owners the compensations granted for tithes suppressed prior
to 1887.[44] The amount of these compensations also increased in
the postwar period. Thus the sum paid by the Fondo to the
Sardinian clergy alone went up from 920,000 lire in 1925 to
1,280,000 lire four years later.[45]

It is not surprising that in these circumstances the Ministry
of Finance developed a tender spot in its heart for the dominical
theory of the tithes. In a circular letter of 1930, addressed to the

---

Giudice, 4th ed., 1939, pp. 322–326, discussed this subject with reference
to later legislation.

[43] Del Giudice, 1st ed., 1933, pp. 248 ff.

[44] A distinction should be made between the supplements to the *congrua* and the indemnities for tithes which had been suppressed by the
governments of the ex-states (*assegni per decime abolite*). The latter were
confirmed by article 2 of the law of 1887. Jacuzio, pp. 447–450.

[45] *Ibid.*, p. 451.

Royal Intendancies of Finance in the Provinces of Venetia, the Ministry officially declared:

After re-examining the question and interrogating the Ministry of Justice, we hold it to be securely established that the tithes [*quartesi*] in Venetia all have a patrimonial character and represent "a reservation of the fruits of the land . . . made on the occasion of the granting of ecclesiastical property in leasehold or as a fief." [46]

Before the outbreak of World War II discontent with the situation was prevalent in two quarters. Some writers of clerical sympathies objected to the fact that the burden of proof rested upon the tithe owners. They pointed out that the existing law, by forcing the tithe owners to prove the dominical nature of the tithes they claimed, indirectly established a presumption in favor of the sacramental nature of the tithes in question. This group endeavored to win from the government legislative or administrative measures that would sanction the doctrine of dominicality once and for all or would at least transfer the burden of proof to the tithe payers. [47]

Tithe payers as well as tithe owners had their grievances. Between the two wars there was a recrudescence of litigation over the tithes in Venetia. Landowners refused to pay the tithes demanded of them. Lawyers became increasingly critical of the precedents by which they were bound. An editorial note appended to a decision of the Appellate Court of Venetia in 1935 was indicative of the new trend of thought:

Lawsuits regarding the nature of the tithes and their incidence upon newly redeemed lands are constantly increasing in Venetia. The question has assumed great importance here, principally because

[46] Quoted by G. Benvenuti, *Le decime ed i quartesi nella storia e nella giurisprudenza* (Treviso, 1933), p. 72, n. 1. I have freely translated *quartesi* as "tithes," since both parties to the dispute agreed that *decime* and *quartesi* were identical in nature.

[47] Del Giudice, 4th ed., 1939, pp. 319–320, recommended the passage of a new law in which possession of the tithe prior to 1887 would be taken as the criterion in deciding cases of this nature.

of the extensive land reclamation carried out in this region since the World War, which has transformed large tracts of malarial marshes into fertile and healthful farming lands.

However, in spite of the legal interest of the controversy and its economic implications, no adequate study has been undertaken either by the interested parties or by the judicial authorities. In substance, the many sentences which have been handed down by the courts on this subject have followed a stereotyped form; they confine themselves to investigating the external features of the tithes and to deducing their essential nature from these features, instead of going back to the historical roots of the institution. Thus there has crystallized on this question a uniform local jurisprudence which, though unconvincing, nevertheless constitutes an obstacle to a more profound examination of the problem. Such an examination would be welcomed by jurists for the sake of scientific accuracy and by the landowners because of the important economic interests involved.[48]

In the late 1930's, as if in response to this wish, several Italian scholars began to take an interest in this question. Champions of a new and heterodox point of view came forward in the persons of two distinguished professors of ecclesiastical law, Arturo Carlo Jemolo of the University of Rome and Mario Falco of the University of Milan. In a masterly monograph, "Considerazioni sulla giurisprudenza dell'ultimo decennio in materia di decime," Jemolo assumed the mantle of his teacher Ruffini as the critic of the Lombardo-Venetian theory of the tithes.[49] This article, unsurpassed in its mastery of legal material and one of the very few studies of the tithe to make use of the decisions of the Roman Rota, made a profound impression and provoked immediate practical repercussions. In 1937 the tribunals of Padua and Venice gave revolutionary decisions in regard to the tithes. The court of Padua defied all precedents by refusing to accept as proof of the dominical nature of the tithes the fact

[48] *FV*, vi (1935), cols. 870 ff., note to *Vianetto vs. Sarretto.*

[49] Published in *Studi in onore di F. Scaduto* (Florence, 1936, 2 vols.), ii, 2–78. In the same year Mario Falco's article, "Questioni decimali," appeared in *Giurisprudenza italiana,* vol. 88, pt. 1, sect. 1, pp. 597–606.

that they formed part of the endowment of a benefice.[50] The
Venetian decision, of the same tenor, was more fully motivated.
In the case of the Parochial Benefice of Santa Maria delle Grazie
in Santa Dona in Piave (diocese of Treviso) *vs.* Janna, the
tribunal categorically declared that the *quartese* claimed by the
plaintiff was sacramental.[51] Its conclusions, summarized briefly,
were as follows: (1) the sacramental or ecclesiastical tithe was
not a voluntary contribution on the part of the faithful but was
a real tax imposed by divine precept and by common law; the
quartese was one-fourth of this tax, assigned by canon law to
the parish priest; (2) all the old presumptions of dominicality
upheld by the Venetian courts were invalid. It was obvious, said
the court, that those presumptions had been dictated by the
peculiar interests of the Church in Venetia. The court then proceeded to set up other presumptions of dominicality which it
believed to be more consonant with the principles of canon
law.[52]

In a note appended to the Venetian decision, Jemolo approved this departure from legal tradition. After observing that
existing regulations in regard to the tithes made up one of the
most incomprehensible branches of Italian jurisprudence, he explained this jurisprudence as an expression of the strong anti-
medieval feeling in Italy (under the Fascist regime) which had
held back research in the medieval field and prevented investigation of Italian medieval institutions. He also stressed the fact that
not only was Venetian jurisprudence on the tithe the result of ig-

[50] *Parish Priest of S. M. di Camponogara* vs. *Bragato,* reported in *DE,*
xlviii (1937), 516–520.

[51] *FV,* viii(1937), cols. 656–677, and *DE,* xlviii (1937), 505–516. A
similar decision in 1938 was reported by *DE,* xlix, 485.

[52] The tithe was to be presumed dominical in the following cases: (1)
when some landowners in a given area paid tithes, while others were
exempt; (2) when landowners living outside the limits of the present and
ancient parochial boundaries paid tithes; (3) when, in addition to the
quartese, the tithe payer owed a rent (*census*) to the bishop or to some
other ecclesiastical person or institution: (4) when the amount of the
quartese varied from one holding to another.

norance of medieval institutions and of canon law, it was also incompatible with the law of 1887. His conclusion, in harmony with that of the court, was that the sacramental tithe was the general rule, the dominical tithe the exception; and like all exceptions the dominical nature of the tithe had to be proved.[53]

The Venetian decision of 1937 was a sensational one. By arousing in the tithe payers of Venetia the hope of a release from their burdens, it stimulated further litigation. The legal journals during the next five years afforded evidence of the renewal of interest in a subject which had long been stagnant.

The history of the Venetian decision is worth recording. The case was taken from the local court to the provincial Appellate Court, which in January 1941 quashed the decision and reaffirmed the traditional doctrine of the tithes. Ultimately the case was carried to the Court of Cassation at Rome, the appeal resulting in another conservative decision confirming the sentence of the higher Venetian court.[54] Undaunted, however, by these two rebukes, the tribunal of Venice did not retreat from the position taken in 1937. At the opening of 1942, in two new lawsuits over the tithe, it pronounced in favor of the sacramental nature of the tithes, restated the views enunciated five years earlier, and declared itself to be unconvinced by the arguments of its opponents.[55]

Some months earlier the Appellate Court of Trieste, which had in the past taken a skeptical attitude toward the dominant theory of the tithes and had rigorously insisted upon proofs of their dominical nature, fell into line with the conservative view and reversed a previous decision of the tribunal of Pordenone, which had recognized that the *quartese* in dispute was sacramental.[56] It is noteworthy that the higher courts, i.e., the Ap-

[53] *FV*, viii (1937), cols. 657–668. For Jemolo's criticism of the new set of presumptions of dominicality, see col. 664. The place of presumptions in Italian civil law is discussed by Coviello, *Manuale*, p. 535.

[54] *DE*, lii (1941), 105; liii (1942), 125–126.

[55] *Ibid.*, liii (1942), 161, 367–371.

[56] *Ibid.*, p. 92.

pellate Courts of Venetia, Bologna, and Trieste, and the Rome Court of Cassation, adhered to the conservative position, while the protest against the dominant doctrine came from the lower courts.[57]

The Venetian and Paduan decisions of 1937 and 1942 were the outcome of a rising spirit of dissent among scholars and practitioners of ecclesiastical law. Within this five-year period a considerable literature accumulated in defense of the new doctrine, most of it from the pens of Jemolo, Falco, and their disciples.[58] But the scientific investigation of the medieval tithe which was so urgently needed remained a desideratum. Some of the obstacles in the way of such an undertaking may be gauged from the contents of a brief article in the periodical *Diritto ecclesiastico italiano* for 1938. The author of this article, a consistent defender of the dominical doctrine of the tithes, after noting that the publications of Jemolo and Falco were encouraging unrest among the tithe payers, expressed his approval

[57] For the relevant Bolognese decision, see *ibid.*, xlix (1938), 146.

[58] In addition to the literature of dissent cited in note 49, see Mario Falco, "Il quartese della parrochia di Grisolera," *Temi Emiliane*, xiii (1936), pt. 2, cols. 17–74; "Sulla natura giuridica dei quartesi del Veneto," *ibid.*, xiv (1937), pt. 1, cols. 242–254; "Ancora sulla prova della dominicalità delle decime," *ibid.* xvi (1939) pt. 1, cols. 246–257; "Ancora sulla natura giuridica dei quartesi del Veneto," *Archivio di diritto ecclesiastico*, iii (1941), 231–246; "La corte di cassazione e i quartesi del Veneto," *ibid.*, iv (1942), 263–272; "Decime e bonifiche," *Rivista di diritto privato*, xii (1942), pt. 2, 247–264; Schiappoli, "Sulla natura giuridica dei 'Quartesi' nel Veneto," *ibid.*, ii (1940), 64–83. See also the brief article by R. Giustiniani, "In tema di prova della natura dominicale delle decime," *DE*, liii (1942), 367–371.

The more recent literature on the subject, including the articles cited above, is listed in the seventh edition of Del Giudice's text, *Manuale di diritto ecclesiastico* (Milan, 1949), p. 231, n. 1, and pp. 177–178, n. 1, and in *DE*, lxii (1951), 119.

The most important book to appear in Italy recently on the tithes is undoubtedly Mario Ferraboschi's *Il diritto di decima* (Padua, 1943). This is a thorough study of the legal doctrines, both canonical and civil, of the tithes, but it contains only a brief historical sketch (pp. 91–119), of which less than seven pages are devoted to the medieval period.

of the recent conservative decision of the Rome Court of Cassation. The new interpretation of the tithes, he wrote, would attain at one stroke the aims pursued by the anticlericals since 1887, namely the total suppression of the tithes. Such a suppression, in his opinion, would produce these results: (1) it would inflict material damage equivalent to spoliation upon church property, a loss which the governmental grants of supplements to the *congrua* would not repair; (2) it would increase the burden resting upon the Treasury, which would have to provide such supplements for the hundreds of ecclesiastical benefices which would lose all or the greater part of their revenues if deprived of the tithe or the *quartese;* (3) it would confer undeserved benefits upon the present owners of the land who had originally paid a lower purchase price because of the tithes with which the land was encumbered; and (4) it would convict the entire Italian magistracy of error.[59] These observations require no comment. They help to explain why the history of the ecclesiastical tithe in Italy remained unwritten when the storm broke over that country in the 1940's.

This chapter has shown that the dispute over the nature of the tithes originated at least as early as the seventeenth century, when the Sacred Roman Rota distinguished between two kinds of tithes, the spiritual and the temporal, thereby setting a precedent which was followed by the civil legislators of the eighteenth century. The law of 1887, which abolished the ecclesiastical or sacramental tithes but retained tithes presumed to be ground rents, belonged in this current of thought.

Venetian jurisprudence after 1895, on the other hand, rested upon foundations provided by the French circular of 1803. Three of Italy's most distinguished jurists, Ruffini, Jemolo, and Falco, clearly demonstrated that the Lombardo-Venetian doc-

[59] G. Benvenuti, "La prova per presunzioni su la dominicalità delle decime e quartesi," *DE,* xlix (1938), 174–176. For other articles by this author in support of the same thesis, see *ibid.,* 1 (1939), 259–261, li (1940), 96–102, lii (1941), 33–38.

trine of the tithes lacked any legal justification and had been invoked purely for economic reasons. In the 1930's Jemolo and Falco urged that a presumption should be set up in favor of the spiritual nature of the Venetian tithes, thus relieving the Venetian landowners of the burden by which their land was still encumbered. Their views were adopted by some of the lower courts in Venetia only to be repudiated by the higher courts and by the national Court of Cassation. By this time it had become evident that a purely legal analysis of the problem was not sufficient to carry complete conviction, that it must be reinforced by a historical study which would place the law of tithes in its context of social and economic history. Only through a historical study into the roots of the institution would it be possible to achieve a real understanding of the nature of the tithes and of the way in which they had been shaped by the accidents of historical development. To this purpose the present work is dedicated.

CHAPTER II

Origins of the Ecclesiastical Tithe

† THE ORIGINS of the ecclesiastical tithe were both remote and complex. Growing out of a series of disconnected local experiments in the early Church, the tithe existed as an idea for several centuries before it crystallized into an institution. It assumed a distinct and recognizable form only towards the end of the eighth century, and even then it exhibited many features alien to the fully developed institution of the thirteenth century and later.[1]

While the primitive Christians were of course familiar with the Jewish tithe for the support of the clergy as prescribed in the Old Testament,[2] they were slow to imitate it. In the intensity of their faith, they did not limit themselves to the fraction of a tenth but gave more generously of their possessions to the clergy and their poorer fellows. Irenaeus, in the second century, regarded the tithe as having been superseded by the gospel precept to sell all one's property and give the proceeds to the poor.[3]

[1] For excellent brief accounts of the primitive tithe, consult Fernand Cabrol and others, eds., *Dictionnaire d'archéologie et de la liturgie* (Paris, 1903—, 14 vols. published), iv, pt. 1, cols. 995–1003; Lesne, *Propriété ecclésiastique*, i, 186–190; Viard, *Dîme avant Gratien*, pp. 9–60. This chapter has been reprinted by permission, with some minor changes, from *Speculum*, xxi (1946).

[2] The classical texts are Lev. 27:30–33; Deut. 14: 22–28.

[3] Cabrol, *Dictionnaire*, iv, pt. 1, col. 995.

Even when the first flush of enthusiasm had declined, the Church did not at once resort to a compulsory tithe. Christians continued to support their indigent brothers by means of voluntary contributions. These were not necessarily fractional in nature and unlike the Jewish levitical tenth were not limited to products of the soil and of animals but might consist of offerings of all kinds. St. Cyprian declared that such offerings were equivalent to the ancient tithe.[4]

In the fourth century a new development occurred. The idea of the tithe was disseminated by the leaders of the Church, notably by Ambrose, Jerome, and Augustine,[5] and by the end of the century the tithing of one's income for religious and charitable purposes was generally recognized as a moral duty resting upon every Christian. Behind this change was, no doubt, the economic pressure created by the needs of a rapidly expanding clergy and by the influx of impoverished city populations into the Church. Towards the close of the fifth century the rhetorician, Pomerius of Arles, intimates that in Provence the tithe had by this time become an established institution into which abuses had already crept.[6]

But if we may be sure that by the late fourth and early fifth centuries the tithe was established in the West as an obligation binding upon the conscience, it is no less certain that the practice had not yet been regulated by church law and was not in any sense a legal due enforced by canonical penalties. It was inculcated by the Church as a moral obligation and was probably more honored in the breach than in the observance. Moreover, there was no agreement among churchmen concerning the employment of the tithes which their exhortations elicited from the laity. It was not yet clear whether the tithe was to be applied primarily for the support of the clergy, as among the Jews, or whether it was to be used exclusively for charity. On the whole,

[4] *Ibid.*, col. 996.   [5] *Ibid.*, cols. 997–998.

[6] Viard, *Dîme avant Gratien*, pp. 42–44. This statement is corroborated for the first half of the sixth century by the sermons of Caesarius of Arles. *Ibid.*, pp. 46–49.

the second purpose seems to have been uppermost in the minds of the leaders of the Church during these centuries of doctrinal elaboration. Caesarius of Arles went so far as to affirm that the Christian who failed to pay tithe was guilty of the death of the poor.[7]

In Gaul during the sixth century the period of experimentation came to an end. The tithe finally took shape as an ecclesiastical tax, regulated by church law, and applied to specific purposes. The provincial synod of Tours in 567 recommended that the faithful of the province should give the Church a tenth of their property, including their slaves, and prescribed that the proceeds should be used by the bishops for the relief of the poor and especially for the redemption of captives.[8] More important still, the second council of Mâcon in 585 transformed the tithe into an ecclesiastical impost, nonpayment of which made the delinquent liable to excommunication. Every Christian, under penalty of exclusion from the Church, was commanded to bring his tithes each year to the clergy, who would dispense them in charity to the poor and in the ransoming of captives as well as for their own needs.[9] Since these assemblies were purely local, their legislation applied only to the territory under their jurisdiction; it is memorable because so clearly symptomatic of the direction in which the tithe was developing.

There is no record of conciliar legislation in Italy similar to that enacted at Tours and Mâcon. It is therefore difficult to ascertain the part played by Italy in the elaboration of the tithe. Precedents, however, may be found which indicate that the Church in Italy by no means stood apart from the main stream of development.[10] Amid the economic distress and impoverishment of the lower classes that accompanied the decay of the imperial power in Italy, the Church assumed a position of

[7] *M.P.L.*, lxvii, col. 1079.   [8] *M.G.H.*, *Concilia*, i, 137–138.
[9] *Ibid.*, pp. 166–167 (c. 5).
[10] Cf. the views of Giuseppe Salvioli, referred to on pp. 12–13.

leadership. In the cities the bishops organized public services for the succor of the indigent, the redemption of captives, and the assistance of refugees from areas overrun by the barbarians. When the resources of the Church failed, these prelates appealed to the more prosperous Christians to contribute alms for their less fortunate fellows.[11] In Rome during the pontificate of Leo the Great (440–461) certain days were appointed on which the faithful were asked to bring their offerings to the churches, where they were to be applied to the needs of the impoverished. This public offering, in which the whole community shared, was termed a *collectio* (or *collatio*) and according to St. Leo had been established in perpetuity by the early Fathers of the Church on the day of a pagan festival. Before each of these "apostolic days" the Pope was wont to preach a sermon exhorting his flock to contribute to the work of charity:

Wisely and piously, dearly beloved [he declared in one of these sermons], did the Holy Fathers ordain that at different seasons there should be certain days to incite the devotion of the faithful to make a public offering. And since all who seek help turn especially to the Church, let there be made, according to the capacity of the community, a voluntary and holy contribution (*collectio*), which the officers of the Church will apply to the necessary charges. The appropriate day is at hand for the fulfilment of this duty, which I know you desire to meet. To the summons of that day we add our admonitions to bring your charitable gifts to the churches of your regions on the approaching sabbath.[12]

In another sermon the Pope suggests some of the uses to which the *collectio* was put: "Men who accumulate wealth are not happy in either their abundance or their frugality, if that wealth serves merely their own uses; if they aid no paupers, help no sick people, redeem no captives, give no solace to pilgrims and

[11] Sergio Mochi-Onory, *Vescovi e città (sec. iv–vi)* (Bologna, 1933), pp. 25–54, 250–265.

[12] *M.P.L.*, liv, col. 166.

the homeless." [13] The contribution enjoined by St. Leo was wholly voluntary and the amount to be given by each individual was determined solely by his capacity and wishes.[14]

Was the *collectio* peculiar to Rome? In view of the leadership of the bishops in charitable activities everywhere in Italy, it seems probable that similar customs existed elsewhere; but there is absolutely no evidence on that score to be gleaned from the sources so far as the present writer is aware. A much more important fact, considering the later history of the tithe, is the voluntary character of the *collectio*. Its optional nature is in marked contrast to the trend towards compulsory contributions which existed in some parts of the Eastern Empire, where, in the generation following St. Leo's, the clergy were trying to compel the faithful to contribute to the Church under penalty of excommunication. This practice was condemned, in respect to Constantinople and its territory, by a law of Emperors Leo and Anthemius (467–471), which refers to such a custom without defining its *locus* or extent.[15]

However, by the end of the sixth century the character of the *collectio* had changed. One of Gregory the Great's letters, dated 599, mentions a *collata* or *collatio*, exacted by the archbishop of Milan from the inhabitants of Genoa, where, thirty years before, many of the Milanese clergy and people had taken refuge from the Lombards. Like the contribution described in the imperial law referred to above, this was a compulsory tax, collected periodically, and was not always just in its incidence. A blind man named Philagrius, compelled to pay the impost, appealed to the Pope and elicited from him this rebuke to the archbishop:

---

[13] *Ibid.*, col. 164.

[14] The phrases used by St. Leo are *secundum sufficientiam, quantum suadet possibilitas et voluntas. Ibid.*, cols. 166, 162.

[15] "Non oportet episcopos aut clericos cogere quosquam ad fructus offerendos aut angarias dandas aut alio modo vexare aut excommunicare aut anathemate damnare aut denegare communionem aut idcirco non baptizare, quamvis usus ita obtinuerit. Transgressor excidit ab ecclesia et administratione ipsius et dat decem libras. Haec vero obtinent in sola regia urbe, et territorio eius, et locis ad metropolitanos, qui a patriarcha ordinantur, pertinentibus, aut ad creatos ab his episcopos." *Codex*

We marvel that one who is more deserving of charity should be oppressed under your very eyes. If this is really true, Your Holiness is not to permit anyone to exact the tax from this man again, because it is exceedingly inhumane to burden with this contribution a man afflicted with blindness, who, were he in material need, would be entitled to a share of the proceeds of the offering.[16]

May these contributions at Genoa and Rome actually be identified with the tithe? The Italian historian Mengozzi identified them both with the ecclesiastical tithe and stated that the *collatio* was a widespread custom in Italy in the time of Gregory the Great.[17] The first hypothesis seems acceptable enough. Though the word *decima* is not applied to either contribution and there is no evidence that Christians gave any definite fraction of their incomes, it seems obvious that both the voluntary offering at Rome and the imposition at Genoa formed part of that complex of practices and experiments in the early Church of which the later tithe was an amalgam. Moreover, in the biography of St. Severinus which Eugippius composed towards the end of the fifth century, the words *decima* and *collatio* are used interchangeably to denote the alms which Christians were exhorted to contribute to the needy.[18] But in view of the reticence of the sources, it would be unwise to accept uncritically Mengozzi's second assertion. There is the possibility that the presence of a large refugee community at Genoa made the *collatio* necessary and that it was an emergency measure rather than a normal institution. Direct evidence for the widespread existence of such a contribution in the fifth and sixth centuries in Italy is

---

Justiniani, ed. Emil Herman (Leipzig, 1848), i, 3, 39, 1. Mengozzi calls attention to this law in *Città italiana*, p. 208, n. 2.

[16] *M.G.H., Epistolae*, ii, 231.

[17] Mengozzi, *Città italiana*, pp. 208–210.

[18] "Pro decimis autem, ut diximus, dandis, quibus pauperes alerentur, Norici quoque populos missis exhortabatur epistolis. Ex qua consuetudine cum ad eum nonnulli erogandarum vestium copiam direxissent, interrogavit eos, qui venerant, si ex oppido quoque Tiburniae similis collatio mitteretur." *M.G.H., AA.*, i, pt. 2, p. 17. For comment on this passage, see Mochi-Onory, pp. 42–43; Viard, *Dime avant Gratien*, p. 45.

pitiably meager, whatever we may think of its intrinsic probability. The word *decima* is rarely used. Gregory the Great, in his *Commentary on the First Book of Kings,* employs it occasionally, but always in a purely allegorical sense.[19] His sole use of the word to denote an offering or contribution occurs in one of his homilies, in which he characterizes the Lenten period as "the tithes of the year" (*decimas anni*): "Wherefore, dearly beloved [the sermon continues], as in the law we are commanded to offer God the tithes of our property (*decimas rerum*), so let us hasten to offer Him the tithes of our days (*decimas dierum*)." [20] This passage, taken alone, would be a slender basis on which to erect any theory concerning the prevalence of the tithe in Italy in Gregory's time. Yet it cannot be denied that the Pope takes for granted a knowledge of the Biblical precept in regard to the tithe and seems to assume that it is still in force. Read in conjunction with the letter about Philagrius, it lends some color to the supposition that at least an equivalent for the levitical tithe was required by the Roman church in the sixth century.

It is a well-known fact that for a century and a half after Gregory the Great the chief impetus towards the development of the tithe came from the British Isles. An Anglo-Saxon canonical source, the *Penitential of Theodore,* believed to embody the decisions of Theodore of Tarsus, archbishop of Canterbury from 667 to 690, is one of our few sources of information in regard to the tithe in the seventh century.[21] It assumes the habit of tithe-paying among the English people and also takes for granted the existence of local customs governing the exaction of the tithe. The poor, pilgrims, and the churches are declared to be the beneficiaries of the tithe, and the clergy are by implication exempted from payment, while the Church is told to exact this

---

[19] *M.P.L.,* lxxix, cols. 228, 241, 242.

[20] *Ibid.,* lxxvi, col. 1137.

[21] The *Penitential of Theodore* is printed in F. W. H. Wasserschleben, *Die Bussordnungen der abendländischen Kirche* (Halle, 1851), pp. 182–219. See also Cabrol, *Dictionnaire,* xiv, pt. 1, cols. 240–241, and Viard, *Dime avant Gratien,* pp. 65–66.

tribute according to the custom of the province and in such a way that the poor shall not suffer hardship.[22] These provisions obviously reflect conditions in Anglo-Saxon Britain. But it seems strange that a provincial custom, implying a relatively long existence, should have grown up in a remote mission church without a corresponding prototype in the older churches on the continent. That prototype of course need not have been a Roman one. Gallic influence may have played a part. But Roman influence seems slightly more probable. It may or may not be significant that Gregory's phrase about "the tithes of the year" was taken up into Theodore's *Penitential* and Gregory thus made a sponsor of the tithe.[23] And it may be purely fanciful to see in Gregory's letter about Philagrius a possible inspiration for the injunction to be lenient to the poor. These are matters of conjecture which do not admit of proof. But of certain facts there can be little doubt. Theodore's *Penitential* strongly influenced the Irish canonical collections [24] which circulated widely on the continent during the first half of the eighth century, and by general agreement, it was those Irish collections that spread the idea of the tithe in that period and paved the way for its general acceptance before the century had closed.[25]

Tithes, expressly denominated as such, are known to have been paid before the end of the seventh century in Gaul, Britain, and Germany. With the conversion of the Lombards to Catholic Christianity, the word *decima* appears in Italian documents also.[26] The tithe now presents itself under a guise very different

[22] Wasserschleben, p. 218. The available facts concerning the tithe in Anglo-Saxon Britain are summarized by F. M. Stenton, *Anglo-Saxon England* (2nd ed., Oxford, 1947), pp. 154–156.

[23] Wasserschleben, *loc. cit.*

[24] The most important of the Irish collections were published in Wasserschleben's *Bussordnungen;* for a discussion of the more recent literature concerning them, see Cabrol, *Dictionnaire*, xiv, art. "Pénitentiel."

[25] Paul Fournier, "Le liber ex lege Moysi et les tendances bibliques du droit canonique irlandais," *Revue celtique*, xxx (1909), 232–233.

[26] I can find no clear and indisputable use of the word *decima* in Italian documents until the seventh century. The charter of 543 in which

from that of the Genoese *collatio,* for it is a voluntary offering
and not a compulsory tax. Among the Lombard aristocracy it
was regarded as a meritorious act to tithe one's revenues for the
benefit of the Church. In 688 King Cunibert confirmed to the
church of San Frediano of Lucca, recently rebuilt by his major-
domo Faulo, the tithes granted to it by its benefactor.[27] The
Lombard noble Pertualdo, returning in 720 from a pilgrimage to
Rome, founded the monastery of San Michele Arcangelo outside
the walls of Lucca and endowed it with the tithes of the produce
of his domains.[28] In 730 four Lombard nobles founded a deaconry outside Lucca and gave it the tithes of all their estates in
Tuscany.[29] This custom spread to all parts of Italy under Lombard domination. It is found near Monza,[30] in the Milanese, and
in the duchy of Spoleto. In 740 Duke Trasimundo of Spoleto
promised to give annually to the monastery of Farfa the tithes
of wine, grain, and oil from one of his estates, including in his
grant a tithe of the rents in kind paid by his tenants.[31] His successor Theodicius in 763 bestowed upon Farfa the tithe of wine
from one ducal manor and the tithe of grain from another estate,
the manor of Amiterna, excepting from the latter a fixed portion
of the tithe of grain which, in accordance with local custom (*per
consuetudinem*), the manorial church of Amiterna was authorized to collect.[32] It is clear from the terms of this grant that the

---

Bishop Euphrasius of Parenzo endows his cathedral clergy with tithes,
cited by Pertile as evidence of the antiquity of the tithe in Italy, is for the
most part spurious. Pertile, *Storia del diritto italiano,* iv, 441, n. 42, quoted
the document on the authority of Pietro Kandler, who had published it in
his *Codice diplomatico istriano* (Trieste, 1847—), i, 37 ff. The apocryphal
nature of the document is demonstrated by F. Cusin, "Il 'privilegio
eufrasiano' e la *charta libertatis* del comune di Parenzo," *AV,* Sixth Series,
xxx (1942), 65–84.

[27] Carlo Troya, *Codice diplomatico longobardo dal 568 al 774* (Naples,
1852–1856, 5 vols.), iii, doc. 352 (p. 11).

[28] Schiaparelli, *CDL,* i, doc. 28 (pp. 101–103).

[29] *Ibid.,* doc. 48.   [30] *Ibid.,* doc. 82.

[31] Ignazio Giorgi and Ugo Balzani, *Il regesto di Farfa di Gregorio di
Catino* (Rome, 1879–1888, 4 vols.), ii, doc. 7.

[32] *Ibid.,* doc. 53.

duke was giving the tithe of his own revenues, and this raises the question of whether the dependent population of the manors also paid tithes. There is no documentary evidence to prove that the masses of the people paid tithe in this period. But it seems highly probable that if the Lombard aristocracy, only recently converted to Catholicism, gave tithes to the Church, the custom must have been previously established among the Roman population of Italy, which had been Christian for centuries. On the other hand, one cannot believe that any tithes in this period were other than voluntary contributions, obligatory only in conscience and certainly unsupported by secular law. Any tendency on the part of the Church to establish a compulsory tithe must have been extinguished by the Lombard settlements, which deprived the bishops of public powers in the cities and kept the popes in constant apprehension for the very safety of Rome. The extension of the tithe in the Lombard period may only be surmised. Its existence, however, is certain.

There continued in the Lombard period a marked emphasis upon the eleemosynary character of the tithe; in giving their tithes to religious foundations, the Lombards thought they were giving them to the poor and to pilgrims and travellers. One of the founders of a deaconry in Lucca in 730 stipulated that the tithe of his domain should be applied to the relief of the poor and the entertainment of pilgrims,[33] and the restorer of the church and hostelry of San Vitale, in the same city, ordained in 790 that the abbess of a nunnery which he had founded should annually tithe the revenue of the nunnery and give the product to the priest of San Vitale, to feed twelve paupers at his table one day each week and in Easter week provide them with a hot bath.[34]

It is clear from the documents that the donors of tithes exercised considerable freedom in designating the churches that were to benefit from their gifts, in itself strong evidence that the tithe in the eighth century was spontaneous and voluntary.

[33] Schiaparelli, *CDL*, i, doc. 48.
[34] *MD*, v, pt. 2, doc. 231.

breadth of their dominions. Whether or not this legislation was aimed specifically at Italy, it automatically extended the civil sanction of the tithe to the Lombard kingdom of the Carolingians.

But the capitulary of Heristal was not exclusively concerned with the ordinary ecclesiastical tithe. Another purpose behind it was the synthesis and clarification of existing legislative measures in regard to a closely related institution: the double tithe, or *decima et nona*. Early in the eighth century Charles Martel had despoiled the Church of a considerable amount of land in order to reward his vassals. The spoliation which he initiated through military necessity was continued by his successors; ecclesiastical estates were assigned by both Pepin and Charlemagne to royal vassals in recompense for needed military service. Martel had originally promised the Church the eventual restitution of its property. But the campaigns and expeditions ceaselessly carried on by the Carolingian rulers made fulfillment of his promise impossible; and therefore, in order to indemnify the dispossessed bishoprics and abbeys, it was enacted, again probably by Pepin, that holders of church property by royal grant (*sub verbo regis*) should pay to the despoiled institution twice the amount of the ordinary tithe. This was called the double tithe, or *decima et nona,* and rested upon the demesne lands (*indominicatum*) of the estates so ceded.[41] Thus on such estates the magnates who held them paid the tithes of the demesne,

---

made the tithe a permanent part of Frankish secular law, the king's motive being the compensation of the Church for the loss of its property through secularization. Viard, *Dîme avant Gratien,* pp. 70–74, adhered to the view that it was Charlemagne who made the tithe permanent and compulsory. The result of Lesne's research, somewhat later, was to push the origin of the tithe back into the reign of Pepin. *Propriété ecclésiastique,* ii, pt. 1, 98–111. Lesne thinks that the Frankish monarchs introduced the compulsory tithe as a means of alleviating the poverty of the churches, especially of those newly founded in the East.

[41] Stutz cleared up the perplexities of earlier writers by showing that the *decima et nona* was merely the ordinary tithe doubled. "Das karolingische Zehntgebot," p. 202, n. 1. Lesne showed that it rested only upon the *indominicatum* of the benefice-holders.

doubled in amount, to the dispossessed institution; the tenants, it may be assumed, continued to pay their tithes to the local churches which had customarily collected them in the past. In all parts of the empire abuses grew up in connection with the double tithe; everywhere the magnates who held church lands as military benefices tried to evade their obligations; and the double tithe, by its very nature, invited misunderstanding.[42] To correct these abuses and to remove all possible misunderstanding was a principal, if not the primary, purpose of the capitulary of Heristal. Chapter 7 of this capitulary commanded every man in the empire to pay his tithe to the Church, the product to be administered in each diocese by the bishop; Chapter 14 regulated the payments of the double tithe, which, together with a *census*, rested upon the demesne lands of the benefice-holders. That the chief preoccupation of the legislator was with the double tithe rather than with the ordinary tithe is suggested by the fact that the obligation to pay the latter is stated in the most general terms, while the former is regulated in minute detail. So far as Italy was concerned, the effect of the capitulary was to extend the double tithe as well as the civil sanction of the ordinary tithe to the Lombard kingdom. To what extent secularizations of church property had been carried out in the interval between the Frankish conquest and the capitulary is a matter of conjecture. It is known that extensive secularizations were operated in Italy before the close of the eighth century and that in Italy as elsewhere the magnates sought to throw off or diminish the burden of their indemnities.

The capitulary of Heristal has been preserved in two forms— a common form and a Lombard form, the second of which is the longer and more detailed.[43] This idiosyncrasy has given rise to much learned discussion. It has been maintained that the second form was a special Italian recension of the capitulary made at

---

[42] The definitive account of the double tithe is Emile Lesne's "La dîme des biens ecclésiastiques aux ixe et xe siècles," *RHE*, xiii (1912), xiv (1913).

[43] *M.G.H., Capitularia*, i, 47–50.

the order of Charles the Great. The generally accepted opinion, however, regards the common form as the basic legislative text for Italy as well as for the rest of the empire and the Lombard form as the glosses of Lombard judges, made sometime between the promulgation of the capitulary and the close of the eighth century. Without examining these questions in detail—and the candid historian will admit that the elements for a definitive solution are lacking—we shall merely point out that the existence of Italian manuscripts of the common form presupposes the use of this form in Italy concurrently with the Lombard form, and that the inclusion of the common form in the *Liber Papiensis*, a codification of Lombard law made in the eleventh century, points in the same direction.[44]

The provisions of the capitulary of Heristal in regard to the ordinary tithe require little comment. No penalty was explicitly attached to nonpayment, but it may be assumed that violation of this command, as of any imperial law, was punished by a fine of six shillings. More complicated are the clauses of Chapter 14 of the capitulary in regulation of the double tithe. Holders of church property *sub verbo regis* were confirmed in their possession of such property unless it was expressly revoked to the uses of the church by the king. Both the double tithe and a rent, or *census,* were to be paid to the dispossessed institution, and the capitulary established a graduated *census* to be taken from land hitherto exempt. In these provisions the legislator was combating the abuse of paying only the *census* without the double tithe or vice versa. Upon the lands torn from the Church was thus placed a twofold burden—a *census* in recognition of the Church's ultimate ownership and the *decima et nona,* roughly a fifth of the produce of the demesne land of the benefice-holder, as an indemnity for the spoliation.

Two years after the promulgation of the capitulary of

[44] The *Liber Papiensis* gives the common form of Chapter 7 but omits Chapter 14, which indicates that the double tithe in Italy had by this time disappeared, either through nonpayment or through assimilation to other charges upon the land.

Heristal, Charlemagne initiated his Italian governmental policy. This was to treat the Lombard kingdom as a constituent part of the Frankish realm and as such subject to the general capitularies, but at the same time to recognize its individuality by giving it a separate administration under its own king. In 781 Charlemagne's son Pepin, still a minor, was created the first king of Italy.[45] The establishment of a separate Italian kingdom resulted in a series of capitularies, drawn up with special reference to Italian needs and conditions. One of the earliest laws issued in Pepin's name, perhaps enacted in council with the bishops of the Lombard realm, commanded that every Christian should offer his tithe to the Church "in accordance with known tradition and sacred custom." [46] This reminder to the conquered people that tithes had been paid in Italy before the coming of the Franks reveals the desire of the Frankish rulers to place the tithe on the basis of existing custom rather than to impose it solely by the legislative command embodied in the capitulary of Heristal.

Judging from the contents of later capitularies, the new legislation concerning both tithe and double tithe met with resistance serious enough to justify special measures for its enforcement. That the legislation about the double tithe was disregarded by the Frankish magnates in Italy even under the strong hand of Charlemagne is evident from a letter which Charlemagne addressed to his counts and vassals there, complaining of their disobedience to the bishops and their failure to observe Chapter 14 of the capitulary of Heristal.[47] An Italian capitulary issued by Pepin between 801 and 810 reaffirmed the obligation of holders of church property not only to pay the double tithe but also to assist in the restoration of the churches,

[45] *Annales qui dicuntur Einhardi,* an. 781, in *M.G.H., SS.,* i, 161; L. M. Hartmann, *Geschichte Italiens im Mittelalter* (Leipzig, 1897–1915, 4 vols.), iii, pt. 1, 13–14.

[46] *M.G.H., Cap.,* i, 189 (c. 9). The editor dates this measure between 780 and 790.

[47] *Ibid.,* pp. 203–204.

the double tithe to be paid to the diocesan bishop and applied
by him to the repair of church buildings and the support of the
clergy.[48]

But we must leave the legislation of Heristal and turn to
the end of Charlemagne's reign, when the ecclesiastical tithe
received its definitive regulation. The *Annals* traditionally attributed to Einhard tell us that in the spring of 813 reforming
councils were held throughout the Frankish realm by order of
the Emperor; five assemblies—at Mainz, Reims, Tours, Châlons,
and Arles—were brought together for the reformation of abuses
in the churches of their respective provinces.[49] The canons of
these councils, which have been preserved,[50] were presented
to the Emperor in September at the diet at Aix-la-Chapelle, and
from their contents a general capitulary was promulgated, sum-
marizing those canons which the Emperor regarded as most
important and desired to have validity throughout the empire.
There is no record of a similar council in Italy,[51] but in the same
year, 813, the ill-fated Bernhard, Pepin's son and successor as
king of Italy, promulgated a capitulary which did for Italy what
the councils had done for other parts of the empire.[52] This
capitulary, believed to have been issued at Mantua, was a provisional measure, subject to the approval of the Emperor and
the diet at Aix. That the intention of the lawmaker was the reform of the Church appears from the prologue, in which the

[48] *Ibid.*, p. 210. The later history and final disappearance of the
double tithe are treated by Lesne, *Propriété ecclésiastique*, ii, pt. 2, 289–
313, and pt. 3, 106–107.

[49] *Annales qui dicuntur Einhardi*, an. 813, *M.G.H., SS.*, i, 200.

[50] *M.G.H., Concilia*, ii, 245–306.

[51] Cf. Hefele-Leclercq, *Histoire des conciles*, iii, pt. 2, 1135.

[52] Alfred Boretius, who edited the capitularies in the *Monumenta
Germaniae Historica*, attributed this measure to Charles the Great and
dated it as of 787, but a manuscript discovered at Vercelli late in the nineteenth century made it necessary to adopt the date 813 and to ascribe
the capitulary to Bernhard. F. Patetta, "Sull'introduzione in Italia della
collezione d'Ansegisio e sulla data del così detto capitulare Mantuanum
duplex attribuito all'anno 787," *Atti della Reale Accademia delle Scienze
di Torino*, xxv (1890), 876–885.

author announces as his purpose the uprooting of the abuses which have grown up in the Church in his day. The capitulary was divided into two sections: one dealing with ecclesiastical, the other with temporal matters. The tithe as part of the internal regiment of the Church was regulated in the ecclesiastical portion of the law, while its enforcement, for which the secular government assumed responsibility, was dealt with in the second part.[53]

It may be assumed that before the advent of the Carolingians, the tithe in Italy had been officially under the control of the bishops, although in actual practice the donors exercised considerable freedom in designating the churches that were to benefit from their gifts. The legislation of the Carolingian period, to the contrary, assigned the tithe to the local churches and their clergy, formulating the rule that each parish must have a definite territory from which it drew the tithe.[54] This innovation is probably to be explained by the growth of rural churches during the eighth and ninth centuries and the necessity of providing an assured income for their clergy. In the Frankish dominions north of the Alps one-fourth or one-third of the product of the parochial tithes, depending upon regional custom, was reserved to the diocesan bishop.[55] This rule the capit-

[53] *M.G.H., Cap.*, i, 194–198.

[54] Important laws assigning the tithe to the parish churches are the capitulary of Mantua itself, the *capitula a sacerdotibus proposita* of 802 (*M.G.H., Cap.*, i, 105–106), canon 19 of the council of Châlons in 813 (*M.G.H., Concilia*, ii, 277), and canon 16 of the council of Tours, also in 813 (*ibid.*, p. 288). The subject is discussed by Perels, *Die kirchlichen Zehnten im karolingischen Reiche*, pp. 49–52; Heinrich Schaefer, *Pfarrkirche und Stift im deutschen Mittelalter* (Stuttgart, 1903), pp. 21–22; Stutz, *Benefizialwesen*, pp. 240–243; Viard, *Dîme avant Gratien*, pp. 110–124.

[55] Methods of dividing church revenues are discussed in Chapter IV. In general, Carolingian legislation favored the Roman system, which allowed a fourth of the parochial tithes to the bishop, but considerable latitude was left to individual bishops in this matter. Witness the capitulary issued by Bishop Hatto of Basel to guide the clergy of his diocese: "The tithe must be paid in full. Of this a third, according to the Toletan canon,

ulary of Mantua flatly contradicted. Chapter 11 states that
no share of the tithes of the parish churches shall be given to
the bishops or the cathedrals.[56] This derogation from the general
rule is thrown into strong relief by several other provisions of
the capitulary: four of its eleven chapters (4, 7, 8, 11) are aimed
against the oppression of the lower clergy by the bishops. The
prelates, the capitulary declares, are appointing clergy in minor
orders as rectors of parish churches; they are encroaching upon
the rights of the parish churches over the lesser chapels of their
districts; they are extorting inordinately large sums from the
parochial clergy during their periodical visitations of their
dioceses; and they are defrauding the parish priests of their just
share of church revenues. Another capitulary, of a few years
later, informs us that in the Lombard kingdom bishops were
practicing what a later period called simony: they were taking
fees from parish priests as the price of their appointment.[57]
While there is abundant evidence to show that these abuses
existed in other parts of the empire, there is some indication
that they were especially rampant in Italy, where many of the
bishops were Franks who cared only for the material emolu-
ments of their office. If the Italian episcopate of this period was
as venal, rapacious, and negligent of its spiritual duties as the
capitulary of Mantua indicates, this is a possible explanation of
the fact that secular rather than ecclesiastical legislation was
chosen as the means of reforming the Church in Italy.

Not only did this capitulary assign the tithes of the rural
districts to the parish churches, it also took stern measures to
compel payment. The second part of the law laid down a special

---

should go to the bishops. We, however, do not wish to avail ourselves of
this power, but intend to take only a fourth of the tithe, in accordance
with the custom of the Roman pontiffs and the observance of the holy
Roman Church." *M.G.H., Cap.,* i, 364.

[56] "De decimis vero quae a populo in plebibus vel baptismalibus aec-
clesiis offeruntur nulla exinde pars maiori aeclesiae vel episcopo inferatur."
M.G.H., Cap., i, 195.

[57] *Ibid.,* p. 278 (c. 16).

mode of enforcement. In each parish four or eight trustworthy
men, according to the size of the parish, were to be elected by
the people to act as witnesses of the payment of the tithe, so
that in disputed cases it would not be necessary to make the
people take an oath that they had performed their duty. At
the actual accounting the presence of two of these witnesses
would be sufficient. Those parishioners who failed to pay the
impost were to be admonished three times by the parish priest;
if they remained recalcitrant, they would be shut out of the
church, then forced to pay the tithe and a fine of six shillings
by the public officials; as a last resort, their houses were to be
sequestrated and any attempt on their part to enter their dwellings would be punished by imprisonment and an additional
fine. These were drastic measures. They mark a radical departure from the mild admonitions previously employed by the
Church and from the laissez-faire attitude of the Lombard kings.
They imply, moreover, a strong current of popular resistance to
governmental attempts to enforce the tithe. The government,
however, determined to leave no loophole by which the tax
could be evaded, used an iron hand. Its one concession to popular sentiment was the vesting of a measure of control over the
payment of the tithe in the hands of the local communities.

That resistance to the compulsory tithe remained constant
for at least half a century after the capitulary is clear from the
contents of later legislation. Capitularies and synodal decrees
continued to reiterate the obligation of the faithful and to
threaten the recalcitrant with penalties. Emperor Lothair, in
the capitulary of Olonna in 825, reaffirmed the provisions of the
edict of Mantua and ordered his *missi dominici* to enforce the
tithe as part of their duties.[58] The synod of Pavia held ca. 850
also demanded the tithe from the faithful and denounced those
who either withheld it or ventured to give it to their private
chapels instead of to the public parishes.[59] A similar decree was

[58] *Ibid.,* ii, 327.
[59] Mansi, *Concilia,* xiv, col. 935 (c. 17).

passed by the Pavian synod of 876.[60] It is noteworthy, however, that in the second half of the ninth century the decrees of church councils were aimed not so much against actual delinquency as against the deflection of the tithes from the parish churches to the private chapels of the large landowners.

From all indications, there was a strong current of resistance to the introduction of the compulsory tithe in Italy and to its regulation by the secular authorities. Nevertheless the institution was firmly established in those parts of the peninsula that were under the direct rule of the Carolingians. In documents of the tenth and following centuries references to the tithe multiply beyond counting. They prove that the tithe took deep root in local customs and that every class of society experienced its impact.

[60] *Ibid.*, xvii, col. 328 (c. 19).

CHAPTER III

The Italian Parish in
the Early Middle Ages

The early Middle Ages in Italy knew only one parish—the pieve; *the period immediately following, the age of the communes, presents two forms: the baptismal church* (plebana) *and another that is without the baptismal font and the greater prerogatives, but which is also recognized as a parish.—Guido Mengozzi,* La città italiana, *pp. 384–385*

✝ SINCE the tithe was assigned by Carolingian legislation to the parish churches throughout the Empire, its evolution in Italy was inseparably connected with the development of Italian parochial institutions. In the following pages, therefore, we shall interrupt the continuity of our central narrative in order to describe the ecclesiastical organization of Italy and especially the organization of the rural parish before the Frankish conquest. We shall then trace the development of the parish under Frankish domination.

Christianity in Italy during the first three centuries of its existence was confined closely to Rome and the South.[1] Ir-

[1] The beginnings of church organization in Italy are summarized by Francesco Lanzoni, *Le diocesi d'Italia dalle origini al principio del secolo vii (an. 604)* (2nd ed., Faenza, 1927, 2 vols.), ii, 1059–1092. The wider background for Lanzoni's account is provided by Adolf von Harnack, *Die Mission und Ausbreitung des Christentums in den ersten drei Jahrhunderten* (3rd ed., Leipzig, 1915, 2 vols.), ii, translated as *The Mission*

radiated from Rome and other cities where there were colonies of Jewish or Syrian merchants, it was gradually disseminated along the military and commercial highways of the southern half of the peninsula. By the end of the second century, each Christian community subject to Rome had a permanent bishop at its head, and the main outlines of episcopal organization in southern Italy had been clearly drawn. But in northern Italy the propagation and organization of the new faith lagged far behind. As late as the third century there were at the most only five resident bishops in the entire North, and only after 325 were bishoprics erected in large numbers in upper Italy.[2]

This inequality of development between North and South reflected fundamental differences in economic and social structure. The North was largely agricultural in its economy and had fewer Oriental communities and trading connections. The land of the North was organized for the most part in large latifundia with but few cities of any size. Consequently, Christianity spread here much more slowly and met with greater resistance from the predominantly agricultural population, which clung tenaciously to paganism. Bishoprics were in course of time

---

and Expansion of Christianity (London and New York, 1908), and by Kenneth Scott Latourette, *A History of the Expansion of Christianity* (New York and London, 1937–1945, 7 vols.), i, *The First Five Centuries*. For Piedmont, Liguria, and Lombardy these general works are supplemented by Fedele Savio, *Gli antichi vescovi d'Italia dalle origini al 1300, Il Piemonte* (Turin, 1898); *La Lombardia*, pt. 1, *Milano* (Florence, 1913); Arturo Ferretto, "I primordi e lo sviluppo del cristianesimo in Liguria ed in particolare a Genova," *ASLSP*, xxxix (1907), 170–431; Felice Alessio, *Le origini del cristianesimo in Piemonte ed in particolare a Tortona, BSSS*, xxxii, pt. 1 (Pinerolo, 1908). Robert Davidsohn, *Geschichte von Florenz* (Berlin, 1896–1927, 4 vols. in 8), i, ch. 2, discusses the evangelization of Tuscany.

[2] The northern bishoprics which may have existed in the third century are Milan, Aquileia, Ravenna, Brescia, and Verona. The evidence is summarized in Harnack, *The Mission and Expansion of Christianity*, ii, 257–260. Lanzoni, *Le diocesi d'Italia*, p. 1061, maintains that there were only three resident bishops in the entire North in the third century—at Milan, Aquileia, and Ravenna.

established in the principal towns of the North, but since the religion was more thinly spread out than in the South, because the estates of the landed proprietors did not offer suitable centers for evangelization, these northern bishoprics were larger and less numerous than those of the more densely populated and urbanized South. Most of the southern bishoprics, founded before the middle of the fourth century, were very small; in the single province of Latium, for example, there were no less than forty-four bishoprics. When the episcopal organization of Italy was substantially complete, at the opening of the seventh century, there were only fifty-three bishoprics in the entire North, as contrasted with one hundred and ninety-seven in the South and Center.[3] This disparity persisted throughout the Middle Ages.

The planting of episcopal churches in Italy was followed by the foundation of rural parishes. This process is impossible to trace, for the history of the earliest rural churches of Italy is irrecoverably lost. The organization of rural parishes with permanent rectors at their heads appears to have begun in the first half of the fifth century. In this and the following century rural churches multiplied, and by the end of the sixth century their condition was regulated by definite custom. Like the bishoprics, which as a rule corresponded territorially to the ancient Roman *civitates,* the parishes tended to conform to the outlines of the Roman civil administration, a parish usually being situated in the principal inhabited center of a *pagus.*[4] This

[3] Lanzoni's estimate, *Le diocesi d'Italia,* ii, 1059. There may have been as many as fifty-seven bishoprics in the North.

[4] Mengozzi, *Città italiana,* pp. 174–175. The rural part of the Roman *civitas* was divided into districts called *pagi,* each of which was in turn subdivided into *vici,* the most important of which served as the administrative center for the whole *pagus.* The *pagus* would normally contain also a number of *villae,* or private estates. The various theories concerning the relation of the rural parishes to pre-existing territorial circumscriptions are discussed by Imbart de la Tour, *Origines religieuses,* pp. 53–59 and more succinctly still by Giuseppe Forchielli, *La pieve rurale* (Rome, 1931), p. 38, n. 1. The view stated in the text appears to be valid for Italy.

is a fact of primary importance for the later history of the Italian parish.

We have called these early rural churches parishes; but at the time of their foundation and for several centuries afterwards the word *parochia* was applied principally to the territory of a bishop, i.e., to the modern diocese.[5] The rural churches founded by the bishops or under their auspices were variously known as *dioceses, baptisteria, plebes,* or *ecclesiae baptismales.*[6] Of these terms, "baptistery" is perhaps the most truly descriptive, since the essential feature of these early rural churches was the possession of a baptismal font, a jealously guarded prerogative which only the bishop could concede. In northern Italy, as in Merovingian Gaul, the term *plebs,* or *pieve,* first used so far as we know in North Africa, became the most common designation for these churches.[7]

[5] The word *parochia* was used in the fourth century concurrently with *diocesis* to indicate the territory of a bishop, and this continued to be the general usage in Italy until the high Middle Ages, although here *parochia* also referred occasionally to the rural part of a diocese as opposed to the *civitas* or city itself. In Gaul, to the contrary, from the sixth century onward *parochia* designated a rural parish. The early history of the word *parochia* is traced by Pierre de Labriolle, "Paroecia," *Bulletin Du Cange,* iii (1927), 196–205.

[6] A Sienese document of 714 is the first in Italy to designate the rural churches as *baptisteria* or *dioceas.* Schiaparelli, *CDL,* i, doc. 17. By the ninth century "diocese" had come to mean normally a bishopric, but as late as the twelfth century Gratian applied the term to the territory of a baptismal church. *Decretum,* C. xxv, *passim.* See *infra,* p. 156, n. 4.

[7] In the course of the eighth century "baptistery" and "diocese" were gradually supplanted by *plebs* (Italian: *pieve*) as the name of the rural parishes, a term first used in this sense by the African councils of the fifth century. Lupi, *De Parochiis,* pp. 53–54. The earliest known use of *plebs* in an Italian document occurs in a Lucchese charter of 724. Schiaparelli, *CDL,* i, doc. 35. The term was generalized throughout the Carolingian Empire in the eighth and ninth centuries as the designation of baptismal churches. The tendency was, however, to restrict it to the rural churches. The nature and history of the rural baptistery is a subject which Giuseppe Forchielli has made peculiarly his own. His views, which are cited frequently in this book, are summed up in his article "Pieve," in the *Enciclopedia italiana,* xxvii, 257–258.

The baptisteries, however, were not the only rural churches. As the number of Christian converts multiplied, other churches were founded in the lesser centers of the *pagus*, but such churches, variously called *oratoria, oracula,* or *tituli,* the result of a secondary diffusion of Christianity emanating largely from the local baptistery, were of inferior status to the baptismal church and were kept in strict subjection to it. Moreover, as Christianity gained adherents among the Roman aristocracy, the great landowners of Italy began to claim the right to found churches in their villas. Such practices were for some time held in check. For the dioceses subject to Rome, Pope Gelasius I formulated strict rules governing the foundation and administration of rural churches: all consecrations of new churches by the bishops had to be approved by the papacy, and if a landowner was permitted to found a church on his domain he was obliged to renounce all claim to its endowment, which the church was to control autonomously, subject to the supervision of the diocesan bishop.[8] The Gelasian rules continued to be enforced during the pontificate of Gregory the Great a century later. By this time numerous laymen were exercising the privilege of erecting oratories on their estates; but such foundations were rigorously controlled; and bishops were instructed by the Pope to deny to private oratories the possession of a baptismal font, a privilege restricted to the baptisteries.[9] The baptisteries, then, were the public parishes of the rural districts, the churches of the local free communities, as distinct from the private oratories of the landed aristocracy.

Concerning the internal organization of the parishes in the Roman period relatively little is known. However, there is some

[8] Nos. 24 and 35 in Thiel, *Epistolae Romanorum Pontificum,* i, 448–449.

[9] Upon application to the pope, the founder of an oratory might obtain an order to the diocesan bishop authorizing him to consecrate the oratory, but on condition that the new foundation should not be a baptistery or have a permanent resident priest. Gregory the Great, *Registrum,* bk. ii, no. 15, in *M.G.H., Epp.,* i, 1, pp. 112–113.

indication that in the parish churches of Italy in the early sixth
century young clerics in minor orders were grouped around the
senior clergy and lived with them under a common roof. This
situation is reflected in a decree of the council of Vaison in 529,
in which the French bishops command that, according to "the
custom which we know to be most salutarily followed throughout Italy, all priests who are established in the parishes shall receive into their houses such junior lectors as are without
wives. . . ." [10] How widespread was the custom recommended
at Vaison it is impossible to ascertain; at any rate the practice
referred to by the Frankish bishops was a prototype of the collegiate organization which was a distinctive feature of Italian
parochial institutions in the high Middle Ages.

The ecclesiastical constitution of Italy in the Lombard
period has been described by Mengozzi in the brilliant essay
cited at the head of this chapter, and we refer the reader to his
pages.[11] The religious center of each city and diocese was the
cathedral, sometimes called the *plebs urbana,* to indicate that it

[10] "Hoc placuit, ut omnes presbyteri, qui sunt in parrochiis constituti,
secundum consuetudinem, quam per totam Italiam satis salubriter teneri
cognovemus, iuniores lectores, quantosque sine uxoribus habuerent, secum
in domo, ubi ipsi habitare videntur, recipiant et eos quomodo boni patres
spiritualiter nutrientes psalmis parare, divinis lectionibus insistere et in
lege Domini erudire contendant, ut et sibi dignos successores provideant
et a Domino proemia aeterna recipiant. Cum vero ad aetatem perfectam
pervenerint, si alequis eorum pro carnis fragilitate uxorem habere voluerit,
potestas ei ducendi coniugium non negetur." *M.G.H., Concilia,* i, 56.
Forchielli took this passage as the starting point for his theory of the collegiate organization of the Italian clergy in the Middle Ages, a theme developed in three remarkable studies: "Una plebs baptismalis cum schola
juniorum a San Giorgio di Valpolicella nell'età longobarda," *Studi Urbinati,*
1927, no. 2; *Collegialità dei chierici nel Veronese* (Venice, 1928), also
published in *AV,* Fifth Series, iii (1928), 1–117; *La pieve rurale* (Rome,
1931; republished at Bologna, without change, 1938). These works supersede the historical portion of an older work by G. Corazzini, *La parrochia
nel diritto italiano* (Turin, 1900).
[11] *Città italiana,* pp. 155–224.

was the sole baptismal church of the urban community.[12] In addition to the cathedral and subordinate to it, there were in each Italian city subsidiary churches, variously called *basilicae, ecclesiae decumanae, tituli, sedales,* and *cardinales,* the status of which was no more uniform than their nomenclature.[13] With the exception of a very few churches which had formerly been episcopal seats, none of these churches had baptismal or burial rights.[14]

The organization of the rural parishes was more complex. Created for the most part by the bishops to serve the local communities, the rural parishes bore the marks of their episcopal

[12] Lupi, *De Parochiis,* pp. 133–266, developed the thesis that except in Rome, the cathedrals were the sole urban parishes in Italy until the eleventh century. This view was incorporated into the work of Paul Hinschius, *Das Kirchenrecht der Katholiken und Protestanten in Deutschland* (Berlin, 1869–1897, 6 vols.), ii, 277 ff., and was accepted by the majority of scholars. It was disputed by H. K. Schaefer, "Frühmittelalterliche Pfarrkirchen und Pfarreinteilung in römisch-frankischen und italienischen Bischofsstädten," *Römische Quartalschrift,* xix (1905), pt. 5, 25–54, who denied that a church had to possess baptismal rights in order to be ranked as a parish; the cure of souls and the right to hold property were, in his opinion, sufficient to acquire that status. *Ibid.,* p. 27. Historical opinion supports, on the whole, Lupi's view that the term "parish" in this early period should be restricted to churches with full parochial rights, hence to baptismal churches. However, research done since Lupi's time has disclosed the existence of a few baptismal churches other than the cathedral in some Italian cities; and the real dividing line in the history of parochial institutions seems to have been the twelfth century, when many lesser urban churches began to share in the parochial functions formerly exercised exclusively by the cathedrals. See Chapter VIII for a fuller discussion of these questions of terminology. In the early part of this book the name "parish" is restricted to baptismal churches.

[13] On these churches see Mengozzi, *loc. cit.;* A. Schiaffini, "Intorno al nome e alla storia del toponimo 'basilica,'" *ASI,* lxxxi (1923), 25–64; Alessandro Colombo, *Milano sotto l'egida del Carroccio* (Milan [1935]), pp. 245–285 and A. F. Frisi, *Memorie di Monza,* i, 55–56 (*ecclesiae decumanae* and the related term *decumani*); Barsocchini, *Dissertazioni,* pp. 46–47 (*sedales*).

[14] Verona had four baptisteries, three of which had formerly served as the cathedral. Forchielli, *Collegialità dei chierici,* pp. 44–47.

origin in their close hierarchical relation to their bishops, who appointed and consecrated the local clergy and gave them the chrism. At the same time the people of the parishes participated in the choice of their rectors, both the lesser clergy and the parishioners being interpellated by the bishops before they proceeded to make a formal appointment. In some Tuscan bishoprics, such as Lucca, Arezzo, and Siena, the people are known to have elected their parish priests with the cooperation of their local officials.[15] This practice, which occurs also in medieval Norway, is thought by some historians to stem from primitive Germanic law and to have been perpetuated in Italy by the Lombard settlements; but it may be attributed with equal plausibility to the continued influence of ancient canon law, which also provided for popular participation in the choice of church officials.

On being invested with his church by his bishop, the rector of a baptistery pledged himself to reside in his parish, to manage its endowment honestly and faithfully, and to labor for his church without thought of personal advantage.[16] In matters of ecclesiastical discipline he was closely subordinated to his bishop, whose annual synod he had to attend and whom he had to entertain on the occasion of the periodical visitation of the diocese. Once appointed, however, he enjoyed considerable independence in the management of the parochial patrimony. By the eighth century the rural churches had become legally sub-

[15] Lucca, 746: the bishop appoints the parish priest of Mosciano "cum cunsensu Ratperti et Barbula centinariis vel de tota pleven congrecata." Schiaparelli, *CDL*, i, doc. 86. Lucca, 819: the bishop appoints a priest in the church of San Donato "una cum consensu Sacerdotum et Aremannos hujus Lucanae civitatis." *MD*, iv, pt. 2, App., doc. 20.

The question of popular participation in the choice of a priest is discussed by P. S. Leicht, *Studi sulla proprietà fondiaria nel medio evo*, i, *La curtis e il feudo nell'Italia superiore fino al secolo xiii* (Verona-Padua, 1903), pp. 154–156; Fedor Schneider, *Die Entstehung von Burg und Landgemeinde in Italien* (Berlin, 1924), pp. 117 ff.; and Feine, "Studien," iii, 71, n. 18.

[16] Schiaparelli, *CDL*, i, doc. 86; ii, doc. 173.

jects of property and possessed landed endowments as well as
the income from miscellaneous fees and oblations. In the day-
to-day administration of this property the rectors acted with a
high degree of independence, although for exchanges of
parochial property a delegate of the bishop had to be present
and to give his consent.[17]

Each baptistery was the center of a cluster of lesser churches
in the outlying villages and on the estates of private landowners.
We have but little direct information concerning the foundation
of oratories in the Lombard period. Some of them were undoubtedly founded from and by the local baptistery to serve the
small communities of the district. Others were originally private
foundations which were brought eventually under the jurisdiction of the baptistery.[18] All new oratories had to be consecrated
by the diocesan bishop, but after this initial act the prelate did
not as a rule govern them directly but placed them under the
jurisdiction of the baptistery.[19] The rector of the baptistery appointed the clergy of the oratories, and celebrated offices in each
oratory on the feast day of its patron saint, when he had the
right to hospitality for himself and his retinue and to a share in
the offerings made by the faithful.[20] The clergy of the oratories
were for the most part recruited from the minor clerics trained
in the baptistery.[21] They do not seem in all cases to have resided in the oratory but merely to have performed church services there on certain specified days.

In addition to the baptisteries, or public parishes, and their
subject oratories, a third group of rural churches existed in the
Lombard period. These were the proprietary churches; or, to
use a somewhat overworked phrase, they were *Eigenkirchen*

---

[17] *Ibid.*, i, docs. 52, 54, 59, 60, 64, 79.

[18] *Ibid.*, i, doc. 19, pp. 70–71.

[19] Deviations from this rule became more common in the eighth century.   [20] *Ibid.*, ii, docs. 181, 292.

[21] Thus the priest of an oratory subject to the baptistery of San Giovanni
of Monza speaks of the patron saint of the baptistery as *nutritor meus.*
Ibid., ii, doc. 218.

(*ecclesiae propriae*), a term which calls for a brief explanation.[22] A proprietary church may be defined as one which is owned and controlled by the owner of the soil on which it stands. The owner may be a bishop, a monastery, a layman, or another church. The owner appoints the priest of the proprietary church and disposes of its revenues; he may bequeath it to his heirs or give it away during his lifetime. The rector of such a church "chants the mass by virtue of the same obligation which compels the ordinary tenant to plough his field or cut his vine." [23] The antecedents of the proprietary church have already been indicated. Laymen were erecting churches at least as early as the pontificate of Gelasius I, without, however, the right to control their endowments. In the disorders accompanying the Lombard settlements, the Roman concepts of public law became attenuated; and the Church found itself impotent to enforce strictly the earlier limitations upon lay founders of churches. By the eighth century proprietary churches in the full sense of the word had become numerous in Italy. Some of these were royal churches; others were oratories founded by private landowners on their estates; still others were on episcopal domains and belonged to the bishopric in a proprietary sense. Sometimes a proprietary church might pass through all these categories, as it was handed from one owner to another. Thus the church of San Pietro in Somaldi, originally a royal church, was given by King Aistulf to the painter Auniperto and eventually came into the possession of the painter's brother, who bestowed it on the bishop of Lucca, reserving the usufruct of it during his lifetime but providing that after his death the bishop was to institute a rector and administer the church.[24] Thus the church was a royal church, a private church in lay hands, and an episcopal proprietary church, all within the span of a few years.

Proprietary churches seem to have been the product of social

[22] See Appendix I, "The Literature of the Private Church."

[23] Paul Fournier, "La propriété des églises dans les premiers siècles du moyen âge," *NRHDFE*, xxi (1897), 492.

[24] Schiaparelli, *CDL*, ii, doc. 170.

conditions wherever they appeared, and not a mystical emanation of Germanic law and the Germanic spirit, as some German historians formerly represented them. In Italy the seeds of the proprietary church had germinated in the last centuries of the Western Empire, but did not fully fructify until the eighth century, when Romans and Lombards had been integrated into one society. Even then it did not assume the same proportions in Italy as in the countries north of the Alps, where the lay proprietary church had become the prevailing type of church by the end of the eighth century. In the North not only had many private churches been founded by lay proprietors, most of the existing parishes had also been reduced to the status of private churches by absorption into the domains of the landowning aristocracy. In Italy, on the other hand, although lay proprietary churches became very numerous in the Lombard period, they remained of minor importance as compared with the baptismal churches.

Thus when the Carolingians conquered Italy they encountered an ecclesiastical constitution which had survived the debacle of the Western Empire. Side by side with the dominant episcopal organization, however, existed large numbers of lay proprietary churches. These two systems were by no means watertight, for the proprietary regime had already begun to affect the episcopal churches. This tendency was accentuated in the Frankish period. Generally speaking, the formal constitution of the Italian parish remained unchanged after the Frankish conquest, but the functional, as distinguished from the structural, aspect of the parish was radically transformed by the growth of the seigniorial regime and by the gradual assimilation of the parishes to the proprietary churches, a process which was already far advanced by the opening of the ninth century.[25]

The remainder of this chapter will analyze, first, the legisla-

[25] The Italian parishes were never secularized to the same extent as those north of the Alps. Their assimilation to the status of episcopal proprietary churches, first discerned by Stutz, *Benefizialwesen*, pp. 326 ff., has been fully documented by H. E. Feine, "Studien," iii, 64–190.

tion of the Frankish period by which both the secular and ecclesiastical authorities strove to strengthen the traditional
parochial organization and, secondly, the growth of abuses in
the parishes, derived largely from the economic conditions of
the ninth century and from the legal ideas which inevitably
flourished in such an economic and social environment.

Soon after the Frankish conquest the condition of the baptismal churches was regulated by a series of capitularies directed
towards the maintenance of the ancient parochial system. The
earliest important capitulary on the subject was a law of Pepin
forbidding laymen to hold baptismal churches, which were expressly confirmed to the ecclesiastical hierarchy; by implication this prohibited lay proprietors from having churches with
full parochial rights on their estates, a measure which, so far
as we know, was without counterpart elsewhere in the Carolingian Empire.[26] At the same time the economic status of the
baptismal churches was improved by the establishment of the
compulsory tithe, designed especially to benefit the rural parishes and the enforcement of which in Italy was to some extent
entrusted to the local village communities.[27]

Church synods of the ninth century usually legislated in
harmony with the capitularies. The Roman synod of 826 confirmed the rights of the local communities in regard to the choice
of their clergy, instructing the bishops to consult the clergy of
the baptisteries in regard to the appointment of new rectors,
who were to be taken from the district of the baptistery with due
regard for the wishes of the parishioners.[28]

The most important landmark in the history of the Italian
parish in the Frankish period is probably the synod of Pavia,
ca. 845–850, the decrees of which defined clearly the status of
the baptismal churches and fixed the terminology of Italian

---

[26] "De ecclesiis baptismalibus ut nullatenus eas laici homines tenere
debeant, sed per sacerdotes fiant, sicut ordo est gubernatae." *M.G.H., Cap.,*
i, 200.

[27] See pp. 43–45.   [28] *M.G.H., Cap.,* i, 373.

parochial institutions. In the thirteenth canon of this council the baptismal church of the ninth century comes fully into view. As in the Lombard period it is the center of a group of lesser churches, here designated as *minores tituli*. At its head is an archpriest, who administers the penitential system and supervises the clergy of the lesser churches subject to the jurisdiction of his baptistery. The bishops are urged to share their administrative burdens with these rural archpriests and to allow them to exercise within their circumscriptions the same authority that the bishops have over their cathedrals.[29]

Was this canon entirely a confirmation of the ancient organization of the parishes or did it embody innovations as well? Here a distinction should be drawn between two different elements in this legislation. The relation of hierarchical subordination between baptistery and minor chapels preserved the lineaments of the system which existed in the Lombard period and almost certainly went back to Roman times. But the archipresbyterate which was here imposed upon all the baptisteries may have been to some extent an innovation. In the Lombard period churches governed by a single rector existed side by side with those governed by two priests, whom the documents call *rectores et custodes*,[30] and there is some indication that the second may have been the more ancient form.[31] The term "archpriest," on

---

[29] Mansi, *Concilia*, xiv, 935. Another canon instructs the rural archpriests to convene all the heads of families in each village in order that "they themselves and all those dwelling in their houses who have committed sins in public shall do penance in public." *Ibid.*, col. 931.

[30] The Veronese basilica, later baptistery, of San Giorgio of Valpolicella in 712 had a clergy composed of two priests, called *custodes*, and a deacon. Forchielli, "Una plebs baptismalis," p. 3. The inscription of 712 discussed by Forchielli in this article contains the earliest known use of the word *custos* to denote the rector of a baptismal church. The term became general in the Lombard period. Lupi, *CDB*, i, 288–289. For examples of churches with two priests, see Schiaparelli, *CDL*, ii, docs. 128, 269; *MD*, iv, pt. 1, doc. 86.

[31] A passage from the writings of St. Ambrose suggests that the Church of Milan, the center for the evangelization of northern Italy, favored the presence of two priests in each church for the safeguarding of clerical

the other hand, first mentioned in the Gallic councils of the sixth century, does not appear in Italy until the second half of the ninth century.[32] Even then it was more fully acclimatized in northern Italy, particularly in Lombardy and Piedmont, which were more strongly influenced by Frankish institutions, whereas in Tuscany, after appearing in Lucchese documents of the last quarter of the ninth century, it yielded in the tenth century to the more ancient *presbiter et custos*.[33] A possible explanation is that in the parishes with two rectors in the Lombard period the senior priest exercised the functions of the archpriest in Merovingian Gaul and that the Pavian decree therefore merely superimposed a terminology developed in Gaul upon institutions long indigenous to Italy.[34]

---

celibacy and the daily administration of the sacraments: "Nunc autem septem diacones esse oportet, et aliquantos presbyteros, *ut bini sint per Ecclesias,* et unus in civitate episcopus; ac per hoc omnes a conventu feminae abstinere debere; quia necesse est eos quotidie praeso in Ecclesia, nec habere dilationem, et post conventum legitime purificentur, sicut veteres. Omni enim hebdomada offerendum est, etiamsi non quotidie peregrinis, incolis tamen vel bis in hebdomada; etsi non desint, qui [quia?] prope quotidie baptizentur aegri." *M.P.L.,* xvii, 471.

[32] Forchielli, *La pieve rurale,* p. 90, says that the Carolingian legislation merely confirmed the ancient archipresbyteral system in Italy. But the *archipresbyteri vicani* mentioned by the councils of Tours (567) and Châlons (650) do not appear in Italy until much later. An eighth-century Lucchese document referring to an archpriest named Sichimundo (Schiaparelli, *CDL,* i, doc. 73) probably refers to the archpriest of the cathedral. An archpriest is mentioned at Monza in 862 (Porro-Lambertenghi, *CDL,* doc. 223) but this is posterior to the Pavian council. The rural archpriests are discussed by Lupi, *De Parochiis,* pt. 1, ch. 8. For a summary of recent scholarship, see *Dictionnaire de droit canonique,* ed. Amanieu, Villien, and Naz (Paris, 1935—), art. "Archiprêtre," i, 1004–1026.

Simultaneously with "archpriest," there appeared in Italy the interchangeable and more popular word *plebanus* to denote the rector of a baptistery; e.g., *MD,* v, pt. 2, doc. 695 (Lucca, 853).

[33] As in the documents relating to the Lucchese baptistery of Sant'Ippolito. *MD,* v, pt. 2, docs. 687, 790, 818; iv, pt. 2, App., doc. 52; v, pt. 2, docs. 998, 1008–1013, 1016.

[34] Cf. the history of the word *capella* to denote the lower churches without parochial functions. *Capella* was not native to Italy but was im-

The Pavian legislation throws further light upon the election of the archpriest. Its fourth canon directs that the priests or other clergy of a baptistery are to choose a suitable rector from their number; the parishioners are then to be asked for their sanction; if a suitable rector cannot be found among the clergy of the baptismal district, then the bishop is to appoint one from among the clergy of the diocese as a whole.[35] That this practice was followed in at least some parishes is shown by several Modenese documents of the late ninth and early tenth centuries, which prove that the clergy of some Modenese baptisteries formed a corporate group which jointly with the parishioners exercised a voice in the selection of an archpriest.[36]

The documents just cited make it clear that some at least of the Italian baptisteries were collegiate churches, i.e., they were served not by a single priest but by a group composed of one or more priests and a number of clerics in minor orders. This corporate organization had existed in Italy at the time of the Vaison legislation in 529, and a case can be made out in favor of the thesis that this was the form of parochial organization favored by the early Church. But granting that many baptisteries had a corporate structure, how far did this involve the observance of the common life at the baptistery? And further, to what extent did the clergy serving the chapels share in any common life which existed?

The documents are too scanty to permit generalization. To sum up briefly the available evidence, it may be said that a small but convincing group of documents from the Lombard period proves that some form of the common life was followed in a number of baptisteries and in some lesser churches, and that the

ported in the ninth century, used by the royal chancery at Pavia, and thence disseminated among the local scribes, eventually superseding the earlier names of the minor churches. Paul Aebischer, "Esquisse du processus de dissemination de 'Capella' en Italie," *Bulletin Du Cange,* v (1930), 5–44.

[35] *M.G.H., Cap.,* ii, 82.

[36] *Regesto di Modena,* docs. 18, 26, 39.

names *monasterium* and *abatia* were popularly applied to such
churches, while the clergy associated in the common life were
sometimes called *fratres* or *monachi*.[37] As for the chapels, it
would probably be accurate to apply to eighth-century Italy the
words applied by a recent authority on the rural parish to
Merovingian Gaul:

The priests who are subject to the Merovingian archpriest are those
who live with him, either as his aides in his own church or as entrusted with the service of the auxiliary chapels in the interior of
the parish. They reside at the oratories only for the time necessary
to accomplish their religious services, then return to the center of
the parish, to the dwelling of the archpriest.[38]

With due allowance for inevitable differences in local circumstances, this was the system followed in Lombard Italy, where
it endured well into the Frankish period at a time when the
archipresbyterate was rapidly dissolving in France. The existence of this corporate organization explains the unity exhibited
by the clergy of the baptismal district, a unity arising from their
early education at the baptistery and manifested in their common action in the election of an archpriest or rector, who was to
be chosen from among their number or at least from the territory
of the parish. Even when distance made it impossible for the
clergy of the chapels to participate in any common life at the
baptistery, they still acted as a unit for certain purposes, notably
for the election of a rector. The baptismal church, as it appears
in the records of the eighth and early ninth centuries, was a self-
regulating cell in the medieval corporative society. But as for
the number of churches in which a full community life was
practiced, it is impossible to speak with assurance. One surmises
that such churches were very few.

Enlightenment on this subject may be sought in the Caro-

[37] The changing terminology may be traced in the baptistery of Monza,
throughout the greater part of its history a collegiate church. Frisi,
Memorie di Monza, i, 43–50; ii, docs. 6, 7.

[38] A. Amanieu, in *Dictionnaire de droit canonique*, i, 1009.

lingian legislation. The early Carolingian rulers supported the reforming elements in the Frankish Church that were fostering the canonical life among the secular clergy; and after the conquest of the Lombard kingdom Pepin applied this policy to Italy. In enjoining upon the Italian bishops the fulfillment of their diocesan duties, he ordained that they should vigilantly watch over the "monasteries" within their dioceses, to ensure that the *canonici* should live "according to the canons," the monks according to the Benedictine Rule.[39] In 816, under the official sanction of Lewis the Pious, the council of Aix-la-Chapelle promulgated a revised form of the rule which Chrodegang of Metz had instituted in his cathedral, and made it obligatory upon cathedrals and collegiate churches throughout the Empire, confiding its enforcement to the *missi dominici*.[40] Somewhat later the Roman council of 826 tried to hold Italian canons to a stricter observance of the common life; it prescribed that cloisters should be erected in the churches and that the clergy should take their meals in common refectories, share common dormitories, and hold and manage in common the revenues of their churches.[41] This decree, repeated by the Pavian synod of 876, no doubt aimed primarily at the cathedral chapters; but while the rural parishes are not explicitly mentioned, neither are they excluded. A French scholar, Monsieur Amann, takes the view that it was the intention of the early Carolingians to extend the practice of the common life wherever possible to the rural parishes, where the priest would lead the "canonical life" with his lower clergy. In Italy, Amann discerned, this would apply to most of the baptismal churches, since they had a collegiate clergy.[42] This opinion, while it cannot be absolutely

[39] *M.G.H., Cap.,* i, 209.

[40] Mansi, *Concilia,* xiv, 315–332 (Chrodegang's rule); *M.G.H., Concilia,* ii, 397–421 (rule of Aix). The two rules are compared and discussed in Hefele-Leclercq, iv, pt. 1, 9–25. Emile Amann, *L'époque carolingienne* (Fliche, *HE,* iv) (Paris, 1937), 261–264, utilizes recent research on the canonical reform.   [41] *M.G.H., Cap.,* i, 373 (c. 7).

[42] Amann, *L'époque carolingienne,* pp. 83–84.

proved, is in accord with recent Italian scholarship and with the evidence of the documents.

Such was the ideal aimed at by the ecclesiastical legislation of the Frankish period in Italy—the maintenance of ancient traditions and practices in the rural parishes, the preservation of old local freedoms, and the strengthening of the parish churches through more adequate revenues, the collection of which was enforced by the state. That the reality fell far short of the ideal goes without saying. If we turn from formal legislation to local records, we are presented with a large body of evidence for the failure of ecclesiastical reform to arrest the growth of abuses and to protect the parishes from the inroads of the seigniorial regime.

Among the disruptive factors must be counted the royal policy itself. The Carolingian rulers extended to Italy the secularizations of church property which Charles Martel had initiated. Concessions of ecclesiastical property made by the Frankish rulers to their vassals were subject, it is true, to a *census* and a double tithe to the original owner, who retained his title to the estates, but for all practical purposes such property was lost to the Church, for the benefice-holders evaded their obligations and seem in most cases to have made their benefices hereditary. Eventually the Carolingians had to abandon the idea of restoring the estates to the Church, as Charles Martel had promised.[43] Not only the lands of churches but the churches themselves were secularized by the government or usurped by laymen. In 879 the important basilica of San Giovanni of Monza, together with the villa of the same name, was the benefice of a royal vassal, Count Liutfred, and the lands of the basilica were

[43] For the Carolingian secularizations, see Emile Lesne, *Propriété ecclésiastique*, ii, pts. 1 and 2 *passim*, and "La dîme des biens ecclésiastiques aux ixᵉ et xᵉ siècles," *RHE*, xiii (1912), 477–503, 659–673; xiv (1913), 97–112, 489–510.

subinfeudated by military tenure.[44] Less than half a century later the basilica had become so impoverished by this kind of exploitation that King Berengar had to come to its assistance.[45]

The royal policy was not alone responsible for the plight of the churches. In Charlemagne's time the central government took special measures to protect the rural parishes against episcopal exploitation.[46] Charlemagne's grandson Lothair, by the capitulary of Olonna in 825, reminded the Italian bishops that they were to appoint as rectors in the baptismal churches ordained priests and not mere deacons or clerics in minor orders, an indication that the bishops were conferring these appointments upon relatives or adherents regardless of their qualifications for the office.[47] Equally serious was the growing habit among the bishops of burdening the baptismal churches with heavy dues. In the eighth century it had been customary for the rectors of such churches to pay their bishops a small recognitive rent; by the opening of the ninth century it had become a common practice for the bishops to demand an annual rent of from fifteen to forty shillings from the rectors. In 806 a bishop of Lucca imposed upon a parish priest a rent consisting of "one repast [when the bishop visited the parish] and a pair of cows and a horse together worth forty shillings; or the forty shillings themselves instead of the cows and the horse." [48] Episcopal requisitions from the rural archpriests when the bishops in-

[44] Porro-Lambertenghi, *CDL,* doc. 289; Frisi, *Memorie di Monza,* ii, doc. 5. Liutfred held the church *de datu domni regis in beneficio.* In 885 two vassals held land from the archpriest by military tenure. Porro-Lambertenghi, doc. 330.

[45] Frisi, *Memorie di Monza,* ii, doc. 12. The church was now officiated by thirty-two canons. Berengar gave them three manors, commanding them to restore the church from the revenues of the manors and from the tithes given by the people to the baptistery.   [46] See p. 44.

[47] *M.G.H., Cap.,* i, 328 (c. 1). Lothair had been crowned king of Italy in 822, and became co-emperor with Lewis the Pious a year later.

[48] *MD,* iv, pt. 2, doc. 7. Other typical leases of baptismal churches are recorded in v, pt. 2, docs. 16, 45, 826, 937.

spected the churches of their dioceses became so excessive that
the synod of Pavia had to limit them to specific amounts.[49] More
and more did the bishops disregard local rights in conferring
the office of archpriest. The Roman synod of 826 warned that
appointments of priests in baptismal churches should be made
"more reverently," that is, with the sanction of the parishioners
and the local clergy; [50] and it forbade the bishops to divert to
their own uses or to those of their cathedrals the landed property of the lower churches.[51]

A Milanese synod of 864 exposed another abuse on the part
of some bishops, who were keeping the parish churches vacant
as long as possible in order to take the parochial revenues themselves, and decreed that any bishop who delayed appointing
suitable rectors in his parishes should be excommunicated.[52]
Numerous Lucchese documents contemporaneous with this legislation show successive bishops of Lucca interfering in the internal administration of the parishes and leasing their property
indifferently to ecclesiastics and to laymen, usually with the
provision that the rents and other dues should be paid to the
central office of the bishopric or to the bishop's local steward.[53]
It is possible that some of these were vacant parishes in which
the bishops deliberately delayed to appoint rectors.[54] Some

[49] Mansi, *Concilia*, xv, 18–19 (c. 15).

[50] *M.G.H., Cap.*, i, 373 (c. 8).

[51] *Ibid.*, p. 374 (c. 16). The phrase applied to the property is *res im-
mobiles.*   [52] *ACN*, doc. 9.

[53] *MD*, v, pt. 2, docs. 670, 672, 709, 817, 957, 976, 981.

[54] An episcopal lease of two chapels subject to the baptistery of Santa
Felicità in 886–887 was made with the consent of the rector of the baptistery. *MD*, v, pt. 2, doc. 949. This suggests the hypothesis that in other
leases where the rector's consent is not mentioned the church was vacant.
It should not be supposed that these practices were universal. Witness
a series of documents for the parish church of Sant'Ippolito which shows
that the rector of this church administered its property independently
from 851 to 898, with the reservation that when he made exchanges of
property, two episcopal *missi* were present, in accordance with the Lombard law. *Ibid.*, v, pt. 2, docs. 687, 818, 998, 1008–1013 (leases); iv, pt. 2,
App., doc. 52; v, pt. 2, doc. 790 (exchanges).

bishops in this period cloaked illegal alienations of parochial property under the guise of leases or contracts of exchange. Sometimes they granted church lands for a purely nominal rent, sometimes accepted for them capital sums not mentioned in the contracts.[55]

No less culpable than the bishops were the local clergy. In the late eighth and early ninth centuries the Lucchese parish of Sesto was the appanage of a kind of sacerdotal dynasty; the office of rector passed from father to son for three generations, in one instance to a married cleric in minor orders.[56] One church, not a parish, remained in the hands of one priestly family for six generations.[57] The Milanese synod of 864 took up the case of those rural archpriests who excused their appropriations of church property by alleging that they were storing church revenues in their own dwellings to protect them from seizure by their bishops. The synod decreed that, if a bishop usurped parochial revenues without the connivance of the rector, he was liable to excommunication; but if the parish priest proved to be the culprit, he should forfeit his church.[58] The capitulary of Pavia in 876 commanded the restitution to the churches of ecclesiastical lands alienated by the rectors "through fear or favor." [59] It is evident from these measures that in some instances bishops and parish priests were in collusion.

Finally, among the factors contributing to the breakdown of discipline in the parishes should be mentioned the continued growth of the private churches and the withdrawal of the wealthier classes from the parishes. This tendency was lamented by the synod of Pavia:

Certain of the laity, especially the rich and powerful, have chapels beside their dwellings in which they hear divine services and are not accustomed to come very often to the mother churches. Seeing that

---

[55] *MD*, iv, pt. 2, doc. 32.

[56] *Ibid.*, v, pt. 2, docs. 214, 281, 282; iv, pt. 2, doc. 8.

[57] Feine instances the church of Brancoli. "Studien," i, 70.

[58] *ACN*, doc. 9 (c. 2). [59] *M.G.H., Cap.*, ii, 102 (c. 10).

diction of his landlord. In the course of time the tenure passed
through a complex development and by the second half of the
ninth century had evolved into two distinct forms. One form,
the characteristic tenure of the serf and the small free cultivator,
carried with it the obligation of residence on the holding, personal cultivation of the soil, and subjection to the lord's court; the
second form, the principal nonmilitary tenure of the upper
stratum of the rural population, lacked these restrictions and
allowed the tenant the free disposal of his holding. The man who
held land under the second form of this tenure was not obliged
to reside on his holding or to render services to his lord; nor was
he subject to the lord's court. He could have his holding worked
by small cultivators or he could sublease it to renters of his own
class. His main obligation was the payment of a rent, usually in
money, sometimes supplemented by contributions in kind. In
other words, an estate so leased passed from the economic sphere
of the legal owner under the virtually complete disposal of the
tenant, subject to the payment of the rent. Contracts in *livello*
were normally made for a period not exceeding twenty-nine
years; but as the contract was usually renewed from one generation to another, the tenure eventually became in effect hereditary.[64]

In the second half of the eighth century the contract of
livello was extended from land to churches. The contracts of
this period and later make no distinction between the tenure by
which a parish priest holds his church and that by which a layman holds an agrarian estate.[65] The church, with its appurtenances, is ceded by the bishop *livellario nomine* to a priest, whose
obligation to hold religious services in the church takes the place

[64] Barsocchini, *Dissertazioni,* pp. 113–144; Pivano, *I contratti agrari,*
pp. 212–213, n. 74. The earliest contracts of this kind sometimes use the
formula *ad resedendum, ad laborandum;* but in Lucca after 820 concessions of this kind use the formula *livellario* (*libellario*) *nomine.*

[65] The term *ecclesia* in contracts of this kind definitely refers to the
church itself, not merely to its property. Pivano, *I contratti agrari,* p. 200,
n. 50; Feine, "Studien," iii, "Die Kirchleihe," p. 77.

of the agricultural work required of an ordinary tenant. Further, by the second half of the ninth century most of the parish priests of Lucca held their churches under the unrestricted form of the tenure. They were not obliged to perform religious services personally if they preferred to entrust this duty to another priest; they could lease the lands and revenues of their churches to tenants of their choice. They could not be deprived of their churches for the duration of their tenure provided religious services continued to be held.

Contracts of *livello* between bishop and rector took the form of a bilateral agreement drawn up by a public notary in the presence of witnesses, and consisting of two documents, one signed by the bishop and given to the parish priest, the other signed by the rector and deposited in the episcopal archives. It is the second group of documents which has survived in large numbers in Lucca.[66] These provide convincing evidence for the virtual assimilation of the rural parishes in the course of the ninth century to the status of episcopal proprietary churches. Bishops treated the baptismal churches as if they were private property; rectors, too, aspired to the tenure in unrestricted *livello*, so that they also might hold their parishes as *ecclesiae propriae*, exploiting their endowments and collecting their revenues.

At the close of the ninth century the parish churches of Lucca possessed landed endowments which varied considerably in size

---

[66] The *livello* was not the sole tenure by which priests held their churches in the ninth century. Some priests held their churches in benefice (*per beneficium*) with only the temporary usufruct of the property, which could not be disposed of freely. In Lucca such contracts seem to have been terminable at the will of the bishop. Barsocchini, *Dissertazioni*, pp. 30–31. When land was held in benefice any alienation by the benefice-holder was forbidden, and exchanges could be effected only by a representative of the proprietary church. Lesne, *Propriété ecclésiastique*, ii, pt. 2, 281. It was the ambition of the parish priests to transform the tenure in benefice into tenure *libellario nomine;* as in the Modenese document of 856 whereby the priest Ariberto asks his bishop to grant him in *enfiteusi* (the Romano-Ravennate equivalent of unrestricted *livello*) the baptismal church which he already held in benefice (*per beneficium vel censitum*). *Regesto di Modena,* doc. 18.

and economic value. The comparatively rich baptistery of Quaratiana was provided with arable land, a vineyard, a meadow, and an olive grove. Seven tenants paid labor-dues to the church, twelve others owed money rents, while still others, listed separately, paid rents totalling seventeen *solidi* and six *denarii*.[67] At the other end of the scale, the poor parish of Atriana had a little arable land, a meadow, and only one tenant.[68] Other baptismal churches in the Lucchese countryside had anywhere from one to sixteen tenants who paid money rents or gave personal services to the priests, those subject to labor-dues contributing from three to five days' work each week. Obviously the average Lucchese parish was land-poor.

The land of a baptismal church consisted usually of a demesne, or glebe, cultivated by the priest with the help of his tenants, and of a number of peasant allotments. The typical peasant holding, designated in the documents as *casa massaricia* or simply *casa et res,* was held under the restricted form of the *livello,* that is, the tenant was bound to the soil and subject, at least in some cases, to the manorial jurisdiction of the church. The tenure was hereditary, although the son of a deceased tenant could choose between renewing the contract or departing with a share of the movables.

In addition to its landed property, each baptistery held tithes. It collected the tithe not only from the inhabitants of its own village but from all the communities within its baptismal area, i.e., from the people who attended religious services in the chapels, often very numerous, under its jurisdiction. To use the same examples as above, the opulent *pieve* of Quaratiana collected tithes from thirty-nine villages, while the less fortunate church of Atriana took tithes from only eleven communities.[69] The wealthier baptisteries of Lucca collected tithes in from twenty-eight to thirty-six villages. The income derived from the tithe may be presumed in most cases to have been considerably

---

[67] P. Guidi and E. Pellegrinetti, eds., *Inventari del vescovado, della cattedrale e di altre chiese di Lucca* (Rome, 1921), doc. 1, p. 4.

[68] *Ibid.,* p. 10.

[69] *MD,* v, pt. 3, docs. 1564, 1568.

more valuable than that from land. It was this lucrative prerogative which made the baptisteries desirable possessions from an economic point of view and the office of rector worth having.

When Bishop Peter II, a prelate with reforming ideas, took office in Lucca in 897, he found that parish priests were making wholesale concessions of parochial property to laymen under the unrestricted form of *livello*. To curb this abuse, he introduced into the acts of investiture a clause stipulating that without the bishop's express consent no parochial land might be leased to other than peasant cultivators.[70] The object of this measure was of course to prevent the passing of church property into the hands of the *milites* of the countryside.

A year after Peter launched his reform, in 898, Emperor Lambert issued a capitulary which "in its brief compass of twelve articles seems to sum up the entire history of the close of the ninth century." [71] Mainly a repetition of previous legislation, this capitulary reflects the ecclesiastical world of the late Carolingian period. The picture disclosed is a depressing one: a grasping and ambitious episcopate, devoted to the pursuit of mundane power; a greedy and cruel military class which seeks to gain control of church property and income and to exploit the rural classes; a parish clergy oppressed or neglected by the bishops, exposed to the encroachments of the lay aristocracy, and too ignorant and weak to resist the abuses of the time; and everywhere an agricultural class which pours rents, tithes, and offerings into the coffers of the Church, only to see them swallowed up by the rapacity of the ruling classes. By the end of the ninth century the bishops were ceding the parishes as benefices to their vassals. "The baptismal churches," Lambert's capitulary

[70] "Nisi illis hominibus, qui super ipsis casis et rebus (resede)rint. Nam aliis hominibus sine vestro consensu livellario nomine . . . dare non debeam." *Ibid.*, iv, pt. 2, doc. 50 (an. 898). For an example of the earlier type of investiture without restraint on alienation, see iv, pt. 1, doc. 50 (an. 759). The formula given in v, pt. 3, doc. 1082 (an. 904) is repeated almost verbatim in almost all appointments of parish priests in the tenth century.

[71] Silvio Pivano, *Stato e chiesa in Italia da Berengario ad Arduino* (Turin, 1908), p. 52.

declares, "shall in no wise be ceded as benefices to the counts, or to the bishops' vassals, or to any laymen." [72]

To judge of the extent to which this evil had penetrated the churches, one has only to turn to an inventory of the bishopric of Lucca which was compiled almost contemporaneously with Lambert's capitulary. The inventory consists of a list of those who held benefices from the bishopric, together with a detailed description of their holdings.[73] As many of these benefices included parish churches, the inventory is a valuable survey of parochial property. It shows that at the turn of the ninth century at least nineteen Lucchese parishes had been ceded as benefices to laymen.

The absorption of the parish into the seigniorial regime that was forming in the Italian countryside was enormously accelerated by the institution of the compulsory tithe, which had effected a revolutionary change in the economic status of the parish. Every parishioner of the baptismal church and its subject chapels now had to pay to the rector of the baptistery a tenth of his income in agricultural produce and in the increase of his livestock. The rural parish, which hitherto had derived a scanty income from its land, supplemented by such tithes as the Biblical precept and clerical exhortation had elicited from popular piety, now exercised a semipublic power over the population of its entire territory. Such an increase of wealth and jurisdiction greatly enhanced the prestige and prosperity of the baptismal churches; but at the same time this new source of revenue exposed them to the violence of the magnates of the neighborhood and excited the cupidity of the bishops. The tenth chapter of Lambert's capitulary should therefore be connected with the acquisition by the baptismal churches of the right to tithe the Christian population of their districts. It provides a last and telling illustration of the failure of Carolingian ecclesiastical policy in Italy.

[72] *M.G.H., Cap.,* ii, 110 (c. 10).
[73] Guidi and Pellegrinetti, pp. 3–11.

CHAPTER IV

Tithe and Patrimony

† FROM AN ACCOUNT of the beginnings of the ecclesiastical tithe in Italy, we turned aside to describe the institutional milieu within which the tithe evolved. We now return to consider the place of the tithe within the fabric of church property and the growth of laws and customs governing its operation. Since the Gelasian rule commanding the quadripartite division of church revenues played an important part in shaping the development of the tithe, we shall devote the initial portion of this chapter to a discussion of its origins.

According to a generally accepted view, ecclesiastical property in the early Church formed in each diocese a single mass administered by the bishop. For the guidance of the bishops under the metropolitan jurisdiction of Rome, the papacy in the fifth century promulgated the rule of quadripartition: the bishop was to divide the diocesan revenues into four parts, one for the lower clergy, according to their merits, one for the poor, one for the maintenance and equipment of church buildings, and one for his own use as the church officer especially responsible for almsgiving and the entertainment of travellers and pilgrims.[1]

---

[1] The first mention of the rule of quadripartition occurs in a letter of Pope Simplicius dated 475. Thiel, *Epistolae Romanorum Pontificum,* i, 176–177. The rule is discussed by Thomassin, *Ancienne et nouvelle discipline de l'église,* vi, 552–553, and Stutz, *Benefizialwesen,* pp. 24–41.

The classical formulation of this rule is a letter addressed by
Gelasius I in 494 to the bishops of Lucania and Bruttium, in
which the Pope orders these prelates to distribute among the
lower clergy the fourth which is their due. In this letter Gelasius
leaves to the bishop the administration of the fourths destined
to charity and the fabric, declaring that the bishop's almsgiving
should be so evident that scandalmongering tongues should have
no cause to reproach him. As for the episcopal fourth, Gelasius
observes in another letter that its purpose is to enable the bishop
to assist pilgrims and captives.[2] The rule of quadripartition thus
laid down continued to be followed in Italian churches during
the Lombard settlements; in 593 Gregory the Great insisted
that it should be applied to newly acquired property as well as
to that of long standing.[3] It was extended from Italy to Roman
missionary areas, notably to Germany and Britain.[4] The churches
in France and Spain also adopted the principle of the rule but
made a tripartite instead of quadripartite division of the diocesan revenues.[5]

The question has been raised as to whether this rule was actually applied to the rural churches. Arnold Pöschl, for example,
denies that the rule was intended for churches other than the
cathedrals, and this point of view was shared by some of the

[2] Thiel, *Epistolae*, i, 378, 381–382 (c. 1).

[3] *M.G.H., Epp.*, i, pt. 1, 244.

[4] Note the instructions given by Pope Gregory II to St. Boniface in
722: "The revenues of the Church and the offerings of the faithful he
[the bishop] is to divide into four parts: one for himself; one for the clergy
according to the diligence with which they perform their duties; a third
for the poor and for strangers; a fourth to be set aside for the maintenance
of ecclesiastical buildings, and of these he is to render an account in the
day of God's judgement." Emerton, *The Letters of St. Boniface*, pp. 43–44.

[5] Georg Schreiber believes that the tripartition was characteristic of
primitive Germanic law and that its presence indicates a Germanic settlement; conversely, the quadripartition was the division officially sanctioned
by the Roman Church and its extension marks the spread of Roman authority. "Gregor VII, Cluny, Cîteaux, Prémontré, zu Eigenkirche, Parochie,
Seelsorge," ZSSR, lxv (1947), *Kan. Abt.*, xxxiv, 95–96.

medieval canonists.[6] If, however, we examine the legislation
of some of the early church councils, Pöschl's challenge to the
accepted view does not seem justified. French and Spanish
synodal decrees of the fifth and sixth centuries, while permitting
the local clergy to administer a portion of the oblations, insist
upon the bishop's right to administer the income from the landed
property of the parishes.[7] It should be observed, before dismiss-
ing this subject, that conditions were not uniform in all regions;
local custom played a large role in determining the relations
between the bishops and the rural churches of their dioceses.
Further, the real point at issue in this early legislation was
whether the revenues of the rural parishes should be applied
exclusively to the uses of the local church and its clergy or might,
at the bishop's discretion, be applied to the needs of other
churches in the diocese, including the cathedral. When any part
of parochial revenues was given over to the administration of
the local clergy, it was understood that such income was to be
spent within the parish and for the needs of the local church,
its poor, and its clergy. In the fifth and sixth centuries the
bishop's supreme jurisdiction over parochial property was un-

[6] Arnold Pöschl, *Bischofsgut und Mensa Episcopalis* (Bonn, 1908–
1912, 3 vols.), i, 19–23. For the views of an important medieval canonist,
see p. 142 of the present book.

[7] The legislation of the first council of Orleans (511) is important in
this connection: "In respect to the donations of land, vineyards, slaves,
and money which any of the faithful shall offer to the parishes, let the
decrees of the ancient canons be followed, that all shall be in the power of
the bishop; of the oblations made at the altar, however, a third shall be
faithfully carried to the bishop." *M.P.L.*, lxxxiv, col. 276 (c. 11), and
Hefele-Leclercq, *Histoire des conciles*, ii, pt. 2, 1012 (c. 14). The third
council of Orleans (538) made a distinction between the property of the
lesser urban churches (*basilicae in civitatibus*) and that of the rural parishes
(*parochiae vel basilicae in pagis civitatum*). Oblations made to the lesser
city churches should be at the disposal of the bishop, who would decide
the amount to be applied to the repair or service of the church in question;
but in respect to the property of the rural parishes, local custom should
be followed. *M.P.L.*, lxxxiv, col. 279; Hefele-Leclercq, ii, pt. 2, 1158 (c. 6).

questioned; church laws which seem to limit that jurisdiction merely forbid the bishop to divert parochial property to his own use or to that of churches other than those designated by the donors of parochial endowments.

A final solution of this problem is not required for the purposes of this narrative. Suffice it to point out that by the eighth century the rural parishes everywhere except in mission territories had acquired the right to receive donations of land and other property and that the endowment of each parish formed a separate complex of property independent from that of the bishopric and administered by the parochial clergy, subject of course to episcopal supervision.[8] The unitary patrimony had disappeared and with it the law of quadripartition. Where traces of the old fourfold division of church revenues still lingered, it was applied exclusively to the tithe. However, when the tithe itself was regulated by the Frankish capitularies, the rule was applied very differently. The division was no longer made by the bishop, except in the case of the cathedral; instead it was made in the parishes by the local clergy. Several capitularies commanded the parish priests to collect the tithes from the people, write down the names of the givers and the amounts, and then divide the product into four parts in the presence of witnesses. The bishop in such cases received a yearly accounting. A few capitularies prescribed a threefold division, the bishop being excluded, and this was the arrangement established in Italy by the capitulary of Mantua.[9] The tendency in the ninth century was to restrict the bishop's share in the income from parochial tithes; but this tendency did not affect the general law of the Church, for a letter from Pope Leo IV to the English episcopate

[8] On the parish churches as subjects of property, see Stutz, *Benefizial-wesen*, pp. 41–66; Imbart de la Tour, *Origines religieuses*, pp. 65–67; Feine, "Studien," iii, 64–67.

[9] *M.G.H., Cap.*, ii, 178 (c. 10). A capitulary of 802 prescribed a three-fold division. *Ibid.*, p. 106 (c. 7). Thomassin's account of the division of church revenues under Charlemagne and his successors is still useful. *Ancienne et nouvelle discipline de l'église*, vi, bk. 2, ch. 18.

affirmed that the tithe was to be paid only to baptismal churches and was there to be divided into the customary four parts.[10] The rule of quadripartition (or tripartition, according to the region) became a recognized tradition in regard to the tithe, never wholly obliterated by the abuses which developed in that institution at a somewhat later period.

At the opening of the ninth century, while the compulsory tithe was taking root in local habits, two rival systems of churches confronted each other in each Italian diocese. These were the episcopal system, consisting of the cathedral, the lesser urban churches, the baptisteries with their chapels, and churches on episcopal estates, and the lay proprietary system.[11] The proprietary principle had for some time been penetrating the episcopal structure, a process which can probably be traced back to the seventh century when the decline of Roman law in northern Italy caused the concept of jurisdiction to become blurred in men's minds and the word itself to disappear from their vocabularies.[12] We have already traced the assimilation of the parish churches to the status of episcopal *Eigenkirchen*. Granted that this assimilation lent itself to grave abuses in the hands of ambitious bishops, it must at the same time be conceded that the accentuation of episcopal proprietary control probably made the bishops fight all the more strenuously against lay appropriation of the tithe during the formative period of that institution.

The lay proprietary churches in Italy continued to increase in number after the establishment of Frankish rule. In 826 they were recognized as legitimate by the Roman synod of that year, which sanctioned the rights of lay proprietors over their

[10] The council of Paris in 829 forbade the bishop to take his share of parochial tithes unless his cathedral was poor. Mansi, *Concilia*, xiv, col. 559 (c. 31). Leo's letter is cited in Gratian's *Decretum*, C. xxv, q. 1, c. 45.

[11] Pöschl, *Bischofsgut und Mensa Episcopalis*, i, 10–48, analyzes the economic and legal relationships of these churches.

[12] The history of the word *jurisdictio* is traced by N. Hilling, "Die Bedeutung der iurisdictio voluntaria und involuntaria im römischen Recht des Mittelalters und der Neuzeit," *AKKR*, vol. 105 (1925), 449–473.

churches, provided that the clergy of such churches were canonically installed by the bishops.[13] It was a peculiarity of Italian
development, however, that the tithe remained the exclusive
appurtenance of the episcopal system of churches.[14] This issue
was fought out in the ninth century, and in the collision between
the two systems, lay and episcopal, the imperial power seems to
have favored the lay proprietors to the extent of permitting them
to pay the tithes of their own demesnes to their private chapels.
In the capitulary of Olonna, Emperor Lothair went further and
conceded that a private person who built a church on his domain with the consent of the diocesan bishop and had a baptismal font also consecrated by the bishop, might have the sacrament of baptism performed in the church.[15] But the Italian
bishops opposed such practices. Another capitulary, issued either
by Lothair or by Lewis the Pious, aimed at striking a compromise:

As for the tithe, in regard to which we have already heard many
arguments between the bishops and the rest of the clergy on the
one hand, and our vassals and other subjects on the other, we decree and grant that if a layman has a church on his domain he may
pay the tithe of his demesne lands to that church and the priest of
the church shall dispense it for the maintenance of the edifice and
for alms. But as for the tenants of the domain, we decree that they
shall pay their tithes to the baptismal church within whose parish
they live; and if they refuse to do so, they shall be compelled by the
public authorities, as we have ordained in our capitulary.[16]

But the Lombard bishops assembled at Pavia about the middle
of the ninth century appealed to Lewis II to correct the very
practices which the earlier measure had sanctioned:

[13] *M.G.H.*, *Cap.*, i, 374 (c. 21).
[14] Stutz, *Benefizialwesen*, pp. 126–132.
[15] *M.G.H.*, *Cap.*, i, 316 (c. 2).
[16] *Ibid.*, i, 336 (c. 8). The phrase "in our capitulary" is thought by
Boretius to refer to Chap. 9 of the *capitula missorum* of 832 (*ibid.*, ii,
64), a date which would harmonize with the conciliatory tendencies
towards the private churches manifested by the Roman synod of 826.

In the sacred canons it is ordained that the tithes shall be distributed as the bishop directs. Some laymen, however, who have chapels on their domains or in their benefices, defying the decree of the bishop, give their tithes, not to the churches where they receive baptism, instruction, confirmation, and the other Christian sacraments, but to their own chapels and clerics according to their caprice. This practice is known to be in every way contrary to divine law and the sacred canons, wherefore we beseech Your Majesty to punish these evildoers.[17]

Later synods made similar provisions, and at the end of the century Lambert's capitulary commanded all tithes to be paid to the bishop or his delegates and the chapels of recalcitrant land-owners to be demolished.[18]

These affirmations of the law favored by the Church were successful in establishing the exclusive right of the baptismal churches of Italy to the tithe. By the end of the ninth century the tithe was recognized as the adjunct of the baptismal font, and any derogations from this rule were known to be exceptions. At the same time, with the collapse of the Carolingian Empire and the agencies by which its legislation was enforced, the tithe entered into the complex of customary usages that made up the effective local law of the rural communities. By that time disputes regarding the tithe were determined, not with reference to the capitularies or to canon law, but solely on the basis of established local custom. This fact is illustrated by a lawsuit submitted to the bishop of Lucca in 892, when the archpriest of the baptistery of San Macario accused the archpriest of Arliano of usurping the tithes and offerings owed him by the inhabitants of eight villages. Sentence was rendered in favor of the plaintiff when witnesses testified that for forty years the *custom of the district* had been to pay tithe to San Macario.[19]

[17] *M.G.H., Cap.*, ii, 82–83 (c. 11).
[18] Synod of Milan, 864: *ACN*, doc. 9; Synod of Ravenna, 877: Mansi, *Concilia*, xvii, 340; Lambert's capitulary: *M.G.H., Cap.*, ii, 110.
[19] *MD*, iv, pt. 2, doc. 48.

Several derogations from the general custom governing the tithe remain to be noted. The bishops exercised considerable latitude in bestowing the tithes of the episcopal manors; usually they granted them to the cathedral chapters. Occasionally, too, they authorized the tenants on such manors to pay their tithes to the manorial churches instead of to the baptismal churches to which they were canonically due. If these churches were later given as benefices to laymen or to clerics in minor orders, according to the customs growing up in the ninth century, the tithe went with the church. Thus in 862 the bishop of Lucca gave to an acolyte the manorial church of Monticello together with the tithes of the manor; and in 897 a later bishop rewarded a notary for his services by granting him the tithes and other revenues of the same church, permitting him, furthermore, to lease the church itself to a third person of undesignated status, who may have been a priest.[20] Such documents disclose the germination of abuses which later denatured the entire system of tithes.

More important was the assignment of tithes to the manors of the royal or imperial fisc. The capitulary *De villis,* issued either by Charlemagne or Lewis the Pious, had assigned the tithes of royal property to the churches in the villas of the fisc.[21] There is no proof that this capitulary was in any way aimed at Italy, and some evidence has been adduced that it was intended only for Aquitaine,[22] but the practice which it sanctioned seems to have been followed in the Lombard kingdom of the Frankish kings. The churches on the imperial manors in northern Italy possessed tithes, which in some cases were their sole revenues. Thus the imperial *missi dominici* who around 835 inspected the manor of Lemonta, near Milan, then held as a benefice by an imperial vassal, found that the manorial chapel had no other

[20] *Ibid.,* v, pt. 2, docs. 917, 1006.

[21] *M.G.H., Cap.,* i, 83 (c. 6).

[22] Walther von Wartburg, "The Localization of the Capitulary de Villis," *Speculum,* xv (1940), 86–91, submits evidence favoring Aquitaine as the source of the capitulary.

income than the tithe.[23] Since royal manors were most numerous
in Lombardy and Piedmont, it is not surprising that in those
regions, unlike Tuscany, the tithe even at a later period was
often the adjunct of a manorial church. It has been estimated
that from 887 to 962, when the crown lands in Lombardy and
Piedmont were at their greatest extent, they included more than
forty-one per cent of the land of those provinces.[24] With the dis-
solution of the royal fisc, these manors with their churches and
tithes passed in large numbers to bishoprics, monasteries, or lay
proprietors, but the tithe was by that time secured by custom to
the manorial church and continued to be paid to it after the
estate itself had ceased to be under royal ownership.

A third and less important derogation from general practice
occurred in connection with monasteries. Both monasteries and
episcopal domains came under the common law of tithes, i.e.,
they were commanded to pay tithe to the baptismal churches
of their districts. But the custom grew up at an early period, certainly before the end of the eighth century, of reserving to the
service of the monastic hospice the tithes of the monks' demesne
(*indominicatum*) and of some of the villas owned by the monastery. This custom was introduced by the council of Aix into
the rule for canons which it imposed upon cathedral chapters and
collegiate churches. By the opening of the tenth century it had
become a general custom in the archdiocese of Milan, and perhaps in the Lombard kingdom as a whole, that the tithes of
monastic demesne lands should be exempt from the jurisdiction
of bishops or rural archpriests and be applied to the expenses
of hospitality and almsgiving.[25]

[23] Giulini, *Memorie di Milano*, vii, 7–8. This manor had a *familia* of
thirty.

[24] Paul Darmstädter, *Das Reichsgut in der Lombardei und Piemont*
(Strassburg, 1896), pp. 4–5, lists 100 royal villas in Lombardy, 105 in
Piedmont.

[25] This appears from the diploma granted by Berengar I in 903 to the
monastery of San Salvator of Tolla: ". . . quia sic prenominatae Ambrosianae ecclesiae cenobia peragere comperimus." Schiaparelli (ed.),
I diplomi di Berengario I (Rome, 1903), doc. 38.

The law which gave the tithe to baptismal churches conferred the tithes of the city dwellers upon the cathedrals, which
in almost all Italian cities were the only churches empowered
to baptize. In the course of the ninth century most of the urban
tithes were granted by the bishops to their cathedral chapters
as part of the disciplinary reform sponsored by the council of
Aix. Bishops in sympathy with this reform tried to reestablish
among their cathedral clergy the practices of the canonical life,
believed to have been followed in the primitive Church; and in
order to provide the clergy with the necessary revenues for the
new observance, they assigned to their chapters, in many instances reorganized under the rule for canons promulgated at
Aix, lands, churches, and revenues detached from the episcopal
patrimony and set up as a separate endowment called the capitular *mensa,* or table.[26] As a result of this movement, the endowment of a cathedral chapter was usually composed of the
following elements, in varying proportions:

1. Landed property
2. Rents, often in kind, from specified episcopal manors
3. Oblations
4. The tithes of the city
5. The tithes of the suburbs
6. The tithes of specified episcopal manors
7. Churches, some of them parishes, and their revenues

[26] Pöschl's *Bischofsgut und Mensa Episcopalis,* vol. ii, is the fullest
account of this movement. Emile Lesne's brief study, *Les origines des
menses dans le temporel des églises et des monastères de France au ixᵉ
siècle* (*Lille,* 1910), has a somewhat different emphasis.

The organization of separate capitular *mensae* in Italian cathedrals,
sometimes in conjunction with the introduction of the canonical life, is
illustrated by the following documents, all including grants of tithes:
Asti, 899: *Antiche Carte di Asti,* doc. 30; Bergamo, 897: Lupi, *CDB,* i,
1059–1060; Como, 803: Porro-Lambertenghi, *CDL,* doc. 77; Cremona,
879: *ibid.,* doc. 475; Milan, 864: *ibid.,* doc. 389; Novara, 840: *ACN,* doc.
6. Piacenza, 883: Campi, i, doc. 26; *Reggio,* 857: *Le carte degli archivi
reggiani fino al 1050,* ed. P. Torelli (Reggio-Emilia, 1921), doc. 12;
Verona, 813: *Cod. dip. veronese,* docs. 101, 102.

Obviously tithes constituted an important part of the normal endowment of a cathedral chapter. Sometimes a bishop reserved a fourth of the urban tithes for his own use but more commonly he gave all the tithes of the city to his chapter. Tithes given to a chapter from an episcopal manor were usually deflected from a rural parish. Italian bishops seem to have had no such limitation on their power as that established by the capitulary of Pitres for France, where the parish priest had a right to at least a minimum of the tithes from episcopal manors.[27]

Some of these capitular endowments included parish churches. For example, in 883 a bishop of Piacenza granted three baptismal churches to his cathedral chapter; and his successor added a fourth, evidently a large church, since it was itself officiated by canons.[28] This practice marks the growth of a clerical proprietary regime side by side with the lay proprietary system; for in respect to legal status an impropriated church was a private church, whether controlled by a cleric or a layman.[29]

By the ninth century, when the canonical reform was carried

[27] The capitulary of Pitres assigned to the cathedral the tithes of episcopal demesne lands and of certain tenures, but gave the parish priest the right to the tithes from hereditary holdings: "De terris censualibus et potestate ecclesiae suae et culturis indominicatis et absitatibus et manufirmatis major ecclesia quae caput episcopatus est decimam recipiat: similiter de carruca indominicata. De mansis hereditatibus presbyter parroaechiae, sicut constitutum est, decimam consequatur." *M.G.H., Cap.,* ii, 336–337. Lesne expresses the opinion that the phrase *de potestate ecclesiae suae* refers to the property of the rural parishes, which has been assimilated to that of the proprietary cathedral church. "La dîme des biens ecclésiastiques," *RHE,* xiv (1913), 492, n. 2.

[28] Campi, i, doc. 26 (pp. 470–471) and doc. 34 (p. 475). The practice of impropriation continued in the tenth century. Asti, 907: *Antiche Carte di Asti,* doc. 37; Florence, 964: *CCF,* doc. 14; Tortona, ca. 945: *ACT,* doc. 3.

[29] Stutz discerned that impropriation, which gave rise to the vicarage system, "was in reality the perpetuation of the essential features of *Eigenkirchentum* under another name." Quoted by David Knowles, *The Monastic Order in England* (Cambridge, 1940), pp. 567–568. Madeleine Dillay also came to this conclusion in "Régime de l'église privée," pp. 260–261.

out in the cathedrals, changed economic conditions had made
the rule of quadripartition clearly inapplicable. The rule had
originated in a period of money economy. By the ninth century
church property consisted mostly of land dispersed throughout
the countryside, and church revenues were made up in large
part of agricultural produce and services. Circumstances called
for a decentralized administration, and the law of quadripartition had already disappeared with the passing of the unitary
patrimony. However, some reforming bishops, in reorganizing
the property of their sees, recognized the continuing validity of
the rule, and some tried to execute it literally.[30] But usually
various expedients were adopted to avoid the awkwardness of
a literal application; some bishops assigned specific lands and
tithes to their chapters in lieu of the clerical fourth of cathedral
income due to them under the rule. Thus the concession of lands
and tithes to the Veronese chapter by Bishop Ratold in 813 was
expressly stated to be a substitute for the clerical fourth.[31]

In the ninth century, generally speaking, references to the
rule of quadripartition, except in regard to the tithe, were purely
academic. In the practical administration of church revenues
the rule had necessarily been abandoned in cathedrals and rural
churches alike. Nevertheless it remained in the minds of the
more enlightened ecclesiastical administrators as an uneasy
recollection of an earlier period in the history of the Church,
when the unity of the diocese had not been broken by the
proprietary system and the conceptions of public law and
jurisdiction still prevailed.

[30] As in the Modenese diploma published by Schiaparelli, *I diplomi di
Ugo e di Lotario* (Rome, 1924), doc. 36: ". . . quartam portionem de
omnibus rebus ad supradictam sedem pertinentibus. . . ."

[31] *Cod. dip. veronese,* doc. 102 (p. 130).

CHAPTER V

Subjection of the Parishes

† THE COLLAPSE of the Carolingian Empire in the last quarter of the ninth century was followed by a series of attempts to set up an independent kingdom in Italy. These ephemeral kingdoms were built upon the Lombard bishoprics, and most of the Italian kings owed their brief triumphs to alliances with the episcopate. The Lombard bishops, having gained control of the cities at the expense of the Carolingian counts, dominated the political scene in Italy and made and unmade kings at their liking. Eventually they joined with the papacy in inviting the German king, Otto I, to come to Italy. After the establishment of the Ottonian imperial dynasty in 962, the secular activities of the bishops continued to increase. Otto I confirmed the bishops in their political powers, and both he and his successors relied upon the episcopate as an instrument, if not the chief instrument, of their rule in Italy. Under these circumstances it is not strange that the political and official character of the episcopate was emphasized. With the growth of feudalism, stress was laid upon the feudal bond uniting emperor and episcopate; the bishops became the vassals of the emperors for their lands, bound by feudal obligations and owing military service. All this, of course, happened gradually, and the process was not completed until the eleventh century.[1]

[1] Silvio Pivano, *Stato e chiesa in Italia da Berengario ad Arduino*

The military activities of the Italian episcopate in the tenth century are vividly portrayed in the *Antapodosis* of Liutprand of Cremona and in other literature of the time. In Milan the archbishop's vassals formed a "militia of Saint Ambrose" which accompanied the archbishop on military expeditions and on ceremonial occasions.[2] Such troops were useful to the imperial government and were often commanded by the bishops in person. There were among the clergy a few conscientious objectors, such as Bishop Rathier of Verona,[3] but most of the bishops seem to have borne their feudal bondage cheerfully enough. Most of them of course were related to the lay nobility and shared the habits and outlook of that class; many of them in the second half of the tenth century were Germans who regarded themselves as primarily imperial officials.[4]

The episcopal vassals were recruited from a social group which first emerged into the full light of history in the tenth century, the *milites*, or knights, who from obscure origins now developed into a hereditary feudal aristocracy. As the central power decayed in the ninth century, the authority of the Carolingian counts in the cities passed to the bishops, while the rural districts were given over to the depredations or the protection, as the case might be, of various local magnates, often loosely organized in clans and entrenched in rude fortified strongholds.

(Turin, 1908) throws light upon political movements in the "age of the Italian kings." The economic aspects of the growth of feudalism are discussed by Gino Luzzatto, *Storia economica d'Italia*, i, pt. 2, *Il Medioevo* (Rome, 1949), pp. 175–186, 209–214, while Salvioli, *Storia del diritto italiano* (9th ed., Turin, 1930), pp. 292–296, 197–217, sketches the highlights of its development as a legal system. For a good discussion of the relations between the German emperors and the Italian feudality, see Geoffrey Barraclough, *The Origins of Modern Germany* (Oxford, 1947), pp. 57–64.

[2] G. Biscaro, "I maggiori dei Visconti," *ASL,* Fourth Series, xvi (1911), 26–27.

[3] *De contemptu canonum,* in *M.P.L.*, vol. 136, col. 500.

[4] L. M. Hartmann, *Geschichte Italiens*, iii, pt. 2, 248; Pöschl, *Bischofsgut und Mensa Episcopalis,* iii, pt. 1, 187.

The men who now rose to power in the countryside seem to have been distinct from the great benefice-holders of the Carolingian period, and few of their descendants attained the position of high feudatories in the fully formed feudal regime of the eleventh century. Employing a French analogy, they might be compared to the petty feudatories of the French royal domain as contrasted with the holders of the great French fiefs. They seem to have been at first a highly mixed group, with no single social or economic status, and certainly without a common ethnic origin, although many were undoubtedly descended from Lombard or Frankish progenitors. The two generations of anarchy following the downfall of the Carolingian dynasty and the disappearance of an effective central government after 888, enabled them to establish their supremacy over the countryside. In the tenth century and far into the eleventh the knights formed a turbulent and anarchical element in Italian society, always antagonistic to a strong central power, whether that of king, emperor, or upper feudatories, sometimes in alliance with the bishops, at other times bitterly opposed to them, always unreliable and unpredictable. This class by its very nature could never pursue a unified policy, nor indeed did it actually form at any time a conscious and unified group. Differences of economic and social status developed within the class, and this chapter will suggest one of the ways in which some of the knights and their families achieved a more privileged position than others.

It was inevitable that in their rise to power the knights should covet the ecclesiastical property dispersed throughout the countryside. At first they strove to gain control of church lands by intimidating the lower clergy; then some of them entered into an open alliance with the episcopate, many of them becoming episcopal vassals in return for the right to exploit the property of the Church in their respective districts. The bishops were thus enabled to play an active political role and after 962 to meet their military obligations to the Empire, while the eco-

nomic and moral position of the *milites* was enormously strengthened.

The relations between the rising rural nobility and the parish churches can be traced in detail only for the bishopric of Lucca. But documents from other Tuscan bishoprics prove that the resulting feudalization of the rural parishes was a general phenomenon. That the same process occurred in Lombardy is attested by later evidence.

In Lucca the absorption of the rural parishes into the nascent feudalism began in the second half of the ninth century and happened in at least two different ways. The capitulary of Lambert in 898, read in conjunction with a Lucchese inventory of the same general period, shows that the Italian bishops were already ceding parishes as benefices to their vassals or to other laymen and that in Lucca at least nineteen parish churches had been so conceded. When a parish church was ceded to a layman in this way, the beneficiary took the rents and services owed by the tenants of the parochial lands and received in addition the not inconsiderable rent due from the rector to the bishop, while the latter collected the tithes and other spiritual revenues of the parish as well as any other income set aside for him by special arrangement.[5] The bishop appointed the priest as of old, but the rent for the parish went to the benefice-holder. It is obvious that the benefice-holder must have rendered services to the bishop, and we may surmise that some benefice-holders performed military service, although it is by no means clear when this practice began.

Concurrently with the cessions of parish churches as bene-

[5] In some documents the priest or layman to whom the church has been leased promises to bring the rent for the church either to the bishop's court in Lucca or to the person who has received the church as a benefice from the bishop. *MD*, v, pt. 2, doc. 1006. That the tithes still remained to the priests until late in the tenth century may be deduced from the fact that numerous documents show the priests leasing tithes to laymen. The intricate subject of the leasing of churches is analyzed thoroughly by H. E. Feine, "Studien," iii, "Die Kirchleihe," pp. 64–190.

fices by the bishops, the parish priests themselves were leasing the lands of their churches to the large landowners of their districts instead of parceling them out in small allotments among peasant cultivators. This practice was by no means confined to Lucca, where it was condemned as an abuse by Bishop Peter II. It was frowned upon by the imperial government and by the upper feudatories.[6]

As the tenth century wore on, all these trends were accentuated and the rural parishes were almost completely engulfed in the feudal regime that was forming in the Italian countryside. Parish priests leased to the knights not only the lands of the churches but also the subordinate chapels and the tithes. The first record of the alienation of parochial property of this kind is a charter of 913, in which the parish priest of Bargi leases to a layman *livellario nomine* a fourth of one of the chapels subject to his baptistery in return for a yearly rent of 90 *denarii* with which to buy a horse and a fat pig for the bishop of Lucca.[7] Soon the parish priests were making more extensive alienations; in 926 the priest of Gurgite leased all the oblations of his church and the tithes of twelve villages for a rent of twelve shillings; and in 936 the priest of Cerbaria leased all the lands of his baptistery and its titularies for eight shillings and the tithes of five villages for seven shillings.[8] Similar alienations were made by other parish priests, usually of all the lands and tithes of their churches.[9]

It appears from these documents that the rectors were profit-

[6] Peter II (897–931) fought in vain against the abuses already rampant in the Lucchese parishes. That church property was going mostly to the lower feudality helps to explain the hostility of the imperial government and the greater feudatories to the break-up of the ecclesiastical patrimony.

[7] *MD*, v, pt. 3, doc. 1146. Tenth-century acts of investiture mention no rent paid to the bishop by the parish priests, but it is probable that such a rent was paid, since in many leases of parochial lands given by the priests to their tenants the rents are paid directly to the bishop's court in Lucca. On this point consult R. Endres, "Das Kirchengut im Bistum Lucca," p. 256, n. 48. Dues in kind, as in this document, were unusual.

[8] *MD*, v, pt. 3, docs. 1210, 1241, 1242.   [9] See Appendix II.

ing by the independence given them by the contract in unrestricted *livello* to alienate their churches for a sizable money rent. With the church went all or part of its landed property and tithes. In some cases the parish priest was probably helpless in the face of the predatory knights. Some priests yielded to the pressure of poverty. But in other instances, the priest, after leasing his lands and tithes to a layman, lived in idleness on the income from the church, while the church itself was served by a hired priest or cleric on a meager stipend from the lay patron. In still other cases, the rector stayed on and performed religious services for a salary.[10]

Until approximately the last third of the tenth century these concessions to laymen of parish churches and tithes in Lucca seem to have been made principally by the parish priests. But shortly after the establishment of German supremacy in Italy and perhaps as a result of it, the bishops of Lucca began leasing their rural parishes directly to laymen. Frequently, as parishes fell vacant, the bishops leased the churches and their property to the local magnates in return for a money rent, sometimes reserving a portion of the property of the parish for the support of a priest, but usually, so far as the documents reveal, making no such provision. Presumably in such cases the magnate who held the church was expected to hire a priest. The tenure employed by the bishops in these transactions was the unrestricted *livello*. The contracts say nothing about military service, and the *livello* of course was not a feudal tenure. There is no way of telling from the text of a document whether the layman who held a parish church was *ipso facto* a vassal of the bishop. Such concessions were regarded by later generations as having established feudal relationships; [11] but in the tenth century Italian

---

[10] Barsocchini, *Dissertazioni,* p. 147. Cf. Albert Dresdner, *Kultur- und Sittengeschichte der italienischen Geistlichkeit im 10. und 11. Jahrhunderten* (Breslau, 1890), pp. 358–362.

[11] This is clear from documents of the twelfth and thirteenth centuries referring to these contracts, as well as from notarial inscriptions on the backs of the original parchments, which designate the leases as fiefs.

feudalism was still in a formative stage and it would probably be inaccurate to designate these holdings of parochial property and tithes as fiefs. At the same time it is clear that the rural parishes of Lucca were being feudalized in the sense that they were falling under the control of those families of the Lucchese contado who were acquiring seigniorial powers in their districts.

Judging by Lucchese records, the absorption of the rural parishes into feudalism was complete by the end of the tenth century. This process, once under way, was consummated very rapidly. A list of episcopal leases of parishes during the last three decades of the tenth century is printed in an Appendix.[12] More impressive than any generalization are the fifty-one concessions, affecting thirty-one parishes, whereby the parish churches with their lands and tithes were handed over to the exploitation of laymen. Some of these leases give the church and all its appurtenances to the beneficiary; others, slightly more numerous, include a fraction of the church and its revenues, always a multiple of a fourth, or designate those villages from which the tithes are to be taken; still others are grants of tithes or lands detached from the total complex of parochial property. It is significant that when a fraction of a church is conceded, it is always a fourth, a half, or three-fourths, indicating the persistence of traditional ideas and practices concerning the fourfold division of church revenues.

Precisely what rights went with the possession of a parish church? To answer this question, we need to remember that the lands of a parish church were organized somewhat after the fashion of a small estate or manor and that some of the larger baptismal churches seem to have exercised court jurisdiction over their tenants. The layman, therefore, to whom a parish church was conceded, stepped into the place of the priest as a landlord; he collected the rent from the tenants of parochial lands and took the customary dues and services. Did he also

[12] Appendix II, pp. 256–259.

exercise some measure of seigniorial jurisdiction over them? It is noteworthy that in the oath which the tenants of the Lucchese parishes took to the bishop during his administration of the property of vacant parishes, they promised not only to reside on their holdings and to cultivate them in person, but also to attend the bishop's court.[13] This seems to indicate that the grant of a parish church carried with it in at least some instances the right of exercising petty patrimonial jurisdiction.[14]

It is also interesting to compare the rentals of these Lucchese *pievi* with those of manors in the same bishopric. In 983 a manor near Capannule, consisting of a demesne and twenty-two peasant holdings, commanded a rent of fifteen shillings; the manor of Vigesimo, with a demesne and ten dependent allotments, brought in a rent of eleven shillings; while a third, the estate of Sugrominio, with thirteen holdings, rented for seven shillings.[15] It would appear that the rental value of one of the larger baptismal churches was considerably higher than that of a manor of moderate size. This difference cannot be explained with reference to the landed properties of the baptismal churches, which were usually not extensive. The value of a parish church was derived from its right to collect the tithes of its district.

When a parish church was ceded to a local knight or to several members of the same clan, provision was sometimes made for the spiritual service of the church by reserving specific portions of the land of the parish for a priest. In a lease of the *pieve* of Loppia in 983, a member of the Rolandinghi clan states that the priest's house and several dependent tenures are ex-

[13] *MD*, v, pt. 3, docs. 1074, 1092, 1143, 1169. The full formula appears in doc. 1092, in which the tenants promise to come if necessary to the bishop's court in Lucca *pro justitia faciendum*.

[14] Gioacchino Volpe, *Studi sulle istituzioni communali a Pisa* (Pisa, 1902), p. 26, n. 3, points out that the formula does not appear when the land is rented to the feudatories (*cattanei*) who do not cultivate it themselves.

[15] *MD*, v, pt. 3, docs. 1527, 1569, 1570.

empted from the grant.[16] A similar reservation was made in connection with a lease of half the parish church of Flesso in 980, but a grant of another portion of the same church three years later included the priest's share also.[17] When the whole parish was conceded to a layman, he had to employ a priest to perform divine services; most of the contracts stipulate that these services must be held and the sacraments duly administered. When merely a part of a parish was ceded, the remainder of the lands and tithes went to the priest. For a complete picture of the fate of the Lucchese parishes in this period, the leases of parish churches to laymen must be supplemented by other records containing the appointments by the bishops of priests in the parishes and confirming the evidence of the leases that priests were often invested with only a part of the revenues of their churches. A document of 975 shows the priest of Cappiano being invested with a fourth of the baptismal church of that place; and in another, of 984, the bishop of Lucca confers half the baptismal church of San Pantaleone upon a rector.[18] It is impossible to compile complete statistics for any one church. On the basis of our fragmentary evidence we may assume that the fractions of the land and tithes of a church that were not included in the investiture of the priest were surrendered to the more powerful lay families of the district.

By the end of the tenth century, as a result of these practices, most of the parish churches of Lucca had been absorbed into a network of private and personal relationships. But even in this dark period the exclusive right of the baptisteries to the tithe was never challenged. In only two or three instances do the abundant Lucchese documents contain examples of the payment of the tithe to a nonbaptismal church or of its detachment from its *pieve*. There are many cessions both to laymen and

---

[16] *Ibid.*, doc. 1538. [17] *Ibid.*, docs. 1515, 1563.
[18] *Ibid.*, doc. 1462, and Muratori, *Antiquitates*, vi, 427–432. Other examples of the same practice: *MD*, iv, pt. 2, docs. 70, 74; v, pt. 3, docs. 1496, 1644.

ecclesiastics of churches other than baptisteries, but the tithe
never accompanies them. Only very exceptionally were tithes
separated from the baptismal churches and made the objects
of special grants.[19] This fact, together with the consistent division of parochial property into fourths, shows that the memory
of ancient church law was not entirely obliterated even by the
triumph of feudalism in Italy.

The social implications of the preceding narrative are impressive. They need to be developed by further research and
reflection, but some tentative conclusions may be stated here.
Episcopal concessions of parishes as benefices to vassals late
in the ninth century and the leasing of parochial lands and tithes
to laymen by parish priests, which began in Lucca somewhat
later, illustrate the growth of Italian feudalism and at the same
time show how the great agglomerations of property built up by
the Church in the preceding period were broken up as a result
of the impact with land-hungry *milites*. The growth of lay
feudalism in the Italian countryside spelled the end of the great
ecclesiastical estates. More vividly than any other documents,
the Lucchese leases of rural parishes show how the countryside
of each Italian town was given over to the predatory activities
of the knights. In the abeyance of a strong central power, individuals and clans fought with one another to impose their
supremacy upon their respective districts. Upon their supremacy
depended their survival; for these Italian knights followed the
Lombard law prescribing equal division of inheritances, and
their phenomenal multiplication tended to reduce their sons
rapidly to poverty. Italian feudalism on the lower levels occupied by the *milites* was always weak, tending to the formation
of splinter fiefs, because property under the Lombard law was

---

[19] The tithes of two villages were transferred from a baptistery to one
of its chapels. *MD*, v, pt. 3, doc. 1188. Cf. docs. 1487, 1536. A few grants
of tithes were made to laymen without mention of any church. *Ibid.*, docs.
1651, 1747, 1567.

not held together by the device of primogeniture. To those who were strong and ruthless enough to bring pressure upon the parish priests or could offer valuable services to the bishops, the church property scattered through the countryside offered itself as a tempting prize. In some cases also, the parish priests and their people may have preferred the protection of a local magnate to that of a distant sovereign or of a bishop immersed in political affairs. Whatever the human motivation behind the process, early in the tenth century some families already towered above others in the rural scene; they were the families which had secured economic control of the parish churches. In Lucca, the clans of the Rolandinghi and Corvaresi, the lords of Vaccoli, Montemagno, and Ripafratta, to mention only a few of the feudatories who waged incessant war with the commune at a later period, all traced their descent from men mentioned in tenth-century documents as recipients of parochial lands and tithes; in fact, with but few exceptions, all the families of the Lucchese contado, who later constituted the *nobiles* so hated by the burghers, first appeared in history in the documents which we have just surveyed.[20] It is evident that the acquisition of parish churches and tithes marked their accession to power. Moreover, it is possible that the very acquisition of the tithe, by giving the knights the right to tax the peasants of their localities, actually helped them to reduce some of the free peasantry to the status of dependents.[21] It has been suggested that the establishment by some knights of the right to tithe the inhabitants of their districts enabled them in course of time to annex other seigniorial rights which did not originally pertain to them.

A further step was taken in the last decades of the tenth cen-

[20] This fact was established by the old but still useful work of A. N. Cianelli, "De conti rurali nello stato Lucchese," *MD*, iii (1816), 81–245.

[21] Cf. the discerning comment of Imbart de la Tour, *Origines religieuses*, pp. 281–282: "The history of the parishes thus serves to explain to us one of the economic origins of feudalism: the concentration of property, the establishment of seigniorial jurisdiction."

tury, when the power of these *milites* over the rural parishes was
sanctioned by the bishops. This consolidation of ecclesiastical
feudalism increased the power of the knights over the rural
population. The possession of a parish church by a knight or clan
made the possessor responsible for the spiritual life of the rural
communities which depended upon the church for the sacraments. With the assimilation of many parishes to the status of
episcopal proprietary churches in the eighth and ninth centuries,
the parish churches had ceased in most cases to be the public
churches of the communities which they served; but they had at
least remained the bishops' churches, part of a great ecclesiastical system which preserved some remnants of the conceptions
of public law. Now they became the lords' churches or the fa-
milial churches of clans which collected their tithes and provided
for their services. Clearly, the acquisition of parish churches by
the knights not only marked the coming of age of Italian feudalism, it also put the seal upon the supremacy of some feudal families by elevating them above the other members of their own
class. The heads of these families became known eventually as
capitanei, or *cattanei,* and constituted a kind of upper stratum
among the lesser feudatories, who did not as a rule hold their
fiefs directly from the sovereign.[22]

The development which can be traced so fully for Lucca occurred in other parts of the Lombardo-Tuscan territory. Episcopal appointments of parish priests in the diocese of Pisa in the
tenth century often conceded to the priest the right of leasing
to others the lands, tithes, and oblations of his parish.[23] In Pisa,
too, around the middle of the century, the bishops were leasing

[22] The term *capitanei,* of which *cattanei* is obviously a corruption,
seems to have meant originally one who held his fief directly from the
ruler (*in capite*). But in Italy, probably in the course of the eleventh century, it also came to mean the more important among the episcopal vassals
and large allodial proprietors.

[23] *Regesto di Pisa,* docs. 38, 40, 43. The leasing of churches in unrestricted *livello* is mentioned even earlier in Pisan documents than in
the Lucchese. *Ibid.,* docs. 22, 28. Cf. *Regestum Volaterranum,* ed. Fedor
Schneider (Rome, 1907), doc. 29.

the lands and tithes of their parishes to the local aristocracy,[24] and about 970, at precisely the same moment as their colleagues in Lucca, the bishops of Pisa began ceding their parishes directly to the lay nobility.[25]

In Lombardy one has to wait until the eleventh century for direct documentary examples of these practices; at last, in 1006 we find the bishop of Novara leasing for twenty-nine years half the lands of the parish of Anzola in return for a money rent.[26] Our most important information as regards Lombardy comes from two Milanese chroniclers, Arnulf and Landulf the Elder. Both date the disintegration of the ecclesiastical patrimony of Milan from the pontificate of Archbishop Landulf (979–998), who "distributed the property of the Church and gave many clerical benefices to the knights" [27] and who, by ceding to some of the city nobles in 983 numerous parishes, benefices, and hospices formerly held by the cathedral chapter and urban clergy, "exalted all the greater knights by giving them baptismal churches, unjustly depriving the clergy of their churches by means of these detestable investitures." [28] The adoption of this policy by Archbishop Landulf, in an effort to steer his way amid the maze of factional strife which then prevailed at Milan, coincided exactly in point of time with the Lucchese and Pisan documents which we have described above. This coincidence offers food for thought.

It is well known that the years after 983 were marked by unrest on the part of the lesser nobility, whose excesses provoked a reaction under Otto III.[29] The political struggles of this period

[24] *Regesto di Pisa,* docs. 44, 50.

[25] *Ibid.,* docs. 60, 62 (970, 975). These practices were by no means confined to the Lombardo-Tuscan territory. See the concessions of baptismal churches in *livello* by the archbishop of Canosa, *Codice diplomatico barese,* i, docs. 7, 12. Concessions of this kind in the South were more often made in *enfiteusi,* as in *Codex Diplomaticus Cavensis,* i, doc. 169.

[26] *ACN,* doc. 119.

[27] Arnulf, *Gesta Archiepiscoporum Mediolanensium, M.G.H., Scriptores,* viii, 9.   [28] Landulf the Elder, *Historia Mediolanensis, ibid.,* p. 55.

[29] Barraclough, *Origins of Modern Germany,* p. 63.

may never be fully understood. Of one result of the struggles, however, we may be reasonably sure: namely, the emergence from the ranks of the lower feudality of a privileged group, the "greater knights," as Landulf the Elder calls them, who formed an alliance with the bishops and as part of their pact secured domination of the baptismal churches.

In the fully developed feudal law of the twelfth and thirteenth centuries, formulated when feudalism as a political institution was already decadent, the feudal classes were organized in a hierarchical structure, distinguished by various gradations. At the apex of the structure were the high feudatories who held their fiefs directly from the emperor; next came the *capitanei*, vassals of bishops and great lay magnates; then followed the valvassors, to whom the *capitanei* had subinfeudated their fiefs; and in Milan from the twelfth century still a fourth class was recognized—the *valvassini*, or *milites*, at the bottom of the feudal structure. But these distinctions had not existed in the formative period of feudalism, and even in the twelfth and thirteenth centuries the name *milites* continued to be used loosely in the generic sense to indicate all the feudatories save the very highest, that is, the bishops, the great marchional houses of northern and central Italy, and a few direct vassals of the Emperor. In the period with which we are now concerned, some of the more powerful *milites* secured concessions of baptismal churches with all the prerogatives attached thereto, which they soon converted into hereditary fiefs.

A redaction of feudal customs drawn up in Milan during the first half of the twelfth century, the *Consuetudines Feudorum*, preserves the memory, possibly somewhat distorted, of this early investiture of some of the feudatories with the lands and tithes of the parishes, and indicates the manner in which the "fief of the tithe," as it was called in a later period, helped to create an upper stratum among the feudal classes. After defining a duke as one who has been granted a duchy by the sovereign, a marquis as the holder of a march, and a count as the ruler of a county, the writer

then goes on: "He who, either by the prince or by another authority has been invested with a baptismal district or part of such a district as a fief, is called a *capitaneus,* though more properly in the olden days he was called a greater valvassor." [30] Turning to the abundant records of the Milanese contado for the twelfth and thirteenth centuries in quest of aid in interpreting this passage, we find ample confirmation of Biscaro's view that in the tenth century the archbishops conciliated the more power-

[30] "Qui vero a principe vel ab aliqua potestate de plebe aliqua vel plebis parte per feudum investitus est, is capitaneus appellatur, qui proprie valvasor major olim dicebatur." For the complete passage see Karl Lehmann, *Das langobardische Lehnrecht* (Göttingen, 1896), pp. 127–128.

I have translated *plebs* as "baptismal district" instead of "baptismal church," because that is what it seems to mean in the *Libri Feudorum.* The objection may of course be raised that *plebs* as there used denotes a civil and not an ecclesiastical circumscription. To this objection two answers may be returned: (1) that in most Italian documents of the high Middle Ages the term indicates the baptismal church or its territory (when, of course, it does not simply mean *populus*); and (2) that the civil authorities continued to use the ecclesiastical divisions as units of administration, thus preserving the connection with the baptismal church or district. In short, the term *plebs,* when referring to a locality, always had some reference to the baptismal church. These statements are best illustrated from Tuscany, where the rural communes often based their organization upon the pre-existing parochial districts, and the urban communes, in extending their supremacy over the countryside, also took over the ecclesiastical divisions. In the Lucchese contado, the officers of the rural communes, in the villages subordinate to the baptisteries, held their meetings at the local churches, while the magistrates of the larger district (*pieve* or *piviere*) including several lesser communes gathered at the baptistery. The *pieve,* in this sense, was made responsible for the tribute levied by the urban commune. But it remained the baptismal area and the unit for the collection of tithes. These practices are illustrated by the statutes of the rural communes; e.g., "Statuti inediti del contado lucchese dei secoli xiii e xiv, tratti dall'archivio degli atti notarili," ed. G. Sforza, *Atti dell' Accademia di Lucca,* xxiv (1886), 489–576. In regions still under feudal control, as in the Milanese contado, the *capitanei* simply retained the power in their local districts which they had acquired as a result of the acquisition of parishes and tithes in the tenth century. As late as the eighteenth century many Milanese *pievi* were still infeudated to a single family or group of families. Cesare Magni, *Il tramonto del feudo lombardo* (Milan, 1937), pp. 216–218.

ful magnates of the contado by ceding them baptismal churches
with their rich revenues in tithes, "thus giving rise to a group
of families who, amid the numerous throng of the archbishop's
vassals, were distinguished by holding the fief of the *caput plebis*
and took the name, first, of *valvassores maiores*, later of *capitanei*." [31] During the twelfth, thirteenth, and fourteenth centuries the Milanese contado was dominated by a number of
powerful families holding fiefs of archiepiscopal origin, of which
the nucleus in each case was the fief of the tithe in the baptismal
district in which the family's holdings were most heavily con-
centrated. The *capitanei,* as the heads of these families continued
to be called, were almost invariably the patrons of the baptismal
church in their district, and normally held three-fourths of the
tithe.[32]

In Milan, as in Lucca, concessions of baptismal churches to
the lay aristocracy were renewed to successive generations and
whatever the original tenure, were assimilated to feudal law.
The heredity of all fiefs was ultimately sanctioned by Conrad II
(the only emperor to ally himself with the lower vassals), who
in 1037 granted to the lesser valvassors as well as to those
greater valvassors who held parish churches the *Constitutio
de Feudis,* which made their fiefs hereditary.[33] Henceforth a fief
could be forfeited by a vassal only through violation of his contract and by judgment of his peers. With the issuance of this
decree the feudalization of parishes and tithes became complete
in law, as it had been for some time in fact. Thus, when the ecclesiastical reform movement was launched a little later, the
advocates of ancient canon law found themselves confronted by
an established system of feudal law in regard to tithes and
parishes as well as by customary rights which they had to respect.

[31] Biscaro, "I maggiori dei Visconti," p. 23.
[32] See pp. 201–203.
[33] *M.G.H., Constitutiones,* i, 89–90.

CHAPTER VI

The Gregorian Reform

† THE CONDITIONS which had originated in the Italian parishes in the tenth century continued unchanged into the eleventh century, when their disastrous effects upon religious life became clearly visible. The monk Donizo, in his versified life of Matilda of Tuscany, tells how the Tuscan bishops sold parish churches to both laymen and priests, to the demoralization of the people.[1] The history of some of these churches can be traced through the century. In 1009 the parish church of Creti in Arezzo was bestowed by the bishop as a prebend upon the archdeacon of his cathedral, with the right of unrestricted alienation; the archdeacon might assign or bequeath the church to another priest or give it as a benefice to a layman, provided the stipulated rent was paid to the bishop. Two generations later the church had become the benefice of a group of nine *milites*. Now practically in ruins, it was retroceded to the bishopric by the knights, who promised to refrain in the future from violence within the church precincts. Of the tithes of the parish, they restored only a fourth, presumably retaining the rest in their possession.[2]

Numerous other examples illustrate the way in which parish churches and their tithes had come to be regarded as objects of

[1] *Vita Mathildis*, c. xv, *M.P.L.*, vol. 148, 981–982.
[2] Pasqui, *Documenti di Arezzo*, i, docs. 95, 278.

proprietary right, to be exploited by clergy and laymen alike. In Lucca, where the concessions in *livello* were in this period being transformed into fiefs, the charges imposed by the bishops upon the parish priests also assumed a more feudal character. One parish was let by Bishop Grimizzo to a priest in return for a money rent and a horse if needed for service in the imperial host.[3] Bishop Anselm I, though he favored ecclesiastical reform, confirmed the grants of parishes to laymen which had been made by his predecessors.[4] In the regions farther north the same practices obtained. Bishops helped themselves to the tithes of their parish churches or shared them with their vassals for political purposes.[5] Marquis Boniface of Tuscany at one time held thirteen parish churches from the bishop of Reggio, who shared the revenues of fourteen others with the local knights.[6] In the Piedmontese bishoprics numerous churches and tithes were held by laymen, although here, to a greater extent than elsewhere in Italy, the tithe was annexed to manorial churches without parochial rights. Ulric-Manfred, count of Turin, and his daughter Adelaide had in their possession many churches and their revenues.[7] When a reformer in the eleventh century used the term "simony," he had before his eyes this whole complex of mercenary transactions which resulted from the growth of the proprietary system of churches and the extension of the proprietary idea to the parishes. It will be noted that the clergy as well as

[3] *MD*, v, pt. 3, doc. 1782. For similar concessions in Lucca, see *ibid.*, docs. 1780, 1781, and iv, pt. 2, App., doc. 74; in Pisa, *Regesto di Pisa*, docs. 80, 91, 104, 161, 164.

[4] *MD*, iv, pt. 2, doc. 107 and App., doc. 87; v, pt. 3, docs. 1793, 1797.

[5] As in the Milanese parish of Varese; Giulini, *Memorie di Milano*, vii, 78.

[6] Tiraboschi, *Memorie modenesi*, ii, doc. 229 (*Cod. dip. mod.*, pp. 50–51).

[7] Ulric-Manfred gave many of his churches and tithes to the Church. His generosity is noted by Damiani, *Opus.*, ix, c. 5, in *M.P.L.*, vol. 145, 218. Adelaide's holdings are illustrated by *Carte d'Oulx*, docs. 32, 33, 34, 37, 38. The status of the tithe in Piedmont is vividly shown by a long document in *Documenti di Scarnafigi*, ed. G. Colombo, *BSSS*, xii (Pinerolo, 1902), App., doc. 5.

the laity exercised proprietary rights over the lower churches, treating them as if they were their private property and disposing of their revenues as if they were private income.

Abuses of a moral order were undoubtedly fostered by these practices. Clerical marriage was of course widespread in Italy, as well as less legitimate relations. Rathier of Verona, late in the tenth century, stated that if he tried to enforce clerical celibacy in his diocese, he would be left without a clergy.[8] In Milan the clergy married according to the forms of civil law and claimed that marriage was a custom permitted to the church of St. Ambrose.[9] Clerical marriage became doubly dangerous to ecclesiastical order when combined with the leasing of churches to the clergy under tenurial forms which gave them complete control of church property; there was a real possibility that church offices and property might become hereditary.

That the first generation of reformers in the eleventh century was disturbed about conditions in the Italian rural parishes is evident from the writings of the two most influential among them—Peter Damiani and Humbert of Moyenmoutier. Both prelates denounced the widespread traffic in parishes and tithes, an abuse for which they held the episcopate chiefly responsible.

There are bishops [writes Damiani] who hand over parish churches to laymen; such prelates sin the more grievously in that they are committing the sacrilege of profaning sacred things; and to those whom they seem to benefit they dispense a mortal poison. For to divert tithes to laymen, is not this to give them a poison of which they will die? Add further that just cause is given to the parishioners of such churches for withdrawing their obedience from their mother churches and not paying them their due tribute of tithes.[10]

Damiani paints a highly colored picture of the Italian bishops of his time, surrounded by armed vassals whom they reward for

[8] *M.P.L.*, vol. 136, 585–586.
[9] Fliche, *La réforme grégorienne* (Louvain, 1924–1937, 3 vols.), i, 32–34.
[10] *Epistolae*, iv, 12, in *M.P.L.*, vol. 144, 323–324.

their services by concessions of church property. The typical
bishop is attended, not as he should be by the divers orders of
the clergy, but by shield-bearers and lancers. When he has given
away all the lands of his see, then he has recourse to parish
churches and tithes as benefices for laymen. This dishonest liber-
ality deprives the poor of their patrimony and discourages the
parishioners of such churches from paying their tithes.[11] While
reserving his fiercest invectives for the bishops, Damiani does
not spare the lay aristocracy which was benefiting from these
abuses, castigating especially the unseemly zeal with which they
seek to transform temporary grants of church property into
hereditary tenures.

What shall I say of the sale of church property? For not only properties which are leased by a contract of *enfiteusi* or originate in such
a right, and those which are granted *libellario nomine*, but even
those which laymen receive under the mere name of benefice cannot
henceforth be revoked or restored to the churches. The hands of the
robbers are so smeared with the glue of devilish tenacity that once
they have acquired property in any way they refuse to surrender it
to the church; and not only hold it themselves by proprietary right
during their lifetime but also transmit it to their offspring. Laymen
beg you for ecclesiastical property, force their importunities upon
you, urge you with entreaties to give them this property, not to be
recorded in a formal contract, but merely as a benefice; which, however, once granted, is just the same as if it had been inscribed on
bronze tablets with a steel pen.[12]

Damiani makes it clear that the taint of the simoniacal heresy
rests upon the mercenary transactions that are taking place in
the rural parishes and that the priest who pays for a rural parish
(*plebs agrorum*) is guilty of simony no less than those who traffic
in the greater churches.[13]

---

[11] *Opus.*, 20, in *M.P.L.*, vol. 145, 445–446.
[12] *Epistolae*, iv, 12, in *M.P.L.*, vol. 144, 323.
[13] "Hinc est plane, quod non solum qui majoribus praeferuntur ecclesiis, sed et illis quoque qui vel plebes agrorum vel canonicales prae-

Cardinal Humbert seems to have shared the contemporary German prejudice against the Italian church as a sink of iniquity and the Italian episcopate as peculiarly corrupt.

Alas! I remember how often I have seen [in Italy] the pavements of noble basilicas ploughed up and pigs and cattle stabled within their walls. And for these atrocities, not the Vandal, Goth, or Hun is responsible, not the Lombard or the Hungarian, but the simoniac. The tithes, too, and the oblations the simoniac sells or gives to laymen in diabolical contracts. Leases of church property flow into lay hands, together with charters and documents bearing the signatures of these simoniacs, so that the ancient rights and canonical privileges of God's churches are conceded to laymen forever.[14]

Since the reformers diagnosed so correctly the conditions in the Italian parishes, it is pertinent at this point to inquire into the place of the lower churches, both baptismal churches and those of a lesser order, in the program of reform that was set forth in 1059.

In April 1059 the Easter synod assembled at the Lateran. During the previous decade the papacy had been purified and regenerated through the action of the lay power, the pious emperor Henry III, the most distinguished member of the Salian dynasty. One of Henry's appointees, Leo IX, had launched the papal reforming movement in a series of synods, mostly in France and Germany, which had condemned simony and clerical marriage. By 1059 the reforming movement was well under way. But political conditions had radically changed. Henry III, sympathetic towards attempts to reform clerical morals, had died three years before, and the new German king, Henry IV, was a minor. Godfrey of Lorraine, a former rebel against the Em-

---

bendas per interventum pecuniae pestilenter accipiunt, simoniacae haereseos tendiculas non evadunt." *Ibid.*, 222–223.

[14] *Adversus Simoniacos*, in *M.P.L.*, vol. 143, 1120–21. This passage has been slightly abridged in translation.

pire and now as husband of Beatrice of Tuscany in control of the
large Canossan domains in central Italy, supported the reformers. The reigning pope, Nicholas II, also from Lorraine and
bishop of Florence before his elevation to the papacy, was Godfrey's protégé. The revolutionary Pataria, led by the deacon
Ariald and the noble Landulf, was agitating for "free elections"
of the archbishops of Milan and attacking the married clergy in
that city. Milan in 1059 was the seat of a veritable civil war. The
Pataria was in open rebellion against the imperialist archbishop,
and Ariald was already negotiating for an alliance with the papacy. This alliance was consummated late in the year.[15]

Against the background of these events 113 bishops met in
the Lateran basilica, their deliberations guided by a brilliant con-
stellation of ecclesiastical statesmen: Nicholas II; Boniface,
cardinal of Sant'Albano, his close adviser, first to sign after the
Pope himself the electoral decree which liberated the papacy
from the control of Roman noble factions; Peter Damiani, recently raised to the cardinalate against his will, the epitome of
the Italian monastic spirit; Hildebrand, the future Gregory VII,
not yet archdeacon of the Roman Church, an Italian but not
of the episcopal aristocracy and perhaps partly for that reason
more accessible to new ideas; and Humbert of Moyenmoutier, a
native of Lorraine and still a comparatively young man, who
had come to Rome as secretary of Leo IX and had steadily risen

---

[15] For the history of ecclesiastical reform in the eleventh century, see
Fliche's monumental *Réforme grégorienne,* the contents of which he has
summarized in more popular form in *La querelle des investitures* (Paris,
1946) and in *HE,* viii (*La réforme grégorienne et la reconquête chrétienne
1057–1125*) (Paris, 1940). Gerd Tellenbach's *Church, State and Christian
Society at the Time of the Investiture Contest* (trans. R. F. Bennett, Oxford, 1940) is a brilliant interpretive study. Recent research is summed
up in *Studi gregoriani. Per la storia di Gregorio VII e della riforma gregoriana,* ed. G. B. Borino (Rome, 1947–1948, 3 vols.). The effects of the
movement on Italy are described by Geoffrey Barraclough, *Origins of
Modern Germany,* pp. 147–153. I have taken the Lateran synod of 1059
as the starting point of my narrative because it was the first important
reforming council held in Italy. In its condemnation of clerical marriage
it had, of course, been preceded by the council of Pavia in 1022.

to influence in the papal curia. Humbert a year before, in his
Three Books Against the Simoniacs, had launched "the first
frontal attack against the whole position of laymen within the
Church," which was soon to give a new direction to the program
of reform.[16]

Three of the decrees passed by the Lateran synod of 1059 are
relevant to our purpose. Canon 3 discloses the organization of
the secular clergy which the reformers proposed to substitute
wherever possible for the abuses of their time. After renewing
Leo IX's decree against the marriage of priests, deacons, and
subdeacons, and forbidding married priests to celebrate mass
(canon 2), the council prescribed that the clergy of those orders
(i.e., priests, deacons, and subdeacons) who in obedience to
the reforming decrees had preserved their chastity, should
henceforth sleep and eat together near their churches, hold in
common the revenues of those churches, and strive earnestly
to realize the apostolic life, namely the common life.[17] Fliche
thus comments: "Nicholas II proposes that the common life shall
be adopted by the universal church. . . . An attempt is made
to prevent the abuse of clerical marriage by making illicit relations more difficult, by organizing mutual surveillance, and by
preventing the clergy from amassing private fortunes." [18] This
comment stresses somewhat too much the negative and disciplinary aspect of the canonical movement which is here un-
veiled. The resurrection of the life of the apostolic Church on
which it was based was the leitmotiv of the Italian reformers
in the eleventh century and was rooted in a tradition of the common life of the clergy which, although almost obliterated in the
darker periods, had never been entirely extinguished. The Carolingian rulers had fostered the idea of the canonical life of the
clergy, and reforming bishops of the ninth century had had a
temporary success in introducing this life into their cathedrals.

[16] Tellenbach, *Church, State, and Christian Society,* p. 111.
[17] *M.P.L.,* vol. 143, 1315–1316.
[18] *Réforme grégorienne,* i, 336–337.

Occasionally canonries were founded in rural parishes, for it would seem that the ideal behind the Carolingian legislation was to extend the reform to at least the larger baptismal churches which had a numerous clergy.[19]

At the beginning of the eleventh century the canonical life was revived in Italy under the sponsorship of eremitical monasticism and evidently was introduced into some of the rural parish churches even earlier than into the cathedrals. Thus in 1005 at Val de Castro, St. Romuald persuaded the local clergy to abandon simony and, instead of living after the manner of laymen, to obey a prior and live in a community.[20] From a monastic milieu the idea spread to reforming bishops and sympathetic laymen. The canonical life was established in a rural parish of Asti in 1024, in Lucca in 1025, where fourteen canons, at the invitation of Bishop John II, united in the common life in the rural baptistery of Santa Maria a Monte.[21] In 1056 some pious laymen gave half of a rural church, evidently a private church and not a parish, to three priests, on condition that they should pursue the common life therein, "dwelling in chastity in houses close to the church." [22] In Milan, Ariald received by gift a private

[19] For the canonical reform, consult Charles Dereine, "Vie commune, règle de Saint Augustin et chanoines réguliers au xie siècle," *RHE,* xli (1946), especially pp. 385–392; Pierre Mandonnet, *St. Dominic and His Work* (English trans., St. Louis, 1944), pp. 241–277; L. Hertling, "Kanoniker, Augustinusregel und Augustinerorder," *Zeitschrift für kath. Theologie,* liv (1930), 335–359. A convenient summary of the literature is given in Fliche, *HE,* viii, 457–461. For the Italian cathedrals an old work by Garampi is still useful: *Memorie ecclesiastiche appartenenti alla storia della beata Chiara di Rimini* (Rome, 1775), pp. 264–314, "Sopra i progressi e decadenza della vita claustrale de' chierici e canonici, specialmente in Italia."

[20] *Vita Romualdi,* by Peter Damiani, cited by Dereine, "Vie commune, règle de Saint Augustin," p. 368.

[21] *Antiche carte di Asti,* doc. 155; *MD,* iv, pt. 2, doc. 88. For comment on the Lucchese example, see Barsocchini, *Dissertazioni,* pp. 233–234. Nanni, *La parrochia studiata nei documenti lucchesi,* pp. 121–122, calls this the first collegiate church in the diocese.

[22] *MD,* iv, pt. 2, doc. 96; Nanni, pp. 131–132. For other Lucchese examples, see *MD,* iv, pt. 2, doc. 101 (San Frediano); doc. 99 (San

church, within which he organized a semimonastic community, where the clergy lived from a common purse, ate at a common board while listening to sacred readings, celebrated the offices seven times a day, and dedicated themselves to a life of individual poverty in imitation of the apostolic community. This church had an irresistible appeal not only for the townspeople but for others who flocked in from the outlying castles and villages, glad to have a church "where they could hear God's word with free minds and partake of the sacraments." [23] In 1058, just before his election to the papacy, Nicholas II, then Bishop Gerard of Florence, had introduced the canonical life into several Florentine parish churches.[24] There is evidence, too, that under the influence of the reforming popes of the 1050's, the Roman clergy also were adopting the common life. Hildebrand is known to have sympathized with the movement and at a later time, as Pope Gregory VII, composed a rule for the canons of such churches.[25]

The most enthusiastic advocate of the movement in Italy, however, was Cardinal Damiani, who devoted to it several of

---

Michele); App., doc. 81 (San Donato); iv, pt. 2, doc. 85 (Santa Reparata); v, pt. 3, doc. 1787 (San Pantaleone). In 1048 the cathedral chapter was reformed and reorganized as a canonry, although the attempt precipitated a struggle that lasted the rest of the century. *MD*, iv, pt. 2, App., doc. 78; Nanni, pp. 122–131; E. Kittel, "Der Kampf um die Reform des Domkapitel in Lucca im xi. Jahrhundert," *Festschrift Albert Brackmann* (Weimar, 1935), pp. 207–247.

[23] Andrew of Vallombrosa, *Vita Arialdi*, in *M.P.L.*, vol. 143, cols. 1453–54.

[24] Pflugk-Harttung, *Acta Pontificum Romanorum Inedita* (Tübingen, 1881–1888, 3 vols.), ii, nos. 121, 123. Nicholas' relations with Florence after becoming pope are discussed by Davidsohn, *Geschichte von Florenz*, i, 210–222.

Canonries in Pisa are mentioned in *Regesto di Pisa*, docs. 120, 173; in Bergamo, Lupi, *CDB*, ii, 663–664, 691–694.

[25] J. A. Macdonald, *Hildebrand* (London, 1932), pp. 55–56; G. Bardy, "Saint Grégoire VII et la réforme canoniale au xie siècle," *Studi gregoriani*, i, 47–64. The rule was published by D. G. Morin, "Règlements inédits du pape Grégoire VII pour les chanoines réguliers," *Revue bénédictine*, xviii (1901) 177–183.

his most eloquent letters. He did not intend to force this life upon all the secular clergy; he states clearly that is only for canons, i.e., the clergy of cathedrals and collegiate churches. But it is evident that he regarded it as the only life possible for a true cleric and desired it to be held up as an ideal for all the secular clergy.[26] Moreover, given the collegiate structure of the Italian rural parish, composed of a central baptistery with its cluster of subordinate chapels, it is permissible to believe that Damiani, writing with Italian conditions before his eyes, wanted the common life of the clergy to be fostered in the rural parishes as a weapon against simony, as well as in resurrection of a traditional ideal. In any case, there is ample evidence in the documents that this was the goal of the leading Italian reformers of this period. The canonical movement, incorporated into the papal program in 1059, remained a vital element in the reform movement in Italy to the end of the eleventh century.[27]

Attractive and inspiring as the canonical reform was as a vehicle for the moral regeneration of the clergy, there were some members of the synod of 1059 who realized that it was not an adequate solution for the ills besetting the Church. Already there were in the Roman curia men who were convinced that the evil lay chiefly not in the corruption of the clergy but in lay control of churches and their revenues. Of this group Humbert had already made himself the spokesman, if indeed he had not created the group, by his *Adversus Simoniacos*. His uncompromising hostility to lay control of the Church was voiced in the sixth canon passed by the synod: "No cleric or priest shall receive a church from a layman, either gratis or for a price." [28] Nothing is

---

[26] *M.P.L.*, vol. 145, col. 482. Mandonnet, *St. Dominic*, p. 259; Bardy, "Saint Grégoire VII et la réforme canoniale," p. 50, n. 8.

[27] In the twelfth century it was absorbed into the monastic movement centering in the Augustinian order. Previously the canonical life had not been identified exclusively with the rule of St. Augustine, nor had the distinction between secular and regular canons existed.

[28] Mansi, *Concilia*, xix, 909.

said here about lay investiture, which was after all a technicality, nor is the prohibition restricted to bishoprics and abbacies. The decree lays the ax at the root of the whole system of lay proprietary rights, whether exercised by the emperor in appointing an archbishop of Milan or by a knight in appointing a parish priest.

However, having enunciated this drastic principle, the Church moved very slowly in enforcing it during the next nineteen years, and it is interesting to speculate as to the reasons why. Humbert died in 1061, having previously refused election to the papacy. Nicholas' successor, Alexander II, while a sincere reformer, seems to have been of a temporizing character, inclined to compromise with the lay aristocracy and with the imperial government.[29] He was the former Anselmo da Baggio, member of a family of *capitanei* which held concessions of parishes and tithes in the Milanese contado.[30] He was one of four candidates for the office of archbishop of Milan in 1045 who were rejected by the Emperor, and was the chief organizer of the Pataria. As bishop of Lucca from 1057 to 1073 he was a zealous promoter of the canonical reform, but local documents still in the episcopal archives of Lucca show that in his relations with the lay feudality he followed in the footsteps of his predecessors. He continued to be bishop of Lucca after becoming Pope in 1061, and we are presented with the curious spectacle of a pope renewing and confirming the "diabolical contracts" denounced by Humbert in his *Adversus Simoniacos*.[31] He made his position clear, however, in a letter which he addressed as Pope to the cathedral chapter of Lucca. For a long time, he wrote, the evil of simony had desolated the church of Lucca; no cleric, however religious,

[29] This is the appraisal of Fliche, *Réforme gregorienne*, i, 340–366, and of H. C. Lea, *A History of Sacerdotal Celibacy in the Christian Church* (New York, 1907, 2 vols.), i, 241–242.

[30] Ca. 1054 a monastery complained that the Da Baggio were encroaching upon a chapel endowed with tithes which had been conferred upon it by a former archbishop. ("Qui propter plebem et praedia quae multa et magna habent circa, sunt conati devastare nos et nostra.") Giulini, *Memorie di Milano*, vii, 67–68.

[31] See p. 107.

educated, or honest he might be, could obtain an ecclesiastical office without the aid of money; on the other hand, if a cleric had the necessary means he could purchase his ordination as priest without passing through minor orders as required by canon law; the church and its property in Lucca were sold by vile traffickers like any earthly object. After condemning simony, the bull then forbade further concessions of church lands to laymen other than leaseholds to peasants and small cultivators. Excepted from the prohibition, however, was property already let out as benefices to laymen.[32] This limiting clause was indicative of the policy which the Church was almost forced to take, and marked out the path in which even the reformers walked for the next few generations. Needing the support of the lay aristocracy in the removal of the most crying abuses, the Church could not afford to estrange them from the cause of moral reform by attacking too vigorously their vested interests in church property.

The most urgent single question in Alexander's pontificate was undoubtedly the affair of Milan, where his election to the papacy had thrown fuel on the flames and confirmed the Lombard bishops in their support of an imperialist antipope, Cadalus of Parma. Alexander, on his side, allied himself with the increasingly radical Pataria and appointed the Milanese noble Herlembald the military leader of the movement in Lombardy. The Pataria is too complex to be analyzed here. A more recent interpretation of this perplexing movement is that it was not a class struggle, an uprising of the depressed classes, but a party struggle in which all classes mingled on one side or the other and in which the major issues were canonical elections and clerical marriage.[33] This primarily religious movement took on a revolutionary guise because necessarily directed against the ruling classes, the Lombard episcopate and the high feudatories, identified with the

[32] *MD*, v, pt. 3, docs. 1794–1795.

[33] For a balanced appraisal of the Pataria, see Alfred Doren, *Storia economica dell'Italia nel medio evo*, trans. G. Luzzatto, *Annali di economia*, xi (1936), 120–121, 169–170.

Lombard *Reichskirche*. In the crises of the movement its chief support came from the poorer classes, the artisans and petty bourgeoisie, but its leaders were nobles and it seems to have been connected in some obscure way with the discontent of the lower nobility.[34] At any rate, with civil war raging in Lombardy and the Lombard episcopate ranged on the side of an antipope, the papacy was scarcely in a position to launch a full-scale attack on lay proprietorship of churches and their property.

Whatever the reasons may be, the Lateran synods until 1078 showed a certain reserve on the subject of the lower churches and their revenues. Canon 6 of the synod of 1059 had not explicitly condemned the holding of churches by laymen, although this principle certainly seems to be implied.[35] In regard to the tithes, the council had merely ordained that they must be paid by the laity to the churches and should be at the disposal of the bishops to be distributed by them according to the laws of the Church.[36] Any right to the tithes on the part of the parish churches and their clergy is not mentioned, and there is no prohibition of lay ownership of tithes.

This reticence on the part of the Roman councils is in contrast to the French synods of the eleventh century, which from 1031 on fought to improve the condition of the lower churches.[37] While refraining for a long time from an express condemnation of lay proprietorship of churches, these French councils asserted vigorously and repeatedly the rights of the bishops to spiritual jurisdiction over the priests of private churches and insisted upon the right of the local church to at least a third of its tithes and

[34] Barraclough, *Origins of Modern Germany*, p. 107, n. 1, goes further and identifies the Pataria as an attempt on the part of the *secundi milites*, or valvassors, to gain control of affairs in Milan by electing one of their own number as archbishop; hence the revolt against imperial control of the archbishopric and the emphasis on "free elections."

[35] See p. 112.　　　　　　　　　　　[36] Mansi, *Concilia*, xix, 908–909.

[37] The legislation of the French councils was first placed in its proper light by Georg Schreiber, "Gregor VII, Cluny, Cîteaux," *ZSSR*, lxv (1947), *Kan. Abt.* xxxvii, 59–67.

oblations.[38] The council of Toulouse in 1056 insisted that in proprietary churches a third of the tithes should go to the priest of
the church to be administered by him for the benefit of the
church under the supervision of the bishop.[39] The synod of Tours
in 1060 threatened with excommunication any layman who possessed, sold, or infeudated the oblations or the third of the
tithes.[40] Similar provisions were passed by the council of Lillebonne (1080) and two councils of Rouen (1074, 1096).[41] This
legislation succeeded in establishing in France the right of the
curé of an impropriated church to at least a third of the tithes,
his *portio congrua,* as it was called at a later period. Since some
of the French councils of the eleventh century were presided
over by papal legates, we may conclude that this practice was
approved by the papacy and constituted part of the papal program of reform.

Not until 1078, however, was the papal policy in regard to lay
proprietorship of churches finally clarified. Gregory VII had in
1075 issued the decree against lay investiture which brought to
a head the long pending struggle between papacy and Empire.
Provoked by Henry IV's appointment of an archbishop of Milan,
it may be regarded as the assumption by Gregory of the Hum-
bertine attitude of uncompromising hostility towards lay control

[38] The council of Bourges in 1031, the first to legislate on the subject,
did not mention the third specifically but forbade laymen to hold "the
ecclesiastical benefices which are called priests' fiefs" (*fevos presbyterales*).
Mansi, *Concilia,* xix, 505. The term "priest's fief" is discussed by Imbart
de la Tour, *Origines religieuses,* pp. 307–308, and by E. Amann and F. Du-
mas, *L'église au pouvoir des laiques,* in Fliche and Martin, *HE,* vii, 288.

[39] ". . . de ecclesiis in alodiis laicorum constitutis, ut tertia pars
decimarum cum primitiis et caeteris in potestate presbyteri, ad servitium
ipsius ecclesiae, sub episcopi vel clericorum ditione permaneant." Mansi,
Concilia, xix, 849.

[40] *Ibid.,* 928.

[41] *Ibid.,* xx, 400; Ordericus Vitalis, *Historia Ecclesiastica,* in *M.P.L.,*
vol. 188, col. 654. The persistence of the system in Normandy is indicated by the eighth canon of the council of Avranches (1172): ". . . de
tertia parte decimarum nihil presbytero qui servit ecclesiae auferatur."
Mansi, xxii, 138.

of church property and personnel, which had been in abeyance during the long pontificate of Alexander II. The investiture decree of 1075 is known to us only through a brief mention by the Milanese chronicler Arnulf, who simply says that the Pope forbade the king henceforth to have any rights in bestowing bishoprics and removed all secular persons from investitures of churches.[42] The decrees of the Lateran synod of November 1078 appear in full in Gregory's *Register*. They threaten with excommunication any knight or lay person who does not surrender to the Church ecclesiastical lands which he has either usurped or received from unworthy priests without the consent of the bishops or abbots. They condemn investitures of churches by emperor, king, or any lay person, whether man or woman. With regard to the tithes, the council took the drastic step of condemning lay possession of tithes even when they had been conceded by the episcopate. The bishops present at the synod were commanded to notify the laity that they were committing sacrilege and endangering their souls' salvation unless they yielded their tithes to the Church.[43] Thus was proclaimed in full the Gregorian program as regards lay proprietorship of churches and tithes. It is noteworthy that this legislation applied to all churches, both upper and lower. It was confirmed in this respect by the March synod of 1080, which, while stressing bishoprics and abbacies, stated that the decrees applied to the lower churches as well. "We ordain similarly concerning the lower ecclesiastical dignities" (canon 1).[44]

In view of the bitter realities facing the reformers, most of the bishops present must have realized the utter impossibility of enforcing these decrees. In fact, it may even be questioned whether the decrees were intended to be more than a statement of principle, to be enforced by reforming bishops and local synods whenever possible. The limits on possibility are illus-

---

[42] *M.G.H., SS.,* viii, 27.   [43] Mansi, xx, 510.

[44] Carl Mirbt, *Quellen zur Geschichte des Papsttums und des römischen Katholizismus* (4th ed., Tübingen, 1924), p. 153.

trated by a decree of the French synod of Gerona in 1078, the
first French synod actually to condemn lay ownership of
churches. Canon 13 declares: "We know that churches do not
pertain to laymen; but where they cannot be taken away from
them, we at least forbid laymen absolutely to possess their oblations and first-fruits." [45] Remembering that the reform movement found a relatively sympathetic reception in France, this
decree permits us to gauge the resistance met by the reformers
when they attacked the lay proprietary system. The synod ad-
mits the impossibility of recovering all the churches from laymen; it condemns the principle of lay ownership, at the same
time making it clear that the practice will be tolerated.

In 1895, in an essay on the *Eigenkirche* which has become
classic, Ulrich Stutz maintained that in 1059 the decision was
taken at Rome to concentrate upon the struggle to free the
bishops and abbacies from lay control and to postpone the
struggle for the lower churches in order not to alienate the lay
aristocracy together with royalty. [46] This thesis contains a large
element of truth. But it requires to be qualified slightly in the
light of our fuller knowledge. It ignores the activity of the French
synods after 1059, of which Stutz seems to have been unaware.
It does not give full weight to the Roman legislation of 1078 and
1080. And it does not take into account a fact unknown to Stutz,
because hidden in local Italian documents, that in the eleventh
century and largely as a result of the activities of the reformers,
the parish churches of Italy established their legal right to a
share in the tithes, a process analogous to that which happened
in France but evidently without the aid of synodal legislation.

There is a considerable body of evidence in existence, both
from the eleventh century and later, to prove that the Gregorian

[45] Mansi, xx, 520, c. 13. For comment, see Feine, "Kirchenreform und
Niederkirchenwesen," *Studi gregoriani*, ii, 507.

[46] *Die Eigenkirche als Element des mittelalterlich-germanischen Kirchenrecht* (Berlin, 1895), trans. in Geoffrey Barraclough's *Mediaeval
Germany* (Oxford, 1938, 2 vols.), i, 35–70.

reformers in their writings and in their practices as bishops of Italian dioceses, claimed for the parish churches a fourth of the tithes, the so-called *quartese*, leaving the remainder at the disposal of the bishops. Since the tithe had been instituted by the Carolingian rulers of Italy to provide the parish churches with an income and since, even during the period when the parishes were being dispossessed of their tithes by the lay aristocracy, their legal title to the tithes had not been questioned, both the theory and the practice of the Gregorian reformers present themselves as strange anomalies, aberrations from canon law. Why did the reformers not demand all the tithes for the parish churches? An answer to this question entails an exploration of local documents showing the appearance of the *quartese* in Italian practice and an examination of the writings of the Roman canonists of the Gregorian period.

Early in the eleventh century there seems to have developed in northern Italy the practice of reserving to the parish church a share in the tithes normally fixed at a fourth. The earliest implied recognition of the right of the parish churches to this fourth occurs in a charter of 1032 in which the bishop of Parma gives as a benefice to a canon of his cathedral the parish church of Malandriano together with a fourth of the tithes, promising that when the remaining three-fourths are restored by the knights who have usurped them, they will also form part of the benefice.[47] This seems to indicate that the church was already in possession of the fourth, presumably reserved to it by previous bishops and evidently respected by the *milites* who held the rest of the tithes. Another example, also without the use of the word *quartesium*, comes from Padua, where in 1045 the bishop impropriated three-fourths of the parish tithes of Pernumia to his cathedral chapter, reserving a fourth to the parish church

[47] Ireneo Affò, *Storia della città di Parma* (Parma, 1792–1795, 4 vols.), ii, doc. 9.

itself.[48] Evidently the custom prevailed, in both lay and ecclesiastical impropriations, of reserving a fourth of the tithes for the exclusive use of the church in whose parish they were gathered. A Placentine document of 1038 varies a little; in receiving from Marquis Hugh, "of the race of the Lombards" (i.e., a local feudatory), a donation of two-thirds of the tithes of Port'Albera to the cathedral chapter, the bishop of Piacenza reserves a third of the tithes of Port'Albera to the local church.[49] The first authentic use of the word *quartese* comes to light in a Paduan document of 1076, in which the bishop of Padua bestows upon a monastery "the entire product of the tithe called *quartese* from the villa of Macerata." [50] This grant of the *quartese* to a monastery was an obvious violation of the custom which seems to have been forming for the protection of the parish churches. Similar violations may have helped to provoke the action of sixteen parish priests in the following year when they appealed to the Emperor's delegates to protect them in their persons and property and especially in possession of their *quartesi*.[51] Anyone familiar with early canon law will immediately recognize in this parochial fourth, as in the French third of the same period, the survival of ancient canonical procedure. The law of quadripartition had evidently survived in this form, with the important modification that the *quartese*, the lineal descendant of the fourth of the clergy, has become the portion of the parish church itself.

The parochial fourth became generalized throughout northern Italy in the course of the eleventh century. In the South, the Normans introduced the threefold division of the tithes which prevailed in France, one third to the local church, the rest under the administration of the bishop.[52] It is of course impossible to fix the precise moment at which these practices originated. In the light of the numerous Lucchese documents of the tenth cen-

---

[48] Gloria, *CDP*, i, doc. 144.
[49] Campi, i, doc. 77 (p. 506).
[50] Gloria, *CDP*, i, doc. 229.
[51] *Ibid.*, doc. 239.
[52] See pp. 232–234.

tury which show that concessions of tithes and parishes to laymen were always in multiples of a fourth, it seems a not
unreasonable suggestion that the parochial fourth may have originated in that century to assure the parish churches at least a
minimum revenue. But this is sheer conjecture. If such a rule did
exist at this early period it was frequently violated; for in many
cases the entire parish and its revenues were ceded to the
knights.

The universality of this practice of reserving either a fourth
or a third of the tithe to the parish churches in the eleventh century leads one to believe that it had a legal basis, which can only
have been ancient canon law. The early dates of some of the
documents mentioning this practice show that it preceded the
papal reforming movement. But it was certainly accepted and
propagated by the Gregorians as part of the restoration of canon
law which they were promoting. Before the Gregorian Reform
there was a great deal of uncertainty as to what the law of the
Church really was. Collections of canons circulated widely but
were permeated with conflicting influences. At the beginning of
the eleventh century there was a marked revival of interest in
canon law, as manifested in such collections as that of Burchard
of Worms. In 1051 this revival took a new direction when Humbert, in compiling his *Sentences,* "the first manual of the reforming movement," adopted as his criterion for the selection of
canons the tradition of the Roman Church.[53] Subsequently a
group of reformers in the entourage of Gregory VII pursued,
with the encouragement of the Pope, an investigation into early
church law and compiled collections of canons. In assembling
their texts, the Gregorian canonists accepted unquestioningly
only laws which had emanated from or been approved by the
Holy See, excluding so far as possible Germanic, Celtic, Frankish, and episcopal law. In this respect the Roman canonical collections of the Gregorian period stand in marked contrast to

[53] Anton Michel, "Die folgenschweren Ideen des Kardinals Humbert
und ihr Einfluss auf Gregor VII," *Studi gregoriani,* i, 71–72.

earlier collections, such as that of Burchard of Worms, which had been much more eclectic in their standards.[54]

The law of the Roman Church before the intrusion of Germanic, Celtic, and feudal influences had laid great stress upon the unity of the diocese and upon episcopal jurisdiction over all the churches, clergy, and church property within it. Roman legislation of the Gregorian period increasingly bears the imprint of these conceptions, and the unity of the diocese, broken both by the growth of the lay proprietary system and by the development of monastic exemptions, became the guiding principle in the administrative reorganization of the Church.[55] Moreover, in the ancient canons the reformers rediscovered the law of quadripartite division of church revenues which had been formulated in the period of the unitary patrimony, and this they applied to the tithes. The most striking feature of Roman legislation of the Gregorian period in regard to the tithes is its emphasis upon episcopal jurisdiction and its corresponding disregard of any rights on the part of the lower church as such.[56] It is hard to generalize from the writings and practices of the Italian reformers, but it seems clear that they believed they were acting in accord with the canons when they assigned only the fourth of the tithe to the parish churches; the law of quadripartition left at the disposal of the bishop not only the fourth reserved for his own use but the fourths assigned to the fabric and the poor which he was authorized to administer.

The interpretation placed upon the law of quadripartition

<hr>

[54] This is the thesis of Paul Fournier, "Les collections canoniques romaines de l'époque de Grégoire VII," *MAIB*, xli (1918), 271–395. On the Gregorian collections in general, see Fournier and Gabriel Lebras, *Histoire des collections canoniques en Occident depuis les fausses Décrétales jusqu'au Décret de Gratien* (Paris, 1931–1932, 2 vols.), ii, ch. 1. Fournier, "Un tournant de l'histoire du droit (1060–1140)," *RHDFE*, xli (1917), 131–154, interprets the Gregorian Reform as essentially a revival and reassertion of Roman legal principles against the Germanic law of the early Middle Ages.

[55] Tellenbach, *Church, State, and Christian Society*, pp. 117–119.

[56] See p. 115. Cf. Mansi, *Concilia*, xx, 510 (c. 8).

by the Gregorian reformers is most clearly illustrated by the *Liber de Vita Christiana* of Bonizo of Sutri. In Book II of this treatise, devoted to the office and duties of a bishop, Bonizo exhorts his fellow prelates not to be remiss in dispensing hospitality:

Because of this duty which rests upon the bishop, canon law has laid down this rule: that of all the revenues of the churches and of the tithes two portions shall be conceded to the bishop, one for the maintenance of his household, the other for the care of pilgrims and guests; the third part is to be assigned to the fabric of the church, the fourth to be divided among the clergy according to the merits of each.[57]

The possibility that Bonizo is here thinking primarily of the cathedral receives support from another passage in which he cites a decree which he attributes to Pope Julius:

Of all the revenues of the church and of the tithes four parts shall be made, one to go to the bishop for the maintenance of his household, a second also to the bishop for the reception of travellers, a third to be applied to the upkeep of the church buildings, and the last to be distributed, according to merit, among those members of the clergy who dwell religiously in their houses in obedience to the bishop and without conjugal ties, being called in some churches canons, in some *ordinarii*, in others, as at Rome, cardinals.[58]

Finally, in Book VIII, Bonizo gives a historical account of the origins of the tithe:

After the time of Constantine, with the continued growth of the Christian faith, it was decreed by the holy fathers and by the authority of the Roman Church that four portions should be made of the tithes: three of these were to be in the power of the bishop; the fourth was to be divided among the clergy according to their merits.[59]

While Bonizo's remarks may be directed especially towards the revenues of the cathedral churches, there is implied in his ex-

[57] Ernst Perels, ed., *Texte zur Geschichte des römischen und kanonischen Rechts im Mittelalter* (Berlin, 1930), i, 50.
[58] *Ibid.*, p. 204.   [59] *Ibid.*, p. 253.

position the claim that the bishop may divide the clerical fourth among the parochial clergy as well as among the canons of his cathedral, giving the preference to those superior in merit who live "religiously in their houses . . . and without conjugal ties," a phrase which may mean those who followed the common life.

It would probably be unwise to attach too much weight to a purely academic discussion of church revenues, written by an exiled bishop in his old age. More important is the evidence of local documents, some of which have already been cited, showing the interpretation of the rule of quadripartition that was actually followed by reforming bishops in administering the tithes of their parishes. We know that in 1058 Bishop Gerard of Florence gave a fourth of the parochial tithes to the clergy of several Florentine baptisteries who had adopted the common life.[60] Ten years later, in judging a lawsuit in Chiusi, Pope Alexander II decided that the bishop of Chiusi must obey the precepts of canon law by giving the priests of the diocese a fourth of their tithes, retaining the other three-fourths under his own control.[61] A third example, from a somewhat later period, should be cited with caution. In 1113 a papal legate, in trying a lawsuit between the archpriest of a Lucchese parish and a local monastery over a fourth of the parochial tithes, decided in favor of the parish church on the grounds that Bishop Anselm had formerly commanded that "all the parishes of his diocese should have a fourth of the tithes." [62]

The practices revealed in these documents, which will be confirmed by later examples to be cited in the next chapter, are clearly contrary both to the system of tithes ordained by the Carolingian capitularies and to that sanctioned in the thirteenth century by the law of the Decretals. The discrepancy is partly to be explained as the result of the revival of ancient canon law

[60] See p. 111 and n. 24.

[61] Pflugk-Harttung, *Acta Pontificum Romanorum*, ii, no. 143.

[62] "Hoc preceptum fuit Anselmi episcopi, quod omnes plebes sui episcopatus quartam portionem omnium decimarum haberent." Muratori, *Antiquitates*, iii, 205–206.

which was then in progress, which stressed episcopal jurisdiction over church property and directed attention towards the ancient rules for the division of ecclesiastical revenues. The Roman rule, favored by the Italian reformers, prescribed, of course, a four-fold division. The assignment of a third of the tithes to the French and south Italian churches in the Gregorian period was based on the Toletan system and permitted by the papacy as a legitimate local tradition. It was also consistent with the legal outlook of the Roman reformers that they should have discarded the system of tithes ordained by the capitularies and councils of the ninth century, for the tithe had been established by the Carolingian sovereigns and the rules which gave it in its entirety to the parish churches were Frankish laws originating with the lay power and therefore suspect to the Gregorian reformers.

In establishing the principle of episcopal jurisdiction over the tithe and requiring only a fourth of the parochial tithes for the parish churches, the reformers could in practice leave most of the tithes where they actually were—in the hands of the laity and the monasteries,—trusting to reforming bishops to recover them from the laity. Since the opening of the century the lay aristocracy had already surrendered many churches and tithes to ecclesiastical institutions. As early as 1019 Boniface of Tuscany and his wife Richelda restored the tithes of four parishes to the bishop of Cremona.[63] Numerous restitutions of churches, mostly manorial chapels, were made by the House of Canossa in Mantua.[64] Ulric-Manfred of Turin and Countess Adelaide made similar donations, the former to the extent of seriously reducing his own resources.[65] After the middle of the century, under the impetus of the ecclesiastical reform, people of lesser rank also began to restore their share of church revenues, sometimes very small. In 1079 a priest in the diocese of Turin gave to the priory of Oulx all his rights in the parish church of Cesena,

[63] Lupi, *CDB*, ii, 497–498.
[64] Torelli, *ACM*, doc. 3; *Regesto di Mantova*, docs. 91, 92, 118.
[65] *Antiche carte di Asti*, doc. 177; *Il libro verde della chiesa di Asti*, ed. Giuseppe Assandria, *BSSS*, xxvi (Pinerolo, 1907), doc. 212.

amounting to a fifth of the church and a twelfth of its tithes.[66]

Almost invariably these restitutions were made to cathedral chapters, to monasteries, or directly to bishops, almost never to parish churches unless they had become seats of the canonical life. The founders and patrons of monasteries liked to endow them with grants of churches and tithes, enriching their protégés and at the same time gaining credit in heaven.[67] The cathedral chapters, in which their sons were often canons, also attracted the gifts of the lay aristocracy. As a result of this preference, monastic churches and tithes multiplied rapidly during the eleventh century, eventually exciting the anger of the bishops and provoking a reaction within the monastic order itself, when the Cistercians refused to hold tithes and churches.[68] The Gregorian

[66] *Carte d'Oulx,* doc. 30. Other typical restitutions are recorded in *MD,* iv, pt. 2, doc. 102; Pasqui, *Documenti di Arezzo,* i, docs. 217, 222, 229, 252, 254, 264; *Carte di Gubbio,* docs. 8, 27.

[67] Most of the monastic churches were minor, nonparochial churches, but a few baptisteries with their tithes passed to the monasteries, e.g., *Cod. dip. di Bobbio,* i, doc. 137. The bishops made numerous grants of tithes to monasteries, thus deflecting them from the parish churches and provoking numerous conflicts, e.g. Gloria, *CDP,* i, doc. 247. In 1033 the bishop of Arezzo tried to extend the tithe to commerce by commanding all merchants of Arezzo to pay a tithe of their gains to the Camàldoli: "How sinful it is not to pay tithe to the monks, when poor rustics devotedly pour the fruits of their toil into the coffers of secular knights!" Pasqui, *Documenti di Arezzo,* i, doc. 153.

[68] For the Cistercians, see Appendix IV. Monastic ownership of tithes was defended on the ground that tithes were intended for the poor and that the monks, as "Christ's paupers," should therefore share in them. Somewhat later Abbot Peter the Venerable of Cluny justified the same practices on the ground of episcopal concession, invoking the episcopal *potestas* over church property. *M.P.L.,* vol. 189, cols. 140–141.

At the Lateran council of 1123 the bishops protested vigorously against what they regarded as the encroachments of the monks upon their rights. The council then passed decrees forbidding abbots and monks to serve parish churches or to receive gifts of churches and tithes from laymen without the consent of the diocesan bishop; in parish churches impropriated to monasteries, priests were to be nominated by the abbot and to be subordinate to the proprietary monastery in respect to temporalities, but to be instituted by the diocesan bishop and to be under his spiritual jurisdiction. *M.P.L.,* vol. 173, 903–904; Mansi, xxi, 285.

reformers themselves did not object to monastic ownership of churches and tithes, provided that it did not disrupt the unity of the diocese. As Tellenbach discerned, the Gregorians were not opposed to the proprietary system as such, but solely to lay proprietorship of churches. Towards the end of the eleventh century the clerical proprietary regime, which had been created by impropriation of the lower churches, was regulated by the papacy in a form modeled upon the old laws governing the lay proprietary regime.[69]

Thus the policy adopted by the Church in Italy in regard to parochial property was not only in accord with canon law as understood by the Gregorians, it avoided alienating the laity and benefited the monasteries who had been the loyal allies of the papacy and whose service of churches was promoting a revival of lay piety. This policy was not, of course, unique to Italy, although applied under somewhat different circumstances there. An incident which occurred at the synod of Reims in 1119 illumines the attitude of both clergy and laity which must have been general during the conflict over investitures.[70] The second decree as proposed by Pope Calixtus II read: "We forbid to laymen investiture of all churches and ecclesiastical possessions." But much opposition arose from the laity and from some of the clergy because they believed that the Pope was endeavoring to take away the tithes and other benefices which the laity had held of old time. The opposition won the day. The decree as finally passed limited the prohibition on investiture to bishoprics and abbacies, excluding the lower churches entirely. The Concordat of Worms, which ended the struggle between Papacy and Empire in 1122, concerned solely the bishoprics and abbacies. The battle against lay proprietorship was essentially won as far as the upper churches were concerned.[71] But the lower churches, namely the

[69] Tellenbach, *Church, State, and Christian Society*, pp. 117–119.

[70] The incident is related by Hesso Scholasticus, *Relatio de Concilio Remensi*, in *M.G.H., Libelli de lite*, iii, 27–28. See also Fliche, *HE*, viii, 383; Tellenbach, *Church, State, and Christian Society*, pp. 122–123.

[71] It should be said that in the relations between bishoprics and em-

parishes and the multitudinous chapels and lesser churches, were
left outside the agreements which ended the investiture controversy. The Church had won in essentials the battle against
simony and clerical marriage; it had virtually destroyed the
Emperor's power over the Church in Italy and had broken the
opposition of the Lombard episcopate. But it had not driven the
laity from their entrenched position in the rural parishes; and it
had not ended the proprietary regime in the lower churches.

---

perors (or kings) other elements than the proprietary were involved.
There were very few bishoprics which were "owned" in the sense in which
the lower churches were owned by laymen or ecclesiastical institutions.

CHAPTER VII

Distribution of Tithes
in the Twelfth Century

† THE GREGORIAN REFORM had eliminated the worst abuses of a moral nature from the Italian Church. Twelfth-century documents yield little evidence of the widespread simony and clerical incontinence characteristic of the previous period, although individual cases continued to occur. The general caliber of the Italian episcopate was improved. But the Italian Church produced few if any leaders of the highest spiritual caliber, and early in the century there was a drop in moral fervor among even the reforming elements in the clergy. The most vital religious movements in twelfth-century Italy were Cistercian monasticism, involving a reactionary asceticism, and the apostolic movement among the laity, inspired by the Gregorian Reform itself, which by the end of the century had joined in large part the stream of heresy.[1] Ecclesiastical records of this century convey an atmosphere of conciliation and moderation,

---

[1] Cistercian monasticism in Italy is treated by Ernesto Buonaiuti, *Gioacchino da Fiore* (Rome, 1931), pp. 97–113 and Catherine E. Boyd, *A Cistercian Nunnery in Mediaeval Italy* (Cambridge, 1943), pp. 19–29. The apostolic movement has been interpreted by Herbert Grundmann, *Religiöse Bewegungen im Mittelalter* (Berlin, 1935), pp. 13–69.

but also one of easy compromise with lay society. It would probably be true to say that the Italian Church in its secular branch was less corrupt than in the preceding age, but in its own way even more worldly. This twelfth-century Church took up the struggle to redeem the parishes and their temporalities from the laity, and the outcome of the struggle, which was reasonably successful in Italy, bears the mark of compromise or, if one prefers, of tolerance.

During the pontificate of the unworldly monk, Paschal II, the papacy had temporarily assumed an intransigent attitude towards lay control of churches and their revenues and had been willing to sacrifice the proprietary interests of its own clergy. Paschal had made to Emperor Henry V the offer embodied in the Convention of Sutri that the Church give up the regalia and live on its tithes and offerings.[2] This Pope also reaffirmed the exclusively spiritual nature of the tithe, forbade laymen to hold churches or their revenues, and branded as simony all traffic in tithes and altars.[3] But the Convention of Sutri proved abortive, and at the synod of Reims under Calixtus II a more moderate attitude towards lay control of churches prevailed. By the time of the Lateran synod of 1123, however, victory on the major issues of the investiture controversy had been assured and the battle against simony and clerical marriage had been won in principle. From this point on, the reforming element in the Church worked more actively for the emancipation of the lower churches, and the lay tithe became more prominent in Roman legislation. The synod of 1123 reiterated the prohibition upon lay possession of church property although it refrained from specifically mentioning the tithe.[4] The Lateran council held under Innocent II in 1139 re-enacted the decree of 1078 which had warned lay tithe holders of their spiritual peril.[5] These decrees seem to have produced results locally. A chronicle

[2] R. W. and A. J. Carlyle, *A History of Mediaeval Political Theory in the West*, iv (London, 1922), 112–128; Fliche, *HE*, viii, 356–364.

[3] Mansi, xx, 1072.   [4] *Ibid.*, xxi, 282 (c. 4).

[5] *Ibid.*, xxi, 528 (c. 10).

quoted by Muratori describes a mass surrender of churches and tithes which occurred in Ferrara during the pontificate of Paschal II:

When Bishop Landulf returned from Rome after his consecration by Pope Paschal, he summoned all the clergy, leading men, valvassors, consuls, and heads of the citizenry of Ferrara, and addressed them as follows: "I will and command all laymen to relinquish their churches with their oblations, tithes, and first fruits into my hands." The laity were indignant and refused to comply. Then the Lord William, the son of Marchisella, declared: "What the bishop asks is right. Laymen ought not to possess churches or share oblations with the clergy, hold tithes and first fruits or demand them from the clergy." . . . Willynilly the laymen then surrendered their churches, oblations, tithes, and first fruits to the bishop, with the promise that they would no longer demand them from the clergy.[6]

A similar campaign against the lay tithe was launched in Genoa by Archbishop Siro, who in an attempt to enforce the decree of 1139 ordered a survey to be made of all the infeudated and leased tithes in his bishopric and then preached so vigorously against the lay tithe that many laymen were frightened and surrendered their tithes to the Church.[7] In his fight against the lay tithe, the Archbishop was supported by the commune of Genoa, which ruled, in a lawsuit of 1151, that the possession of tithes by laymen was "contrary to the sacred canons and the ordinances of the Holy See." [8]

In this way many churches and tithes were recovered by the Church. But the mode of their recovery is indicative of the spirit of the age. Restitutions by the laity were rarely gratuitous. Even in the eleventh century pious laymen had preferred to call their restitutions of church property "concessions" or "donations." Bishops, monasteries, and cathedral chapters, occasionally a parish church, now simply bought back parochial tithes from the laity. Ecclesiastical archives abound in documents recording

[6] *Antiquitates,* vi, 261–262.
[7] Genoa, *Registro I,* p. 28.   [8] *Ibid.,* pp. 114–115.

purchases of tithes by the churches, and while no statistical summary is possible, it is almost certain that purchases exceeded gratuitous restitutions in number. Conscientious bishops who purchased or received donations of parochial tithes saw to it that the parish churches were provided with the *quartese;* the rest of the tithes they kept under their own control.

For the distribution of tithes in the first half of the twelfth century it is possible to draw upon two episcopal inventories of tithes, from Pistoia and Genoa respectively, which unfold a vivid picture of the workings of the tithe and also serve as an exposition of the ideas and principles animating the more exemplary bishops during the aftermath of the Gregorian Reform.

Bishop Hildebrand of Pistoia, whose pontificate dates approximately from 1104 to 1133, was a member of the orthodox reforming party under Calixtus II. His personal integrity was unimpeachable; but he was typical of his generation of reformers in that he avoided conflicts with lay society and sought accommodation instead. His policy was not to excommunicate usurpers of church property but to buy back that property if possible and thus to rebuild the patrimony of his see.[9] Around 1132 Hildebrand had an inventory drawn up of the lands and tithes actually in the possession of his see. The inventory is worth quoting in detail. In the parish of Montemurlo the bishop held three-quarters of the tithe, twice usurped by the knight Guido Guerra and finally recovered by Hildebrand. In the parish of Montemagno he held an undefined share of the tithe which had previously been infeudated to Count Ugolino dei Cadolingi, from whom Hildebrand had garnered them in as the result of a death-bed repentance on the Count's part. In the parish of Greti the bishop had various tithes which he had recovered from the *lombardi,* and a fourth of which he had duly given to the parish priest (*plebanus*). In the baptismal church of Lamporecchio

[9] Romolo Caggese, "Note e documenti per la storia del vescovado di Pistoia nel secolo xii," *BSP*, ix (1907), 133–185. The inventory is printed in full on pp. 179–185. The date 1132 is conjectural.

he again held three-quarters of the tithe, which had been restored by Count Ugolino and the abbot of a local monastery, who
had held them in *livello* from the bishopric. In the parish of
Limite the bishop also had three-quarters of the tithes, which
he had purchased at much trouble and expense from the laymen
to whom they had been leased. In this parish a few scattered
individuals also paid tithes to the bishop, who kept an agent in
Limite to collect his tithes. Half the tithes of the parish church of
Furfalo had been usurped by the local count. The tithes of the
parish of Spannarecchio belonged to the bishop, save those of
the few individuals who paid their tithes to the almost ruined
baptistery. The bishop also collected the tithes of a number of
villages and scattered individuals throughout the diocese. Occasionally the tenants of episcopal lands paid their tithes to the
bishop instead of to the local baptistery.

It is clear that Hildebrand did not feel obliged to remit to the
parish priests more than a fourth of the parochial tithes, and that
in some instances he felt no hesitation in administering all the
tithes himself. In the six parishes mentioned in the inventory,
the bishop held the preponderant part of the tithes. In one parish
he held all the tithes, in three others three-fourths of them, and
in the remaining two the larger part. The inventory also shows
that Hildebrand had purchased most of his tithes from laymen
to whom they had been infeudated or leased by his predecessors
or who had taken advantage of the prevailing chaos in Pistoia
to usurp the tithes of the parish churches. The sacrifices which
he had had to make—for Pistoia was a poor bishopric—explain
the proprietary attitude which Hildebrand took towards parochial tithes acquired by purchase.

Hildebrand's inventory is merely a list of the tithes and other
property which he had recovered for his church. The Genoese
inventory is a comprehensive survey of the tithes of a whole
bishopric.[10]

[10] *Il registro della curia arcivescovile di Genova*, ed. L. T. Belgrano,
ASLSP, ii, pt. 2 (1862), 15–25 [*Registro I.*]

Archbishop Siro of Genoa, a contemporary of Hildebrand of
Pistoia, was an able administrator bent on reconstituting the
patrimony of his church. When he became bishop, most of the
tithes of Genoa were held by the laity, who freely sold or alienated them and even gave them as dowries to their daughters. In
the course of his campaign against the lay tithe after the Second
Lateran Council, Siro summoned the parochial clergy of his diocese and asked them for a precise statement as to the disposition
of the tithes in their parishes, then commanded that all tithes held
as fiefs or leaseholds should be listed in a register of church property with the names of all tithe holders in the diocese. The resulting inventory is nearly complete. After enumerating the oblations
belonging to the archbishop in the local churches, it proceeds to
an account of the tithe of shipping which the archbishop gathered in the port of Genoa, and ends with a list of parochial tithes
ascertained by inquest among the clergy of the diocese. Of the
twenty-eight Genoese parishes, twenty-one are included in this
list. The list itself is summarized in an Appendix at the end of
this volume.[11] A perusal of this unique document, the only sur-
viving inventory of the tithes of a whole bishopric, shows that
the greater part of the parochial tithes were in the possession
of laymen. In sixteen of the twenty-one parishes listed, the parish
church had a fourth of the tithes, in accordance with the principles of the reform; the remaining three-fourths were for the most
part held by laymen, although some had been acquired by the
archbishop and in one parish the cathedral chapter had acquired
tithes. Siro did not feel obliged to give to the parish churches
tithes surrendered or sold by laymen within their districts, provided the parish had the usual fourth. Except in a few cases the
chapels subject to the baptisteries had no tithes at all. Sometimes
a place was detached from the rest of the baptismal district and
paid its tithes to the archbishop or some other tithe owner.

[11] Appendix III. There is an admirable account of the Genoese parishes
by Arturo Ferretto, "I primordi e lo sviluppo del cristianesimo in Liguria
ed in particolare a Genova," pt. 2, "Le pievi battesimali e le chiese minori,"
ASLSP, xxxix (1907), 435–855.

Noblemen were not the only lay possessors of tithes; in one parish tithes had been acquired by serfs.

In both Pistoia and Genoa the prevailing disposition of the tithe was that only a fourth should go to the parish church. The remaining three-fourths, which in most parishes were held by laymen, were regarded as legally belonging to the bishop if he could obtain their restitution or acquire them through purchase. It is impossible to believe that these two surveys reveal a purely factual situation without legal sanction. The legal basis of these arrangements has been indicated in the preceding chapter. Numerous twelfth-century documents prove that the rule assigning the *quartese* to the parish churches was the prevailing law in regard to the distribution of tithes until the very end of the twelfth century, while the *quartese* itself survived long after that time. We shall cite only a few of the more interesting documents showing the law that was enforced during approximately the first three-quarters of the century.

Lucca, 1127. In judging a dispute between a baptismal church and one of its chapels, the bishop of Lucca decided that according to law (*de jure*) the baptismal church was entitled to take a fourth of the parochial tithes.[12]

Genoa, 1139–1143. In regulating the distribution of the tithe of olives in the baptismal district of Sori, Archbishop Siro ordained that the baptismal church should take the fourth of the tithes as in the past; the remaining three-fourths, then under his own administration, he assigned also to the baptismal church and its chapels in return for an annual rent of twelve shillings to be paid to his curia at Christmas. If the baptismal church and its chapels failed to pay this rent, the tithes would revert to the archbishop or his successors. The document concludes with the

---

[12] ". . . de quarta parte decimarum eiusdem capelle ac ceterarum totius plebis, que tota quidem plebano de iure pertinebat, ut dissentio tamen nulla sit inter eos, medietate plebanus sit contentus, altera vero capellanus medietate minime privetur." Nanni, *La parrochia studiata nei documenti lucchesi,* p. 155. This incident illustrates the growing demand on the part of the chapels to share in the tithe.

statement that if the archbishop gives the larger part of the tithes to the local churches, justice requires and the canon law decrees that he and his successors should share in the product of the tithes in order to help the poor and pilgrims—an obvious invocation of the earlier law of quadripartition.[13]

Genoa, 1148. The people of Nervi paid the archbishop a special tithe of olives. They wanted to give this tithe to their baptismal church instead of to the archbishop, but the consuls of Genoa decided in favor of the archbishop, giving a fourth to the baptismal church in deference to canon law and to the fact that the church had for some time been collecting it. Of the ordinary tithe in this parish the baptismal church likewise held a fourth, the remaining tithes being divided in equal parts between the archbishop and some laymen.[14]

Como, 1162–1189 (?). This diocese, in a document of uncertain date, provides us with the clearest statement of all concerning the law enforced in the Lombard bishoprics in the third quarter of the twelfth century. A set of episcopal ordinances for the churches of the diocese, issued sometime after the middle of the century, contains this clause:

Concerning the tithes, which are granted for the use of the churches, we command the observance of this rule: laymen shall not be permitted to possess the fourth part assigned to the churches, but each baptismal church shall have the fourth in its diocese. If anyone encroaches upon the fourths belonging to the churches, let him be held guilty of sacrilege and excommunicated as a violator of church property.[15]

This edict seems to have been an adaptation of the Lateran decrees to local custom and is similar in content to the legislation of the eleventh-century French synods. It is a matter of some interest that the ordinance does not forbid laymen to hold the remaining three-fourths of the tithes, in which it was entirely

---

[13] Genoa, *Registro I*, pp. 14–15.   [14] *Ibid.*, pp. 83–85.
[15] *Cod. dip. della Rezia*, ed. F. Fossati, *PC*, vi (1888), doc. 167.

in accord with local practice if not with the principles laid down by the Roman legislation.

Analogous practices in the repartition of the tithes in the twelfth century may be cited for the bishoprics of Bergamo, Brescia, Bologna, Ferrara, and Lodi.[16] In the Piedmontese bishoprics, Turin, Vercelli, Ivrea, and Novara, a third of the tithes was reserved to the parish church, in accordance with the Gallo-Spanish method of division.[17] The most completely documented example of the functioning of the tithe in this region comes from Revello, in the diocese of Turin, where the parish priest collected a third of the tithes of Revello and the Val del Po, the remaining two-thirds being held by the bishop's vassals until 1220, when the nunnery of Rifreddo acquired them by gift or purchase.[18]

The uniformity of the practices just described shows that the Italian episcopate had some legal basis for their conduct. Their ultimate inspiration came, of course, from the canonical collections prescribing a fourfold division of church revenues. Possibly there may have been in Italy a synodal decree, since lost, corresponding to the earlier French legislation, or it may be that the Italian episcopate by general consent adapted to their traditions the laws of the French councils. Furthermore, it is entirely possible that the canonists and episcopate alike simply developed and generalized a local custom which antedated the Gregorian Reform and which was legally justified by an appeal to ancient

[16] Lupi, *CDB*, ii, 1373–74; *Brescia Sacra*, ii, (1913), 4–6; Augusto Gaudenzi, "Sulle enfiteusi e sulle decime vescovili," *BISI*, xxxvi (1916), 242–243; *M.P.L.*, vol. 200, col. 1153; Vignati, ii, doc. 101.

[17] *LI*, docs. 50, 124, 125; *Documenti biellesi di archivi privati, 1039–1355*, in *BSSS*, xxxiv (Pinerolo, 1908), doc. 33; *Carte d'Ivrea*, doc. 294. The bishopric of Acqui was exceptional in making a fourfold division. As late as 1434 the bishops of Acqui were granting three-fourths of the parochial tithes to nobles and reserving only a fourth to the parish churches. J. B. Moriondi, *Monumenta Aquensia* (Turin, 1789–1790, 2 vols.), i, 395–398. Cf. cols. 244–245, 301–303, 320–321.

[18] Catherine E. Boyd, *A Cistercian Nunnery in Mediaeval Italy*, chs. 3 and 7.

canon law. The answer to this question is hidden in the mists of the tenth century. We shall probably never know in complete detail the way in which the *quartese* originated. But the practice has now been traced to its roots and the nature of the *quartese* clearly demonstrated. It remains to trace the development of the canon law of tithes from Gratian to the Decretals and to show the form and conditions under which the *quartese* survived.

The work of the eleventh-century canonists was crowned, about 1148, by Gratian's monumental *Decretum*, in which he not only assembled but clarified and harmonized all the canonical texts bearing upon specific problems. Studied and glossed by canonists of the twelfth century, the *Decretum* prepared the way for the classical formulation of canon law which culminated in 1237 in the Decretals of Gregory IX.[19] At the hands of Gratian and the Decretists a law of tithes finally emerged which superseded the conflicting views and doctrines of the pre-Gratianic period. This was the law of tithes sanctioned by the Decretals,

[19] On the development of canon law in this period J. F. von Schulte's standard work, *Die Geschichte der Quellen und Literatur des canonischen Rechts von Gratien bis auf die Gegenwart* (Stuttgart, 1875–1880, 3 vols.) should be supplemented by Stefan Küttner's *Repertorium der Kanonistik* (*1140–1324*) (Vatican City, 1937). Some of the works of Gratian's commentators, the Decretists, have been published: e.g. *Die Summa Magistri Rolandi*, ed. F. Thaner (Innsbruck, 1874); *Die Summa des Paucapalea über das Decretum Gratiani*, ed. J. F. von Schulte (Giessen, 1890); *Die Summa Decretorum des Stephanus Tornacensis über das Decretum Gratiani*, ed. Schulte (Giessen, 1891); and *Die Summa Decretorum des Magister Rufinus*, ed. H. Singer (Paderborn, 1902). Still unpublished is the most important commentary of all, the "Summa Decretorum" of Huguccio of Pisa, teacher of Innocent III, who wrote at the end of the twelfth century and profoundly influenced the development of canon law. I have used the "Summa" in the MS. Vaticanus Latinus 2280. Also essential to an understanding of the evolution of canon law in the high Middle Ages are the glosses on the *Decretum* made by Johannes Teutonicus and Bartholomew of Brescia, which appear in most of the early printed editions of that work; e.g., *Decretum sive Gratiani auctoris vel compilatoris cum apparatibus Johannis ac additionibus Bartholomei Brixiensis* (Nuremberg, 1493), Harvard Law School.

included in the *Corpus Juris Canonici*, and therefore the authoritative statement of the law in De Luca's time and later.

In the course of the twelfth century, and as a result of the Gregorian Reform, the constitution of the medieval Church took the form of a papal monarchy built upon the ruins of the older episcopal and federative system. The formulation of canon law, as developed by Gratian and brought together in the Decretals published under the auspices of Gregory IX, was part of this centralizing process. But just as many remnants of the episcopal organization of the Church remained, so did local customs tenaciously survive, sanctioned by long usage. Canon law was not at first imposed *à force majeure* upon the local churches. It was indeed the general body of laws accepted and promulgated by the universal Church, the common law or *jus commune;* but it was not regarded as necessarily incompatible with local customs which did not conflict with it too flagrantly, especially if such customs were to the advantage of the local church. "As Thy Discretion is not unaware," wrote Innocent III to the archbishop of Cosenza, "different churches follow different customs, which the Roman Church does not reject or condemn unless they are contrary to the canon law." [20]

In the twelfth century, then, the ancient polity of the Church was changing. We shall merely summarize, without detailed discussion, the changes in the law governing the repartition of the tithes.

Four sections, or Cases, in Gratian's *Decretum* (X, XIII, XVI, and XXV) are hypothetical lawsuits over the tithe. In addition, Case XII is directly concerned with the distribution of church revenues.[21]

Particularly important for later law is Gratian's discussion

[20] *M.P.L.*, vol. 215, col. 254.

[21] The *Decretum* forms the first volume of the *Corpus Juris Canonici* (2nd rev. ed., by E. Friedberg and E. L. Richter, Leipzig, 1928, 2 vols.). The second part of the *Decretum* is divided into Cases (*Causae*), in which Gratian discusses hypothetical lawsuits in illustration of controversial points.

of a question much debated in his day: Shall the tithe be paid
to the church of the place where the believer lives and receives
the sacraments, or to the church within whose parochial boundaries his lands are situated? Case XIII concerns the hypothetical case of the parishioners of one church who because of warfare
have shifted their dwellings to another parish but continue to
cultivate their lands within their old parish. Must they pay their
tithes and be buried in the former parish or not? Gratian decides
that the church in the old parish has the right of the case; that is
to say, the believer must pay his tithe to the church in whose
parish his lands are situated rather than to the church where he
receives the sacraments. This decision, widely commented on
by the Decretists, established once and for all the essentially
predial nature of the tithe and divorced it from the administration of the sacraments.[22]

Gratian followed the Gregorian canonists in stressing episcopal jurisdiction over the parish churches and their revenues. In
Case X he exalts the episcopal *potestas* as the antithesis of lay
control and the best means of preserving the integrity of church
property.[23] Any danger of falling into the confusion between
ownership and jurisdiction which had prevailed in the preceding
period was lessened in Gratian's time by the current revival of
Roman law with its clear distinctions and categories.

Case XVI bears the imprint of the system of distributing
tithes then practiced in Italy. In treating the question of the
service of parish churches by monks and the monastic exemption
from the tithe, Gratian declares himself in favor of these practices. To the objection that the monastic exemptions were depriving parish churches of their ancient rights, Gratian replies

[22] The Decretists, however, did distinguish between predial tithes, resting upon the land, and personal tithes, i.e., those from revenues derived
from industry or business (*de artificio, de negotio*), the second of which
were to be paid to the church in whose parish the believer resided and received the sacraments. Singer, *Die Summa Decretorum des Magister
Rufinus,* pp. 332–333.

[23] See especially *Decretum,* C. X, q. i, c. 15 and q. ii, cc. 7, 8.

that according to the canons all the tithes are at the disposal of the bishops; therefore the bishop who has founded or permitted the foundation of a monastery can give it the tithes of the lands tilled by the monks themselves; for just as the pope can unite or sever bishoprics, so can a bishop divide one parish into several and distribute the tithes among them. In this case, Gratian quotes Leo IV's decree that tithes shall be paid only to baptismal churches, at the same time qualifying this statement by demanding that the baptismal church must have legally designated parochial boundaries.[24] Case XVI clearly shows the impact of the two laws, old and new, in regard to the tithes.

Finally, in Case XXV, Gratian debates the question of whether a papal privilege can overthrow the established rules of the Church, and uses as his illustration the attempts made by the clergy of a baptismal church, on the basis of a papal privilege, to collect all the tithes of the baptismal area instead of the fourth allowed them by the law of quadripartition. Gratian here assumes that the clergy of the baptistery are entitled under the old law to only a fourth of the tithes. He concludes that the pope can grant a privilege to a baptismal church permitting it to collect all the tithes of its district, even if the law of quadripartition dictates the division of the tithes into four portions.[25]

In Gratian's time the old discipline was changing, and his treatise exhibits traces of both rules for the distribution of tithes. The final triumph of the new rule, actually a revival of the law of tithes in the Carolingian period, was largely due to the Decretists, and especially to Huguccio of Pisa and his pupil, Innocent III. The Decretists struggled bravely with the contradictions in the ancient canons, formulated under different historical condi-

[24] *Decretum,* C. XVI, q. i, cc. 45–49, 56. Gratian's doctrine in regard to the episcopal *potestas* obviously favored both the monastic exemption from tithes and monastic ownership of tithes. In this period monastic apologists often appealed to the principle of episcopal jurisdiction over church property to justify the growing power of the monasteries over parish churches and their revenues.

[25] Friedberg-Richter, *Corpus Juris Canonici,* i, 1006–1019.

tions than their own, and Huguccio finally reached the conclusion that the rule of quadripartition was intended for the cathedral revenues alone and that in the rural districts each baptistery should have all the tithes of its district.[26] By Huguccio's time, however, another problem had emerged, that of dividing the tithes between the baptisteries and their chapels. Of this, Huguccio remarks that the baptistery should make four portions of its tithes; keeping one for itself, giving another to the chapels under its care, and assigning the other fourths to the poor and the repair of the fabric respectively. But in fact, he continues, the avarice of the bishops has led them to seize for themselves in many places three-fourths of the tithes, leaving the baptisteries in possession of only the remaining fourth, while the chapels have no tithes at all.[27] Thus Huguccio rejects the customs prevalent in Italy and accepted by the canonists until his time on the basis of a mistaken interpretation of the rule of quadripartition. His view that the tithes were the exclusive patrimony of the baptismal churches became part of canon law in the thirteenth century through its affirmation in the Decretals.

The principle that the tithes belonged to the parish churches was written into the canon law by two canonist popes—Alexander III, who as Cardinal Roland had wrestled with the problem of the tithes while composing a commentary on Gratian's *Decretum*, and Innocent III, the pupil of Huguccio of Pisa.

During the pontificate of Alexander III the tithe became in-

[26] For the comments of the Decretists, see Thaner, *Die Summa Magistri Rolandi*, pp. 421–423 and Singer, *Die Summa Decretorum des Magister Rufinus*, pp. 301–302. Huguccio's conclusions are expressed in the "Summa Decretorum," MS. Vat. Lat. 2280, fol. 215 r.

[27] "Et sic episcopus non debet nisi de decimis que dividuntur in quattuor partes, ut xii, q. ii, Vobis concesso quattuor, que omnia loquuntur tantum de episcopalibus ecclesiis. Similiter quelibet plebs ruralis debet habere omnes decimas de sua parrochia et dividere in quattuor partes. Una sit baptismalis ipsius ecclesie, secunda capellarum, tertia pauperum, quarta fabrice. Sed modo avaritia episcoporum occupavit sibi in multis locis tres partes decimarum, tantum quarta relicta plebi, capellanis existentibus siccis." *Ibid.*

creasingly prominent in legislation and adjudication. Two problems were especially pressing: the lay tithe and the noval tithes. The Third Lateran Council, held in 1179 under Alexander's presidency, for the first time attached ecclesiastical penalties to lay ownership of tithes, condemning not only traffic in tithes among laymen but also transmission by inheritance. The decree "Prohibemus" declares: "We forbid laymen who at the peril of their souls hold tithes to transfer such tithes in any way to other laymen. If any layman receives such tithes and does not restore them to the Church, let him be denied Christian burial." [28] Viard has pointed out that this decree merely tried to prevent the infeudated and leased tithes from becoming an object of commerce among laymen; it did not expressly condemn the holding of tithes by their present owners; but by forbidding laymen to transmit their tithes to their heirs, it implied that lay ownership of tithes was intrinsically wrong. No doubt the leaders of the Church hoped that the lay tithe would be extirpated within a generation, but their expectations were destined to be disappointed.

The noval tithes were those resting upon newly cultivated or "assarted" lands, defined in the Decretals as "land never before known to be cultivated." The internal colonization of Europe in the twelfth century had resulted in a great deal of land reclamation and reduction of waste to tillage. From such lands, designated as *novalia,* as from the older settled lands, the Church claimed the tithe. From about the middle of the twelfth century a distinction appears in the documents between the ancient tithes (*decimae antiquae*) and the noval tithes (*decimae no-*

[28] Mansi, xxii, 226 (c. 14). This was taken up into the *Decretales Gregorii IX*, III, xxx, "De decimis," c. 19. Viard, *La dîme ecclésiastique dans le royaume de France aux xiie et xiiie siècles (1150–1313)* (Paris, 1912), p. 125. In France from this time on, the ecclesiastical courts recognized the legitimacy of tithes held by laymen prior to 1179 but refused to consider as canonical infeudations made after that date. Joseph Declareuil, *Histoire générale du droit français* (Bordeaux, 1926), p. 328, n. 62. This had certainly not been the intention of the Third Lateran Council.

valium). For the latter, there were no established rules in canon law, and many bishops were uncertain as to the course they should take. To an inquiry from the bishop of Brescia, Alexander III replied that if the noval land was within the boundaries of an existing parish, the bishop was to assign the noval tithes to the parish church, retaining his own share, i.e., the episcopal fourth; otherwise he was to assign the tithes to another church or retain them himself if he wished.[29] Alexander's interpretation of this general principle appears in a privilege which he granted in 1177 to the parish church of Montechiari in Brescia, confirming the church in possession of all the noval tithes of its parish together with a fourth of the ancient tithes.[30] The principle laid down by Alexander was a reforming innovation arising from the reinterpretation of canon law. Less than a generation earlier, in 1145 and again in 1154, the papal legate in Lombardy, Cardinal Aribert, had assigned to the cathedral chapter of Cremona only a fourth of the noval tithes of its parishioners and for that concession had made them pay a rent of seven *librae* as compensation to the bishop.[31] This decision was obviously an application to the noval tithes of the old rule favoring the bishops and was soon superseded, in canon law at least, by the new rule stated by Alexander.[32]

[29] *Decretales Gregorii IX*, III, xxx, "De decimis," c. 13. Arnold Pöschl has studied the noval tithes, with special reference to Germany, in "Der Neubruchzehnt," *AKK*, xcviii (1918), 3–51, 171–214, 333–380. Noval tithes are mentioned as early as the council of Tribur in 895 but were not important until the twelfth century. The classification of tithes into ancient and noval was important in Italy and Germany; though known in France, it did not play much part in the evolution of the tithe in that country. Viard, *Dîme avant Gratien*, pp. 159–160.

[30] G. Bonelli, "Una bolla grande di Alessandro III per Montechiari," *Brescia Sacra*, iii (1912), 4–6.

[31] Kehr, *IP*, vi, pt. 1, 277.

[32] The European countries diverged considerably in regard to the noval tithes. In France the parish priest succeeded in establishing his exclusive right to the noval tithes. J. Declareuil, *Histoire générale du droit français*, p. 328, n. 64. In Germany, to the contrary, the bishops made good their pretensions to the tithes of assarts. Stutz, *Beneficialwesen*, p. 240, n. 16.

The new law in regard to the distribution of tithes was finally declared by Innocent III, who gave the parish churches the ordinary right to collect the tithe. To a question concerning the ever-recurring problem of the noval tithes, Innocent replied:

Since in some parishes the collection of the tithes belongs by ancient custom to certain churches or ecclesiastical persons, and recently new lands have been created in these parishes, you ask us to whom the tithe of these new lands belongs. We answer your question as follows: Since the collection of tithes belongs to the parish churches by common law, the tithes of lands newly reduced to cultivation in those parishes also belong to the parish churches, unless a reasonable cause is shown by those who own the other tithes [i.e., the ancient tithes] that the tithes of the new lands also belong to them.[33]

In a letter to the bishop of Beauvais, about monastic tithes, the Pope affirmed the same doctrine.[34] Both these letters were included in the Decretals of Gregory IX and thus assured the triumph in the newly forming canon law of the principle that tithes were a distinctively parochial revenue.

Still another letter of Innocent's, addressed to the bishop of

---

In this respect Italy resembled Germany. A Milanese custumal compiled around 1216 declared that the archbishop had the exclusive right to the noval tithes according to canon law. Berlan, *LCM*, p. 60. Vested in the bishops in Italy, the noval tithes underwent the same fate as the ancient tithes; they were infeudated or leased to laymen, conferred upon monasteries, and sometimes, though exceptionally, granted to parish priests. For examples of concessions of noval tithes by bishops to monasteries, see *Cartario di Pinerolo*, doc. 51; *Documenti di Scarnafigi*, doc. 7. Concessions of noval tithes to parish priests were usually leases for a limited period of time. Turin, 1271: the bishop granted for twenty years to the *plebanus* of Castellar a third of the ancient and noval tithes of the district, subject to an annual rent in kind. *Cartario di Pinerolo*, doc. 139. An isolated concession which followed the canonical form was the granting of all the noval tithes, less the episcopal fourth, to the parish priest of Peire. *LI*, doc. 12. In 1194 a parish priest of Asti claimed the right to a fourth of the noval tithes of his parish, although in canon law he was entitled to all such tithes. *ACA*, doc. 130.

[33] *Decretales Gregorii IX*, III, xxx, "De decimis," c. 29.
[34] *Ibid.*, c. 30.

Spoleto, shows the Pope's attitude toward the old law. Deciding a dispute between the bishop and a parish church in 1202, Innocent confirms the parochial clergy in the traditional fourth of the tithes, then goes on to say: "The other two portions, which canon law assigns to the edifice and to the poor, we reserve to the disposition of the bishop in order that, *according to the approved custom of the diocese of Spoleto,* he may dispense them faithfully, since he will render account for them to God." [35] Thus the law governing the distribution of tithes in the first half of the twelfth century had become merely an approved custom a century later. The old law of quadripartition assigning all the tithes except the parochial fourth to the disposal of the bishop was permitted to exist as a local custom, whereby the fourths of the fabric and the poor were administered by the bishop, leaving only the clerical fourth under the direct jurisdiction of the parochial clergy.[36] But the law of the Decretals assigned the tithes by common law to the parish churches, and with the passage of time this became the classical system of tithes.

Needless to say, the older system of tithes was not abrogated in northern Italy, nor did most bishops divide the tithes in the manner enjoined by Innocent upon the bishop of Spoleto. Thus in the Lombard bishopric of Lodi, feudal concessions of tithes continued in the thirteenth century, although always with the reservation of the parochial fourth.[37] Episcopal leases of tithes

[35] *M.P.L.,* vol. 214, col. 955.

[36] The transition is illustrated by a document of 1159 from Gubbio, in which the bishop confirms the canons of a baptismal church in their fourth of the tithes and oblations, assigns the fourth of the fabric to one of the canons to administer, but retains in his own power the fourth due to the poor. The document contains the provision that the bishop and his successors may not alienate the fourth of the poor nor give it away as a fief or benefice. *Chartularium Imolense,* ed. S. Gaddoni and G. Zaccherini (Imola, 1912, 2 vols.), doc. 187.

[37] In 1263 the bishop invested three laymen *per gentile et legale feudum* with a third of the ancient tithes of Castelnuovo, excepting the fourth due to the local church and all the noval tithes. Another feudal concession of

in the Piedmontese bishoprics continued to reserve a third to the local churches. Examples could be multiplied from practically every bishopric in Italy. The most obstinate resistance to the new law seems to have come, however, from the bishoprics composing the later Republic of Venetia. This is the region which has preserved the clearest traces of the ancient system of tithes on which the law of the Decretals was imposed. It is, moreover, the section of Italy more especially characterized by the use of a distinct name for the parochial fourth—*quartisium* or *quartesium* in the Latin documents, *quartese* in the vernacular.[38]

Throughout the high Middle Ages in Venetia the *quartese* continued to be the normal portion of the tithe belonging to the parish church and its clergy, guaranteed to them by common law and sanctified by usage. The parish churches of this region usually had only the *quartese* of the old tithes, although they sometimes received from their bishops the right to take all the noval tithes.[39] When grants of tithes were made by the bishops to monasteries, the *quartese*, not always called by name, was reserved to the parish churches by common law.[40] Eventually in this region, the *quartisium* was distinguished from the rest of the tithe and was spoken of as if it were a separate entity.[41] The *quartese* was administered and collected just like the rest of

---

tithes, in 1284, carried the reservation "deducting the fourth of the church." Vignati, iii, docs. 356 and 394. Cf. docs. 393, 396, 423.

[38] In spite of its name the *quartese* was not invariably a fourth of the tithe; it was sometimes a third (*tercesium*). Thus the bishop of Padua in giving a church to a monastery excepted "the third of the tithes which is called the *quartese*" customarily held by the archpriest of the local baptistery. Gloria, *CDP*, ii, doc. 157. Du Cange, *Glossarium*, v, 551–552, comments on *quartisium* and its variants.

[39] The *pieve* of Monselice in Padua had all the noval tithes of its territory and the *quartisium* of the old tithes. Kehr, *IP*, vii, pt. 1, no. 5.

[40] Padua, 1144: in giving a monastery three-fourths of all the tithes of Scodosia, the bishop explained that he was reserving the fourth which belonged to the churches ("Nam quartam portionem quibus competit reservamus ecclesiis"). Gloria, *CDP*, ii, doc. 431.

[41] *Ibid.*, ii, doc. 743 ("decima cum toto quartisio").

the tithes in ecclesiastical hands.[42] In Padua during the twelfth century the urban parishes won the right to share in the *quartese* with the cathedral chapter, and in 1170 they pooled their rights in the *quartesi* of Padua and its district.[43] The statutes of Padua, in addition to throwing light upon the collection of the *quartese,* show that the commune enforced the payment of the *quartese* as well as of the rest of the tithes to their respective owners.[44] The *quartese* also prevailed in the diocese of Concordia.[45]

In Verona the *quartese* was the normal portion of the parish church, the remainder of the tithes usually being owned by laymen or monasteries.[46] In this bishopric in the thirteenth century the word *quartisium* was also applied, although very exceptionally, to the portions of the tithe held by laymen, showing the confusion that was beginning to creep into the institution.[47] In some documents the word tended to become interchangeable

[42] Throughout this region the churches commonly leased out the collectorship of their *quartesi* indifferently to clerics or laymen. Gloria, *CDP,* iii, doc. 1445.

[43] *Ibid.,* docs. 1002, 1087, 1169.

[44] *Statuti di Padova,* p. 217, no. 662.

[45] Ernesto Degani, *La dominicalità delle decime della diocesi di Concordia* (Portogruaro, 1889), p. 62. That abuses had come into the *quartese* is indicated by the fact that many of the prebends held by the cathedral clergy included both tithes and *quartesi. Ibid.,* pp. 158–159.

[46] Witnesses in a lawsuit over the tithes of Trebenciolo testified that the tithes belonged to two laymen "excepto quartesio quod intelligitur esse plebis illius terre trevenzoli." ACNV, San Giorgio in Braida, doc. 8447. Doc. 8424 is similar.

[47] ACNV, San Giorgio in Braida, doc. 8417. Here *quartisium* obviously means simply a fourth of the tithe, not the parochial fourth. A witness testified: "Scio quod Facinus et alii habent medietatem maioris decime super totam curiam trevenzoli praeter quartesium et novales et decimam predictorum mansorum. . . . Item scio quod dominus Balduinus de Jacolo Drago iudice habent quartesium maioris decime curtis trevenzoli et aliud quartesium habet quondam Opidinus . . . et dico quia ecclesia trevenzoli habet aliud quartesium maioris decime." In doc. 8418 the Facinus mentioned in the previous document states that the church had the *quartesium,* while the remainder of the tithes was divided between himself and some other laymen. This was the more general usage.

with *decima,* losing its narrow significance of the fourth of the tithe reserved to the parish church.[48]

During the high Middle Ages the *quartese* was not indeed confined to Venetia. It occurs sporadically in the documents of Mantua and Parma. Some landowners and tenants in Mantua had managed to free their lands from the tithe but continued to pay the *quartese* to the local church.[49] Tenants usually paid their tithes to laymen or monasteries, often their landlords, their *quartese* to the parish church.[50] That the entire *quartese* was sometimes infeudated to laymen appears from a document of 1222 in which a layman bestows upon the cathedral chapter the entire *quartese* of the ancient tithes of a village, with the consent of the archpriest of the local baptistery from whom the layman held the *quartese* as a fief.[51] This infeudation of the *quartese* by a parish priest was of course an extreme abuse and seems to have been uncommon. In Parma the cathedral chapter and the local monasteries seem to have been encroaching upon the *quartesi* of the rural archpriests.[52]

But it is in the bishoprics within the Venetian orbit that the *quartese* survived most tenaciously into modern times. It is interesting to note that in Treviso the provincial government reported to the Austrian government in 1817 that in many, if not all, of the parishes there existed in favor of the local priest "the tax called the *decima* or *quartese,*" and also noted that in some places in Treviso there were lands which paid tithes to ecclesiastical corporations and even to lay families by virtue of episcopal investiture.[53]

Most revealing of all, however, is the situation in the diocese

---

[48] After stating that the local church held the *quartese* of the tithe, a witness testified that the other three parts of the *quartese* (*alie tres partes quartisii*) belonged to a layman. ACNV, San Giorgio in Braida, doc. 8423.

[49] Torelli, *ACM*, doc. 34.   [50] *Ibid.,* doc. 42.

[51] *Ibid.,* doc. 59.   [52] *Carte di Parma,* docs. 571, 664.

[53] G. Benvenuti, *Le decime ed i quartesi nella storia e nella giurisprudenza,* p. 21.

of Vicenza. In the first half of the nineteenth century, the custom in this diocese still was that in each parish the local clergy held a fourth of the tithes while three-fourths were in the hands of laymen who held them as fiefs from the bishops. Vicenza clung tenaciously to the ancient discipline as regards the division of the tithes. In 1834 Todeschini wrote:

In Vicenza there never was established the rule concerning the collection and disposition of the tithes which came to form the common law of the more recent canonical discipline. The collection and administration of the tithes never passed to the parish priests. In founding and endowing parishes, the bishops left the parish priests only the fourth part of the tithe granted by the ancient canons to the lower clergy and kept the rest in their own power. The common law of this diocese was and is that to the parish priests belongs the so-called *quartese*.[54]

This statement is confirmed by numerous documents referring to the *jus commune* of this region. Thus one bishop of Vicenza in confirming to a parish church in 1262 all the tithes of its territory which were not held by others as fiefs, excepted the *quartese* which belonged to the parish church by common law.[55] And the customary clause in episcopal investitures of tithes was "saving the right of the baptismal church in regard to the *quartese*." [56]

In Vicenza in the nineteenth century there was a marked disproportion between the *decima* and the *quartese*. The latter

---

[54] G. Todeschini, *Le decime feudali del vescovado di Vicenza* (Vicenza, 1882), p. 79. This work, first written in 1834, is probably the ablest of the nineteenth-century accounts of the problem of the tithes, thanks to the author's knowledge of canon law. For a concise exposition of his views, see pp. 12–57.

[55] ". . . quarum quartisium spectat ad eamden ecclesiam de iure comuni." Gaetano Maccà, *Storia del territorio vicentino* (Caldogno, 1812–1815, 14 vols.), vii, 147.

[56] Feudal investitures of tithes made by the bishop of Vicenza in the early eighteenth century (1716, 1718) all contain the traditional clause ". . . saving the right of the baptismal and parochial church in regard to the *quartesi* and other accustomed dues." *FV*, 1920, col. 334.

extended over much land that was not subject to the tithe, and in some communes the product of the *quartese* exceeded that of the *decima*. Todeschini explains this by the fact that much new land never did pay the noval tithes, but paid the *quartese:*

The fate that overtook new lands legally subject to the *decima,* that is to say, the three-fourths of the tithe under episcopal jurisdiction, did not equally affect the *quartese* of the parish priests. This payment was very small, and of a nature not to arouse opposition; it was difficult not to admit the justice and the convenience of providing for the maintenance of the parish priest with a slender portion of the revenues from land and thus to let him share in the greater prosperity which gradually became the lot of his parish.[57]

Moreover, the parish priest was always on the spot to collect. Thus in Vicenza survived the ancient system of dividing the tithes, under which three-fourths of the tithes were at the disposal of the bishop. The ultimate right of the bishop over the tithes was a general fact in this diocese. To maintain the dominical nature of the tithes in Vicenza it would be necessary to maintain that there was a time when all the lands of the diocese were the property of the Church.[58]

We shall conclude this chapter on the distribution of the tithes by a brief account of the tithes of Pirano. From the archives of the church (now the cathedral) of San Giorgio have been extracted more than fifty documents recording in great detail a lawsuit over the tithes dating from the pontificate of Innocent III.[59] This collection of documents affords a perfect local example of the conflict of laws in Istria at the turn of the twelfth century.

[57] Todeschini, pp. 80–81.

[58] This is true of the eight Venetian provinces and of Ferrara, where the *quartese* also survived. The right of the archbishop of Ferrara over the tithes was justified by the Rota in 1787 on the ground that he was "universal parish priest" of his diocese. *DE,* i (1890), 795, n. 2.

[59] In *Chartularium Piranense,* ed. C. de Franceschi, *Atti e memorie della società istriana di archeologia e storia patria,* xxxvi (1924).

The small commune of Pirano, on a promontory of the Gulf
of Istria, lay within the bishopric of Capodistria. Its principal
church was the baptistery of San Giorgio, a collegiate church,
which held the *quartese* of the town and which received, in
addition, from the people of Pirano a special tithe of oil, the
product of the olive groves in the hinterland. The tithe of oil had
been for some time a cause of strife between the Piranesi and
their bishop when, in 1201, the bishop tried to collect this tithe,
together with the fourths of the poor and the fabric, from the
people and met with resistance so strong that he laid the town
under an interdict.[60] This incident provoked a lawsuit which
lasted for four years and the records of which prove conclusively
that the parish clergy and their people were solidly united
against the bishop. A significant fact emerging from the testimony given in this lawsuit was the information that of the ordinary tithe of Pirano the clergy had only the *quartese;* the remaining three-fourths had been infeudated by the bishop to his vassals.[61] It was for his vassals, then, that the bishop was so strenuously demanding the fourths of the poor and the fabric. The most
interesting moment in the case came when it was transferred to
Padua. The advocates of the Piranesi came before the bishop
of Padua, now papal judge delegate, armed with a battery of
citations from Gratian's *Decretum;* they showed themselves to
be familiar with the inconsistencies in Gratian's texts, rejected
the distribution of the tithes described in Case XII and rested
their claim to the tithes upon the decree of Leo IV cited in Case
XVI; then reinforced their argument by citations from papal
decisions since Gratian's time and from Justinian's Code. True,
they said, the Twelfth Case prescribes the fourfold division of
church revenues to be made by the bishop; but Gratian's texts
referred not to what was actually done at Rome but what *ought*
to be done; by the same token, they, the defendants, were not
basing their claims upon the customary practices of Pirano but
upon what *should* be done. And obviously what should be done

[60] *Ibid.*, i, docs. 11, 12, 13, 15.   [61] *Ibid.*, doc. 22.

was to give the fourths of the local poor and the fabric to the parish church of Pirano, to be administered by the local clergy for the benefit of the parish.[62] This was a flat repudiation of the whole theory of customary law and established rights.

The case was ended in Ferrara, in 1205, by two papal judges delegate. The baptistery won the tithe of oil and was confirmed in possession of the *quartese;* but the remaining three-fourths of the tithe were left with the bishop's vassals.[63] The net result of the decision was the confirmation of the status quo. This lawsuit at Pirano was a local application of the policy formulated by Innocent III, in sanctioning the possession of ancient tithes by laymen if they held them as fiefs.[64]

[62] *Ibid.,* doc. 44.   [63] *Ibid.,* doc. 65.   [64] See p. 170.

CHAPTER VIII

The Italian Parochial System
in the High Middle Ages

† THE TWELFTH CENTURY witnessed the gradual emancipation of the lower churches of Italy from the lay proprietary
system. By the middle of the century, as a result of restitutions
of churches, the aims of the Gregorians as regards lay domination
of churches were on the way to fulfillment; before the century
had ended, lay ownership of churches had dwindled to a mere
right of patronage, whereby the lay patron simply presented a
priest to the bishop for appointment. The noble families of Milan,
Lucca, Turin, and other places continued for many generations
to be the patrons of the parish churches of the countryside, to
collect their tithes, and to exercise all the rights accompanying
an advowson. But after the twelfth century the exclusively
spiritual nature of the priest's office and its subordination to
episcopal authority were never questioned. Gradually the noble
families seem to have lost interest in their rights over the rural
churches; when they did not return their churches outright to
the ecclesiastical authorities, they sold their rights or lost them
to the communes which sprang up all through the Italian countryside in the high Middle Ages.

This is not to say that the proprietary idea was immediately obliterated. In the early twelfth century the Italian episcopate tended to treat the churches restored by laymen as if they were the private churches of the bishopric. But with the growth of canon law, the misconceptions on which these practices rested gradually ceased. Furthermore, the clerical proprietary system, which the Gregorians had not challenged, was preserved in the form of incorporation, as the impropriation of churches to monasteries and cathedral chapters was now called.[1] Impropriation usually involved nonparochial churches, mostly churches on the domains of laymen or founded by monasteries; among the hundreds of churches whose priests were nominated and whose revenues were administered by cathedral chapters or monasteries, comparatively few were baptisteries. But the distinction between parish churches and chapels was beginning to break down in this period, and an understanding of the Italian parochial system requires a summary of the main outlines of this development.

In the twelfth century Italian parochial institutions began to lose their original unity and to evolve into a more complex system. Hitherto the word "parish" has been synonymous with "baptistery" or "baptismal church" (*plebs* or *pieve*), an institution which in its organization and structure was somewhat different from the modern parish. The baptismal church was the apex of a hierarchical structure including a cluster of lesser churches; it alone could baptize and bury the people of its district and celebrate certain solemnities. It alone possessed the tithe, or such part of it as had escaped the laity. The baptismal church, therefore, was the only church which before the twelfth century can properly be called a parish church, with the cure of souls. But in that century some churches of a lesser order also began to exercise parochial rights, and from this time on such churches in respect to social function may be regarded as parishes. This change is reflected in the terminology of local

[1] Fliche, *HE*, viii, 411–413.

documents. Some Genoese documents of the twelfth century distinguish between the *plebeium,* or baptismal district, the entire area subject to the prerogatives of the baptistery, and the *parochia,* or parish, where its parishioners, in the modern sense, resided.[2] In this sense many chapels also had their parishes, and as time went on, the phrase "a chapel with its parish" became not uncommon.[3] This Italian use of the word "parish" was noted by the canonist Stephen of Tournai, in connection with the phrase "sicut et parochiales" in Gratian's Thirteenth Case:

This phrase is more intelligible to those who are familiar with the customs of the Italian Church. For in Italy there are some churches called *plebes,* in which archpriests reside, and these baptismal churches, as they are called, have under them other lesser churches, which are called chapels, or parishes.[4]

With the attainment of full parochial rights by some of these lesser churches, the modern parish came slowly into being. In the rural districts this was a village church of which the priest was charged with the cure of souls, a church with the right to baptize and bury its parishioners and under the immediate jurisdiction of the bishop. This change took place very gradually in Italy; the chapels did not supersede the ancient baptisteries until after the Middle Ages had ended. But signs of their ultimate emancipation from the baptisteries appear in the documents of the twelfth and thirteenth centuries.

[2] Genoa, *Registro I,* p. 21: "Ipsa plebs habet totam decimam sue parrochie pro quarta totius plebeii."

[3] E.g., ". . . capellam de trivino [Trino] cum parochia sua de burgo novo." *Le carte del monastero di Rocca della Donne,* ed. F. Loddo, BSSS, lxxxix (Turin, 1929), doc. 5.

[4] J. F. von Schulte, ed., *Die Summa des Stephanus Tornacensis über das Decretum Gratiani,* p. 218. Both in the Thirteenth and the Twenty-fifth Cases, Gratian distinguishes the baptismal church and its "diocese" from the parochial church with its parish; e.g., "Constat unamquamque baptismalem ecclesiam habere diocesim sibi legitime assignatam, sicut et parochiales ecclesias habent parochias sibi distributae." *Decretum,* C. XIII, q. 1 (Friedberg-Richter, *Corpus Juris Canonici,* i, col. 717).

The elevation of chapels to the status of baptismal churches had indeed been going on all through the Middle Ages. While some baptisteries went back to remote antiquity, others had originally been chapels themselves. This movement was greatly accelerated in the twelfth century as the population grew and new lands were cleared. At the same time the whole hierarchical structure involving baptisteries and chapels began to crack.

The issue between baptisteries and chapels was sharply joined early in the century, when partisans of the chapels tried to break down the ancient discipline which made the baptismal church the center where various ceremonies had to be performed and to which tithes were paid from the whole circumscription.[5] This demand for autonomy on the part of the lesser churches and the people of their communities was the religious aspect of the general movement towards local independence which had begun to animate the people of rural Italy. Many villages, already organized as rural communes, were ambitious to have their own parish churches, to choose their own priests, and to keep the product of their tithes and offerings within the district. Other factors played a part in bringing about change. Some bishops saw in this movement a chance to secure more complete control over the rural clergy by destroying or weakening the mediate jurisdiction of the baptisteries and entering into direct relations with the chapels and their clergy. Numerous monasteries also strove to win parochial rights for their impropriated churches. But even with these collaborators, the lesser churches had a hard struggle to establish their independence of the baptisteries. Very slowly indeed were the exclusive rights of the baptismal churches whittled away and their daughter churches recognized as the parishes with cure of souls of the local communities. As early as the twelfth century some churches without the rank of

[5] The controversy between partisans of the chapels and those of the ancient system left its mark upon one of the recensions of the canonical collection, "Polycarpus," studied by Paul Fournier, "Les deux récensions de la collection canonique romaine dite le Polycarpus," *Mélanges d'archéologie et d'histoire de l'école française de Rome*, xxxvii (1918–19), 89–97.

baptisteries won the right to administer baptism,[6] and in the same period chapels here and there began to share in the product of the *quartese*. But in this and the following century the authority of the baptisteries was outwardly at its height, and most of the legal decisions of the high Middle Ages maintained the rights of the ancient baptisteries against the lesser churches. Thus, while a duality had manifested itself within Italian parochial institutions, and we may speak of two kinds of parish during the high Middle Ages and later, this duality did not seriously affect the distribution of tithes among the churches, on which the supremacy of the baptisteries by this time largely rested.

The internal organization of the parishes in the high Middle Ages was substantially the same as in the past. Collegiate churches multiplied. The evidence gathered by Forchielli with regard to collegiate organization in the baptismal churches of the bishopric of Verona is so abundantly confirmed from the records of other dioceses that one may hazard the surmise that in Upper Italy in the high Middle Ages collegiate churches were in a majority.[7] The common life in the sense understood by the

[6] Such seems to have been the status of the collegiate church of Faido, described by G. P. Bognetti, "Le pievi delle Valli di Blenio, Levantina, e Riviera," *Archivio storico della Svizzera italiana*, iv (1929), 40–46. Very rarely in the twelfth and thirteenth centuries did subordinate churches attain the baptismal font. Such concessions became much more general in the fourteenth and fifteenth centuries; but the right of all parishes to the baptismal font was actually not proclaimed as a principle until the new code of canon law went into effect in 1918. Nanni, *La parrochia studiata nei documenti lucchesi*, p. 185.

[7] Forchielli, *La pieve rurale*, pp. 121–156, proves that the majority of the Veronese baptisteries were collegiate in the high Middle Ages. Numerous other examples of collegiate baptisteries may be cited; e.g., San Giovanni in Revello, Catherine E. Boyd, *A Cistercian Nunnery*, pp. 54–56; San Giorgio of Pirano, *infra*, pp. 151–153; San Lorenzo of Chiavenna, which in 1179 had an archpriest and seven canons (three priests, three clerics, and an acolyte), *Cartario di Chiavenna, PC,* xxi (1914), doc. 85; San Giorgio in Braida, ACNV, especially docs. 6880, 6886; the baptistery of Verdeto in Piacenza, where the archpriest and canons were living the common life prior to 1243, when a division of property was effected, Campi, ii, 176; the baptistery of Olubra, also in Piacenza, *ibid.*, ii,

Gregorians had indeed been abandoned. The clergy of collegiate churches simply preserved some form of capitular organization, not necessarily involving real community of property or of life. The collegiate organization seems in some cases to have included the priests serving the chapels subject to the baptistery; but the core of the organization consisted of the priests and clerics directly attached to the baptismal church itself. The senior priest in each baptistery, designated either as archpriest or *plebanus,* exercised the powers of a petty bishop throughout the baptismal area. Within this district he conferred all minor orders, appointed to all ecclesiastical benefices, and tried certain kinds of lawsuits.[8] Periodically he inspected the chapels subject to his baptistery, which were often very numerous.[9] Under his jurisdiction were the clergy of the chapels, who had to be selected from the clergy of the baptistery, to which they repaired when the time came to elect a new *plebanus.*[10] The clergy of the baptistery, sometimes those attached to the chapels, are fre-

doc. 81 (pp. 393–394); the baptistery of Castelluchio in Mantua, which had in 1258 an archpriest, two priests, a deacon, subdeacon, and a cleric, Torelli, *ACM,* doc. 148; San Giovanni of Monza, Frisi, *Memorie di Monza, passim;* the *pieve* of Agno, below, n. 11; the baptistery of Lonigo, where the cure of souls was entrusted to an archpriest and four canons, while fifteen other canons chanted the offices, G. Maccà, *Storia del territorio vicentino,* i, 55, n. iv.

[8] Some Veronese baptisteries had the *plebania,* or pleas involving church law and discipline, and the *jus adulterii,* or right to try cases of marital infidelity. Antichi Archivi Veronesi, Clero Intrinseco, i, 19 v. In some bishoprics of Friuli the baptisteries held the *placita christianitatis,* defined in one document as *jus synodandi.* Thus in 1119 the patriarch of Aquileia impropriated three baptisteries to a monastery, two of them *cum omni jure plebis et placiti christianitatis,* the third *absque jure placiti christianitatis.* E. Degani, "Il placito di Cristianità," *Memorie storiche Forogiulesi,* viii (1912), fasc. iv, p. 286.

[9] San Giovanni of Monza in the twelfth century had twenty-one chapels and in addition had an impropriated baptistery with seven chapels. Frisi, *Memorie di Monza,* ii, doc. 68. In 1178 San Lorenzo of Chiavenna had eighteen chapels. *Cod. dip. della Rezia,* doc. 150, in *PC,* vi (1888), 92–94.

[10] This was the organization of San Giovanni in Revello, which I studied in *A Cistercian Nunnery,* pp. 54–56.

quently designated as canons, although they did not follow the
canonical life as the Gregorians had defined it.

In the communities served by the chapels the people heard
mass and received most of the sacraments in the chapels themselves; but for the sacrament of baptism they had to take their
children to the baptistery, where they also had to attend certain important festivities. On Palm Sunday the olive or palm
branches were blessed at the baptistery, and here, also, solemn
processions known as litanies and important ecclesiastical ban-
quets were held. When the chapels celebrated the holy days of
their patron saints, the *plebanus* officiated in the chapel, bringing
with him a retinue of specified size to whom the chapel had to
furnish hospitality.

Less picturesque but economically more valuable were the
financial prerogatives of the baptistery. A large share of the
revenues of the chapels went to their baptisteries, which in the
high Middle Ages usually maintained their exclusive rights to
the tithes of their districts. How extensive the rights of a baptistery might be, may be gauged by a glance at the baptistery
of Agno, between Lakes Maggiore and Lugano, in the bishopric
of Como. Early in the present century the area of this baptistery
contained thirty-five parishes and eleven vice-parishes. In the
twelfth century it constituted one large ecclesiastical unit, in
which the *plebanus,* with the assistance of a single priest, had
the cure of souls throughout the entire district.[11]

In some regions the local communities regarded the baptisteries as oppressors and tried to escape from their jurisdiction.
The exclusive dominance of the baptistery was especially resented by the villagers if their village was at some distance from
the baptistery. The parishioners of the chapels, as we may now
call them, wanted also to choose as their priests local men who
were not necessarily members of the clergy of the baptistery.[12]

[11] Enrico Maspoli, *La pieve di Agno* (Como, 1917).
[12] The ecclesiastical courts in the twelfth century usually upheld the
right of the baptisteries to supply their subordinate chapels with priests.

They also desired that such of their tithes as had escaped the rapacity of laymen should be expended in the places where they were gathered, instead of swelling the revenues of a distant and relatively affluent baptistery. To some extent the local communities obtained redress of their grievances in the course of the high Middle Ages, but their most serious grievance, the financial one, was never fully alleviated. The majority of the baptisteries maintained their right to the tithe as late as the Council of Trent. Until the mid-fourteenth century in the bishopric of Treviso, each *plebanus* had the sole right to the *quartese* of his baptismal district and gave the chaplains only a stipend, while in the mid-fifteenth century the *plebanus* of a baptistery in Concordia was disputing with the rectors of the chapels their respective shares of the *quartese* of his district.[13] Conditions in the monastic chapels were similar in respect to the division of the tithes. According to canon law, the tithes of such churches went in their entirety to the baptistery within whose district the chapel was situated. In many instances this rule was followed; but in some cases baptistery and monastery together shared the tithes of impropriated churches. If the baptistery itself was impropriated to a monastery or cathedral chapter, as occasionally happened, the ecclesiastical patron took all or most of the tithes.[14]

The position of the chapels and of impropriated churches in regard to the tithes was discussed by the canonists in the twelfth century and regulated to some extent by the papacy. Considerable influence in this connection seems to have been wielded by

Manaresi, *Regesto di Monte Velate*, doc. 105; Vignati, i, doc. 155; *Cod. dip. della Rezia*, doc. 145, in *PC*, v, pp. 400–401.

[13] Carlo Agnoletti, *Intorno la dominicalità delle decime nel diocesi di Treviso* (Treviso, 1891), pp. 17–54; E. Degani, *La diocesi di Concordia* (2nd ed., Udine, 1924), pp. 354–356. In Treviso after the middle of the fourteenth century the tithes were divided among the chaplains; in Concordia the bishop set aside seven villages from which the disputants were to take the tithes in equal portions.

[14] The nineteen impropriated chapels of the baptistery of San Zeno (diocese of Camerino) paid a third of their tithes to the baptistery, two-thirds to the monastic impropriator. Romani-Feliciangeli, p. 320.

Huguccio of Pisa. Huguccio wished to deny to cathedral churches any share in the tithes of the rural parishes. He attributes to some canonists of his own day the opinion that the tithes of the rural districts should go only to the baptisteries, but that the rector of the baptistery should then divide them between himself and the priests of the chapels in such manner as to provide the latter with an adequate stipend. He himself recommends the division of the tithe into four parts, one for the baptistery itself, one for the chapels, a third for the poor, and a fourth for the repair of church buildings. He then notes the fact, no doubt gleaned from his observation of Italian conditions, that in many places the avarice of the bishops has led them to seize three-fourths of the tithes, leaving the baptistery in possession of only one-fourth and the chaplains with nothing at all.[15]

Before the end of the twelfth century the papacy took some action to relieve the plight of the lesser churches. During the pontificate of Alexander III the Church seems to have made an effort to assure the rural chapels the *quartese* of the noval tithes of their parishioners. Somewhat later, the Fourth Lateran Council, which tried to carry out Innocent III's program of reform, took steps to assure an adequate income to impropriated churches. Canon 32 demanded that a suitable portion of church revenues (the *portio congrua*) should be assigned to the priests who officiated such churches. This canon was aimed at the abuses in the vicarage system which had grown out of the practice of impropriation. But it had a relevance to parochial institutions in general that justifies quotation here:

An abusive custom that must be destroyed has grown up in some regions, whereby the patrons of some parish churches and some others [the allusion is probably to the bishops] claim for themselves the revenues of such churches and leave to the priests appointed for their service only a meager portion of the income insufficient to support them in decency. We have ascertained it to be a fact that in

[15] See p. 142, n. 27.

some regions the parish priests receive for their maintenance only a fourth of the fourth, that is to say, one-sixteenth, of the tithes. Hence it comes to pass that in those regions scarcely a parish priest can be found who has even the rudiments of learning. Wherefore . . . we decree that, notwithstanding any custom established by a bishop, patron, or any other person, a sufficient portion shall be assigned to the priests. He who possesses a parish church must officiate in person and not through the intermediary of a vicar, unless the parish church is annexed to a prebend or to a dignity. In this case the titulary of the prebend must designate a vicar for the parish church and leave him a sufficient part of its revenues, under penalty of losing the church. . . .[16]

It is clear that some phrases of this canon mirror quite precisely the situation in Italy as regards the distribution of the tithes. It was not merely the lay and monastic patrons of churches who deprived them of their revenues; the bishops also were guilty of keeping three-fourths of the tithes; and there were certainly many chapels, or parish churches in the new sense, in Italy, in which the clergy had only a "fourth of the fourth," and in some cases not even that.

Alexander III, who was much concerned over this problem, attempted to define the conditions under which new parishes could be carved out of the domains of the baptisteries. His decretal "Ad audientiam," while maintaining in principle the territorial integrity of the ancient parishes, also recognized that legitimate reasons could exist for the dismemberment of old parishes and the creation of new ones.[17] This decretal opened the way for the ultimate emancipation of the chapels from the baptisteries; but the new law in Italy did not finally triumph until the Council of Trent.

Such were the main outlines of the Italian parochial system of the high Middle Ages. The reader will have observed that the ancient hierarchical system was strong enough to withstand successfully the impact of new social forces and that the lesser

[16] Hefele-Leclercq, *Histoire des conciles*, v, pt. 2, 1359–1360.
[17] *Decretales Gregorii IX*, III, xlviii, "De ecclesiis aedificandis," c. 3.

churches had made comparatively little progress towards legal emancipation by the end of the thirteenth century. Especially were they unsuccessful in breaking the tenacious hold of the baptismal churches on the tithes of their districts. It should be noted, however, that the monopoly of the baptisteries as regards the administration of the sacraments and the performance of purely spiritual functions was being gradually undermined, and that from the point of view of social function and the cure of souls many of the chapels had become *de facto* parishes.

CHAPTER IX

Transformation of the Lay Tithe

† ROMAN legislation of the twelfth century against the lay tithe culminated in the decree "Prohibemus" of 1179.[1] In practice, however, the Church in Italy had to condone the continued existence of the lay tithe, contenting itself with the mitigation of the worst abuses and with the safeguarding of the parochial fourth. The universality of the *quartese* throughout the northern half of the peninsula proves that the Church was eminently successful in establishing the fourth (or third) of the tithe as a minimum revenue for the parish clergy, a success which must have been due in large measure to the cooperation of the laity, who saw not only the justice but the advantage of a reform which left the greater part of the tithes of many parishes in their own hands.

The comparative moderation of the twelfth-century Church in pressing the attack against the lay tithe must be explained not only by the temporizing character of many bishops but also by the Church's position within the economic system. As the largest single property owner in the medieval world, the Church could hardly attack too severely property rights sanctified by long usage and confirmed by secular law. Many lay tithe holders held

[1] See p. 143. The term "lay tithe" as used in this chapter and elsewhere in this book refers to the ecclesiastical tithe in the hands of laymen.

their tithes by virtue of contracts granted by the episcopate in earlier centuries and renewed through successive generations. Most of the feudal investitures of tithes and parishes which were made in Italy during the twelfth century were renewals of such long-standing contracts; for the tithes were regarded as fiefs, governed by feudal law. It says much for the prestige of the Church that most of these contracts reserved the parochial fourth.[2]

Feudal law was not the only obstacle to the destruction of the lay tithe. In the high Middle Ages the Italian communes were also compiling and codifying their local customs; and the two systems, ecclesiastical and communal, conflicted on more than one point. The customs of the Lombard communes recognized and enforced the lay tithe.[3] The customs of Milan, assembled by a private jurisconsult around 1216, stated clearly that while canon law forbade the lay tithe, regional custom permitted its existence.[4] In the twelfth century, lack of respect for canon law, still in a fluid state, did not necessarily indicate lack of respect for the Church. Thus in 1176 the consuls of Chiavenna tried a lawsuit over the tithes between the local church and some laymen, in which the church cited the prohibition of the lay tithe by canon law, but the consuls upheld the rights of the laymen on the grounds that hitherto the Roman Church had permitted laymen to hold tithes.[5]

The worst abuses in the tithe during this period undoubtedly resulted from the survival of the proprietary concept in regard

[2] As in the following examples: Brescia, 1158: In investing two members of the noble Martinengo family with the tithes and advowsons of four parishes, to be held according to feudal tenure, the bishop in one case excepts the fourth of the tithe due to the local baptistery. Odorici, *Storie bresciane*, v, doc. 90, pp. 111–112. Lodi, 1228: The *capitanei* of Mellegrano hold all the tithes of the parish of Strata, except the fourth reserved to the local baptistery. Vignati, ii, docs. 286, 288. Cf. doc. 112 for an advowson held as a fief.

[3] Alessandro Lattes, *Il diritto consuetudinario delle città lombarde* (Milan, 1899), pp. 322–331.   [4] Berlan, *LCM*, p. 58.

[5] *Cod. dip. della Rezia*, doc. 146, *PC*, v (1885), 402–404.

to it, a concept shared by clerical and lay tithe owners alike. While the churches busily purchased tithes, sought to persuade pious laymen to restore them, or simply acquiesced in existing conditions, the laity were doing a flourishing commerce in this supposedly spiritual revenue, selling their tithes to one another, bequeathing them, or giving them as dowries to their daughters.[6] Those who held tithes as fiefs often subinfeudated them to other laymen.[7] Feudal investitures of tithes were practiced without hesitation, and on occasion bishops judged lawsuits between laymen over infeudated tithes.[8]

Through the legislation of 1179 the Church had tried to suppress commercial transactions in tithes among the laity. But the fate of tithes which were restored by the laity to clerical hands was not always encouraging. A previous chapter has shown what happened to tithes which were purchased by bishops or voluntarily surrendered to them by lay tithe owners. In the case of tithes gathered in the rural parishes of their dioceses, the bishops felt no obligation to restore them to the parish churches, provided the latter had the parochial fourth. This was particularly true of tithes acquired by purchase. Sometimes the bishop, after assuring himself of the title to the tithes, would give the usufruct or collection of them to the layman who had formerly held them.[9] Strange anomalies are to be observed in connection with these redeemed tithes. In 1173, for example, the bishop of Verona infeudated to a parish priest some tithes raised within

[6] Milan, 1135, 1178: Manaresi, *Regesto di Monte Velate,* docs. 100, 193; Genoa, *Registro I,* p. 15.

[7] Vignati, ii, docs. 286, 288; *Regesto di Mantova,* doc. 605; *Chartularium Piranense,* doc. 97.

[8] For an application of feudal law to tithes, see the investitures, with consent of both clergy and vassals, by the bishop of Lodi in 1147, *de omni feudo et benefitio,* formerly held by some of his vassals in the parish of Mulazzano. Vignati, i, doc. 123 (pp. 153–154). An investiture of 1165 carried elaborate provisions for inheritance according to feudal law. *Ibid.,* ii, doc. 17.

[9] Genoa, *Registro II,* doc. 1. In Genoa the office of collector of tithes tended to become hereditary; in 1180 the widow of a tithe-collector inherited his rights. Genoa, *Registro I,* App., doc. 76.

his parish which had been restored to the bishop by their lay owners. For these tithes the priest paid the handsome sum of 325 *librae*.[10] The documents record cases of priests surrendering tithes to bishops, who promptly grant them out as fiefs to laymen.[11]

Occasionally, of course, the tithes found their way back to the parish church within whose district they were gathered. This rarely happened as the result of a free gift. When the redemption of tithes through purchase was formally sanctioned by the papacy in the twelfth century, some of the more prosperous parish churches utilized the opportunity to increase their endowments in tithes. There is a whole series of documents showing how the Milanese *pieve* of Monte Velate redeemed the tithes of its district from laymen. Thus, in 1189 the archpriest of this church sold a mill in order to raise thirty-eight *librae* for the purchase of infeudated tithes.[12] When the tithes were bought from episcopal vassals, the archbishop had to consent to the transaction before it was valid.[13] The parish churches themselves, after receiving restitutions of tithes, applied to them the standards of secular law and private ownership and sometimes leased them forthwith to laymen.[14]

The documents make it all too evident that clergy and laity alike had come to regard the tithe as a conservative long-term investment, guaranteed by the prestige of the Church and the long-suffering endurance of the agrarian classes upon whom the tithe rested. In some documents the economic motivation behind the struggle for tithes thrusts itself into the foreground. A count of Parenzo, attended by a large troop of knights, complained

[10] ACNV, San Giorgio in Braida, no. 7222.

[11] Antichi Archivi Veronesi, Bevilacqua-Vescovo, no. 10.

[12] Manaresi, *Regesto di Monte Velate*, doc. 305. Docs. 228, 322 record other purchases of tithes by the archpriest. Sometimes he gave land in exchange for the tithes. *Ibid.*, docs. 309–312. Sometimes he rented tithes from laymen. *Ibid.*, doc. 315.

[13] *Ibid.*, docs. 169, 170.

[14] Giulini, *Memorie di Milano*, vii, 118–119; *Carte di Gozzano*, doc. 32; Antichi Archivi Veronesi, Esposti, no. 42.

to the bishop of Parenzo ca. 1183 that the five hundred tithe payers with whom he had been invested by the bishop's predecessor had diminished to two hundred. When the bishop requested proof that the count was entitled to take the tithe from five hundred people, the count seized the tithes of Rovigo, which the bishop had previously ceded to another layman, and held them as equivalent to the tithe payers demanded.[15]

This was the situation as regards the lay tithe in northern Italy at the close of the twelfth century, when Innocent III mounted the papal throne. The next section will be devoted to an account of his policy in respect to the lay tithe, followed by a discussion of the forms assumed by the lay tithe as it survived into the thirteenth century.

According to some writers, the pontificate of Innocent III marked a new era in the history of the lay tithe, in that Innocent was the first pope to abandon the struggle against the lay tithe and to tolerate an institution condemned by earlier popes as an abuse. The silence of the Fourth Lateran Council in regard to the lay tithe lends color to this point of view.[16]

The fullest statement of Innocent's policy in this matter at the beginning of his pontificate occurs in a letter which he addressed to the bishop of Vercelli in 1199, later included in the Decretals of Gregory IX.[17] The bishop had complained that the laity of Vercelli and the neighboring dioceses were resisting the payment of tithes. Some deducted the expenses of cultivation and paid tithe only on the net product; others took the tithe of the rents in produce paid by their tenants and gave it to their chaplains or to other churches and clerics, sometimes even giving it directly to the poor; some refused to pay tithe because of the immoral life of the clergy; others asserted that they had been exempted from tithe by imperial concession; still others were

[15] Kandler, *Codice diplomatico istriano*, i, 204.

[16] Thomassin, *Ancienne et nouvelle discipline de l'église*, vi, 61; Viard, *Histoire de la dîme ecclésiastique dans le royaume de France*, p. 149.

[17] *M.P.L.*, vol. 214, cols. 802–804.

usurping the noval tithes by virtue of their possession of the
ancient tithes, which they claimed that the Church had conceded to them. All these practices the Pope condemns as abuses.
With regard to the lay tithe, he replies to the bishop that it is
not permissible for laymen to usurp the noval tithes of a region
in which they hold the old tithes as a fief, since the license permitted them in such matters should not be extended but to the
contrary restrained.[18] In another letter referring to the same
subject, Innocent says that a lay tithe holder is to be admonished
to restore his tithes to the church to which they belong; but
if he cannot be persuaded to do this and with the consent of
the diocesan bishop gives them to another church, especially
to a monastery, the donation is to be permanently valid.[19] The
Pope then justifies this diversion of tithes from the legal owner
by distinguishing between the alienation of property actually
possessed by a church and the redemption for ecclesiastical uses
of property usurped by laymen. In the same letter, Innocent
cites the Lateran decree of 1078 requiring monasteries to secure
the consent of the diocesan bishop before accepting churches
and tithes from laymen, and interprets this to mean that the
bishop's consent was sufficient to authorize this diversion of the
tithes, adding the qualification: "This provision we understand
to refer to tithes which have been conceded as perpetual fiefs." [20]

These two letters, viewed in conjunction with Innocent's
other decisions, do not justify the opinion that this pope was the
first to sanction the lay tithe; for Innocent was in no sense
introducing a new policy of toleration. If his words do not have
the ring of the ardent reformer, they are stamped with the mark
of the trained lawyer, concerned above all with bringing order

[18] ". . . nec occasione decimationis antiquae, licet in feudum concessae, decimae sunt novalium usurpandae, cum in talibus non sit ex-
tendenda licentia, sed potius restringenda."

[19] *Ibid.*, col. 273.

[20] "Haec autem de eis decimis intelligimus quae perpetuo sunt in
feudum concessae." For the decree, see Mansi, *Concilia*, xx, 510 (c. 8).

and clarity into existing practices. The reformers of the early twelfth century had been compelled to leave to the lay aristocracy tithes which had been in their families for generations. Throughout the twelfth century the local churches had been active in purchasing tithes which had been alienated by their own pastors as well as actually usurped by the laity. If the Lateran Council of 1215, generally agreed to represent Innocent's program of reforms,[21] was silent in regard to the lay tithe, this did not indicate any withdrawal from principles previously enunciated. In the eyes of the leaders of the Church, the total and immediate extirpation of the lay tithe was impossible; it was too deeply rooted in secular law. The council therefore limited itself to regulating such abuses in the existing system as were amenable to immediate reform, questions, for example, such as the monastic exemption from the tithe and the abuses in the vicarage system. Moreover, if the Church seems to have retreated from the battle before it was completely won, the reason is that the lay tithe, while by no means uprooted, was under control. The Church had vindicated her legal title to the ancient tithes while permitting them to remain in large part in lay hands. It was not yet evident that the noval tithes would undergo the same fate. The lay tithe became part of the working compromise which the Church effected with lay society in the twelfth and thirteenth centuries. It was deplored by the canonists; but it was so deeply embedded in the legal and social structure of the period, so ingrained in men's habits and interwoven with their material interests, that to attempt to extirpate it completely would have involved a revolutionary attack on property rights. Confronted by a rising tide of heresy and secularism, the Church refrained from throwing down the gauntlet to lay society. Instead, the lay tithe was transformed wherever possible into an instrument which the Church utilized for her own purposes.

[21] See the recent study by Augustin Fliche, "Innocent III et la réforme de l'église," *RHE*, xliv (1949), 87–152.

By the opening of the thirteenth century the Church had given her sanction to lay tithes that were ancient fiefs. Did she go further and permit new concessions of tithes to laymen? In principle she did not deviate from the view that the tithes were exclusively ecclesiastical property; but in practice she could not prevent new grants of tithes to the laity. Here the canonists came to her aid with a neat distinction; a cession of the usufruct of the tithe, they maintained, was not illegal, provided that it was made for a limited period and the title of ownership was retained by the Church.[22] This distinction between the *jus decimae* and the *fructus decimae* proved a fertile one; the bishops used it to justify the farming of tithes to laymen, usually for a period of twenty-five or twenty-nine years. This was the dominant form of the lay tithe in the thirteenth century.

The best available source of information about the lay tithe in its new form is the *Libro delle investiture* of Goffredo di Montanaro, bishop of Turin from 1264 to 1294.[23] This collection of one hundred and twenty-eight documents is not an inventory of tithes in the bishopric of Turin, but a record of episcopal investitures, mostly of tithes administered directly by the bishop and included in the episcopal *mensa* as distinct from the endowment of the cathedral chapter. Monastic tithes do not appear in the record, and the tithes of parish churches figure in it only indirectly. The *Libro* therefore does not give a complete picture of the tithes in the diocese of Turin, nor does it lend itself to a statistical analysis.[24]

In a minority among Bishop Goffredo's investitures are renewals of tithes to the lay patrons of parish churches. This

[22] Hostiensis says of the *jus decimandi*: ". . . although this is a civil right, it can be conceded to a layman not as property but as the right to collect the fruits [of the property]." Quoted by Gaudenzi, "Il monastero di Nonantola," *BISI*, xxxvi (1916), 254.

[23] *Il "libro delle investiture" di Goffredo di Montanaro vescovo di Torino (1264–1294)*, ed. F. Guasco di Bisio, *BSSS*, lxvii (Pinerolo, 1913), 129–276, hereafter cited as *LI*.

[24] Turin is described because it is the most fully documented example of conditions widely prevalent.

peculiarity probably arises from the nature of the *Libro* itself. When the advowson of a church is mentioned, it usually appears as the holding of a family or clan rather than of an individual, and when the tithe accompanies the advowson it also is the possession of a group, or *consorteria.* The family church, more properly perhaps the clan church, was characteristic of both Lombardy and Piedmont, where it left numerous survivals in ecclesiastical organization of the later Middle Ages.[25] Goffredo's investitures show the manner of its survival in Piedmont. Such concessions, which occur but rarely in the *Libro delle investiture,* invariably take the form of infeudations, indicating that these tithes and advowsons were ancient fiefs. Frequently two-thirds of the tithes were infeudated in this way, the remaining third being reserved, either explicitly or by implication, to the local church.[26] These investitures were obviously renewals of ancient infeudations of *pievi* and their tithes, in which ownership has been transformed into patronage. Such grants were always made in feudal forms, *nomine recti, nobilis, gentilis et antiqui feudi,* and were accompanied by an oath of fidelity. The recipients of the grants were episcopal vassals. In most cases the bishop was simply confirming ancient infeudated tithes, which by this time had been sanctioned by canon law.

Far more numerous than the infeudated tithes were concessions of the tithes of a district, either in whole or in part, for a limited period. These were grants of the usufruct of the tithes pertaining to the episcopal *mensa.* The tenure indicated by this contract diverges sharply from the feudal investitures; there is no oath of fidelity and the whole transaction is simple and businesslike.[27] The concedee may not alienate the tithe without

[25] Fr. Niccoli, "I consorci nobiliari ed il commune nell'alta e media Italia," *RSDI,* xiii (1940), 310 ff.; Feine, "Studien," ii, 44–45 and n. 118.

[26] *LI,* docs. 10, 42, 49, 54, 57, 58, 72, 93. The oath of fidelity is defined more closely in doc. 64.

[27] The term episcopal *mensa* as used here denotes the property of the bishopric administered directly by the bishop. That the bishop was operating on the new theory of the lay tithe is shown by the formula "decima,

the bishop's knowledge and consent, and if he violates the contract, the bishop may grant the usufruct of the tithe to another
person. Usually the product of the tithe was divided in equal
portions between the bishop and the grantee. Customary also
were payment in kind and in installments from the product of the
tithe and the deduction of a tenth of the product for the expenses
of collection and storage. The average term of the contract was
twenty-five years. These arrangements are repeated in a whole
series of documents, although single factors varied. There was
some tendency to substitute a money rent for payments in produce; and where the latter method prevailed, payment might
consist of a fixed amount of the produce rather than a percentage.[28]

Although this type of concession was merely an administrative device for gathering the tithes, it lent itself to abuses.
In such contracts the Church preserved her title to the tithe, but
by handing over the collection to laymen, such contracts tended
to obscure the ecclesiastical character of the impost. The bishops
found themselves on the horns of a dilemma; either they had
to admit their inability to enforce payment of the tithe or they
had to run the risk of destroying its religious nature by confiding its administration and collection to local landowners, of

hoc est, proventus [seu fructus] decimae," which appears in numerous
documents. *Ibid.*, docs. 20, 22, 23, 25, 43, 85, 90.

The type of the leases described in this paragraph is set by a concession of the yield of the tithe (*proventus decimae*) of Cabalario Leone
(doc. 95).

[28] In Turin in the second half of the thirteenth century the tendency
was either to substitute money payments for the tithe or to stipulate
fixed amounts of produce in lieu of the tenth. Both practices are amply
illustrated in the *Libro delle investiture*.

The most common term of the contract was twenty-five years; contracts for this period are more numerous than all the others put together.
Doc. 63, exceptionally, records the concession of tithes for forty years in
enfiteusi, a type of concession which violated canon law. Viard notes
similar practices in the territory of Bugey and in the bishopric of Basel.
"La dîme ecclésastique dans le royaume d'Arles et de Vienne au xiie et
xiiie siècles" *ZSSR*, xxxii (1911), *Kan. Abt.*, i, 155.

whom laymen seem to have been regarded as the most efficient.[29]

Despite the canonical legislation, the noval tithes suffered the same fate as the ancient tithes. A majority of the grants listed in the *Libro delle investiture* refer to new lands. Canon law left the bishops considerable discretion in regard to the noval tithes raised outside the boundaries of established parishes; customary Lombard law gave them such tithes in their entirety. In most of the cases recorded in Goffredo's book the noval tithes were simply farmed out by the bishop, usually to laymen. In a few instances even noval tithes were held by a nobleman as a "tithe conceded of old as a fief." Probably these instances represent the usurpation of noval tithes by virtue of possession of the ancient tithes which Innocent III had condemned in his letter to the bishop of Vercelli.[30] The most extensive grant of this kind noted in Goffredo's book was the investiture of the marquis of Saluzzo with the fief of the noval tithes of all his lands within the diocese of Turin.[31] Other grants show that the threefold division of the tithes was extended to the noval tithes. Thus in 1286 the bishop invested three noblemen with two-thirds of the noval tithes of Vallesperga, Cornato, and other places, while simultaneously he granted to the parish priests of those communities one-third of the noval tithes; in both concessions the term was twenty-nine years and there was a money rent. Incidentally, the rate charged the parish priests was higher than that charged the noble laymen, although canon law in the preceding century had assigned the noval tithes to the parish clergy.[32]

The contents of the *Libro delle investiture* make it clear that the transition to a money economy in rural Piedmont was affecting the administration of the tithes. In 1291, for example, the inhabitants of Cervasca reached an agreement with their parish priest whereby fixed payments were to take the place of a tenth of the produce. The priest was here acting in the name of the

[29] *LI*, doc. 6.
[31] *LI*, doc. 49.

[30] See p. 170.
[32] *Ibid.*, docs. 105, 106.

bishop, to whom he was obliged to remit two-thirds of the tithe, retaining, according to Piedmontese custom, a third for himself and his church. On the same day the bishop of Turin ceded to a group of nobles of Vignolio, adjacent to Cervasca, the usufruct of his two-thirds of the tithes for twenty-five years in return for a money rent of fifteen Astensian *librae,* stipulating that the previous contract with the people of Cervasca was to be respected by the lease-holders.[33] Obviously it was more convenient for the bishop to lease the tithes to local proprietors for a money rent than to try to collect the tithe in kind. Under this arrangement the priest of Cervasca gave the episcopal thirds to the nobles of Vignolio, who then paid their rent to the bishop.

The documents in Goffredo's book, because of their nature, tell us nothing directly about the maintenance of the rural churches. It seems likely that in the case of the infeudated tithes, which were usually connected with a church of which the tithe owners were patrons, the lay aristocracy who held the greater portion of the tithes may have contributed to the upkeep of the church. But in other instances, when the two-thirds of the tithe are leased to laymen in contracts stating in detail the terms of the concession, one is forced to the conclusion that the third allotted to the local church had to meet the maintenance charges of the edifice as well as pay the salary of the parish priest.

The evidence of the *Libro delle investiture* as regards the disposition of tithes is confirmed by numerous documents from the archives of practically every Italian bishopric. Although the worst abuses in the lay tithe had been eliminated, it was still an important element in the organization of the Italian Church in the thirteenth century. There were many reasons for its survival. Laymen, of course, made every effort to render their fiefs of the tithes perpetual and to increase their holdings of tithes, especially from new lands. The bishops, too, had reasons for preserving the lay tithe, at least in a modified form. In some instances they ceded the collection of tithes to laymen because

[33] *Ibid.,* docs. 124, 125.

of the difficulty and expense of collecting them through their own officials. A Vicentine diploma of 1260 states that the bishop was ceding tithes to laymen because their power in their districts would enable them to recover church property which had been usurped.[34] The investiture of a layman with tithes sometimes gave him an incentive to improve the condition of the land. Finally, it was through investitures with tithes that the bishops often rewarded the services of local gentry.

Tested by the evidence of Piedmontese and other documents, the prevalence of the lay tithe in the rural districts of thirteenth-century Italy may be regarded as an established fact. It is impossible to avoid the conclusion, moreover, that the parish churches had lost beyond recall a large part of the ancient tithes and been despoiled of many noval tithes as well. A large part, if not the greater part, of the tithes in Italy was in the hands of laymen, monasteries, or cathedral chapters, or administered directly by the bishops. Thus, in spite of the efforts of the Church to combat the lay tithe, it continued to flourish in those rural areas which were subject to feudal influences. Within the orbit of the greater communes, however, where a money economy displaced feudal and agrarian survivals in the course of the thirteenth century, the evolution of the tithe followed a somewhat different course.

[34] Todeschini, *Sulle decime feudali del vescovado di Vicenza,* pp. 84–85.

CHAPTER X

The Communal Revolt

† ONE of the less-known conflicts between Church and State in the high Middle Ages was a struggle between the Italian episcopate and the communes over the tithe. In the course of the twelfth century the communal governments gradually absorbed the once extensive public powers exercised by the episcopate in the Italian cities. Deprived of imperial support by the outcome of the investiture contest in Italy, the bishops were too weak to resist. They ended by yielding to the communal authorities temporal powers conceded or sanctioned by the emperors and consolidated by an alliance with the lay aristocracy of the countryside. Yet at the close of the twelfth century they still possessed remnants of their once great political power, and the clergy as a whole enjoyed numerous immunities and privileges. Above all, the increasing agricultural wealth of Italy, attested by the many references to new lands in the cartularies, lay under the incubus of the tithe, symbol of the close cooperation between the bishops and the *milites*. In the thirteenth century, with the arrival in power of the Popolo, or bourgeoisie, many communes launched an attack upon the tithe and upon the immunities of the clergy. As this struggle progressed in the thirteenth century, it took on a violently anticlerical bias, its

inheritance from the radical, anti-sacerdotal heresies which had racked the communes in the preceding century.[1]

The hostility of the communes towards the tithe is explained by the historical development of that institution. A large part of the tithes in Italy had been ceded by the bishops to the feudatories, and in the thirteenth century still remained in the hands of their descendants. Tithes formed part of the wealth of the hated magnates, whom the Popolo strove to reduce to submission. The magnates, nobles, and other powerful people of the cities, we learn from a Bolognese statute of 1288, also held tithes and in their efforts to collect them often seized or damaged the property of the mercantile and artisan classes as well as of the peasants.[2] Small landowners or peasants who had migrated to the towns tried to escape payment of tithes. Townsmen who bought lands in the country also resented the tithe. It had become an irritating burden upon landed property, divorced from its original spiritual significance. Moreover, in many communes lawsuits over the tithe had to be tried in church courts, which enforced the provisions of canon law.

In most communes the attack on the tithe coincided with changes in the class structure of their governments. During the greater part of the twelfth century, generally speaking, there had been few signs of resentment against the tithe, and some communal governments, as at Genoa, cooperated with the bishops in enforcing payment. The communal governments of that period were oligarchical regimes, made up of nobles who had moved into the city and associated themselves with the upper mercantile element; in some instances, as at Bergamo, the ruling oligarchy consisted of episcopal vassals. Only toward the end of the twelfth century does evidence of friction come to light. In the thirteenth century the accession of the bourgeoisie and

[1] For a pioneering study of this subject, see Gaetano Salvemini, "Le lotte fra stato e chiesa nei comuni italiani durante il secolo xiii," *Studi storici* (Florence, 1901), pp. 39–90.

[2] *Statuti di Bologna dell'anno 1288*, ed. G. Fasoli and P. Sella (Vatican City, 1939), pp. 312–313.

the supremacy of the artisan classes in many cities unleashed long-standing resentment against the Church and bore fruit in anticlerical legislation. In some cities, as at Parma, Bologna, and Reggio, the ensuing struggle was open and violent; in others it was quieter and more concealed, manifesting itself in the steady growth of customs unfavorable to the tithe owners and in the progressive curtailment by communal statutes of ecclesiastical jurisdiction over the impost.

Parma was one of the bishoprics where the bishop had received from the emperor the authority of a count.[3] The tithes of the city and its suburbs were gathered by the cathedral chapter.[4] The attack upon the tithe began in 1219, when Frederick II, at the request of the citizens, confirmed the privileges received by the commune in the Peace of Constance. This act was interpreted by the communal government as an abolition of the temporal rights of the bishop, and it forthwith enacted statutes curtailing clerical immunities before the law and drawing the tithe under the jurisdiction of the commune.[5] The clergy appealed to the Pope to annul the statutes. Honorius III complied; and when the commune refused to submit, he excommunicated the podestà and magistrates and laid the city under an interdict. Frederick, then in Rome for his coronation, approved the papal act.[6] In the following year, 1221, the commune came to an agreement with the bishop, who apparently gave up his exclusive jurisdiction over the tithes, a compromise which the Pope refused to sanction. The bishop himself either did not or

[3] *M.G.H., Diplomata Regum et Imperatorum Germaniae,* i, doc. 239.
[4] *M.P.L.,* vol. 130, cols. 1111–1112.
[5] ". . . de clericis conveniendis sub communi Parmae, bannendis, privandis necnon decimis et quarteriis hominum non solum diocesis sed et civitatis." G. Drei, "Le decime del vescovo di Parma," *ASSP,* New Series, xx (1920), 3, explains the word *quarteria* as meaning rents owed by the tenants of church lands. Other documents make it clear that what was really in question was the *quartese,* or parochial fourth.
[6] Frederick was for the moment a docile son of the Church. This was one of several acts which he took this year in favor of ecclesiastical institutions.

could not observe the agreement, because the legist Uberto Bobio in 1227 told him that he must not interfere with the ancient tithes but yield his jurisdiction over them to the commune. In 1231 the bishop anathematized the usurpers of clerical authority who, without his consent, heard lawsuits over the tithes and other matters which were properly within his jurisdiction. Gregory IX supported the bishop's stand and laid another interdict upon Parma—a fate which the city seems to have borne with equanimity. Finally the bishop yielded and agreed to appoint two lay judges each year to hear lawsuits over the tithes and to try the clergy in criminal cases. In the same year the Pope ordered two of his delegates to investigate the situation in Parma, and it is believed that the disgrace involved in a papal investigation, added to the obstinate resistance of the commune, hastened the death of Bishop Grazia of Parma, a distinguished canonist who had formerly taught canon law at Bologna.

The communal statutes of 1255 contain several provisions in regard to the tithe. They provided (1) that the tithe should not be levied upon land which had not paid it in the past, thus decreeing the extinction of the noval tithes in Parma; (2) that a layman who owed tithe to another layman might redeem it by a gift of land or money, the estimation of its value to be made by two burghers and two peasants, and the agreement to be sanctioned by the communal authorities; and (3) if the tithe in question was held as a fief, the land given in compensation to the tithe owner was likewise to be held from him by feudal tenure.[7]

As late as 1261 the commune of Parma was still insisting upon the observance of the compact made with Bishop Grazia in 1221; it again declared that no innovations were to be made as regards the tithe and the *quartese*.[8] Involved in this conflict at Parma was not so much a refusal to pay the old tithes as a

[7] A. Rhonchini, *Statuta Communis Parmae* (Parma, 1856–1860, 4 vols.), i, 232–233.

[8] ". . . nec aliquid auctum nec imminutum episcopatui sit et speciali nihil super decimis et quartesiis innovatum."

question of preventing the institution of new tithes. Above all, the commune insisted that it should have jurisdiction over lawsuits arising from disputes over the tithe.

An equally intense struggle took place at Bologna in the same period. Bologna was not an ecclesiastical seigniory like Parma, but the bishop of Bologna did have temporal jurisdiction over a number of towns and castles in the contado. The cathedral chapter collected the tithes of several rural parishes as well as three-fourths of the tithe of the city; early in the thirteenth century it acquired by gift from the bishop of Bologna his share of the tithes of the city, presumably the remaining fourth.[9] Up to this point, relations between the bishops of Bologna and the commune had been amicable, but now the commune became ambitious to extend its dominion over the countryside and thus came into conflict with the temporal rights of the bishop. Bishop Gerard, at the opening of the century, was so somnolent a prelate that the papacy forced him to resign. Enrico da Fratta, his successor, defended his rights against the commune more energetically. In 1220 Frederick II confirmed the sovereignty of the bishop over ten castles in the contado, thereby frustrating the attempts of the commune to bring them under its own jurisdiction.

Strife between bishop and commune came to a head in 1231, just after the commune of the Popolo had been established in Bologna.[10] The ire of the Popolo seems to have been aroused by a determined effort on the part of the bishop to collect the tithe. On being informed of the revolt against the tithe in Bologna, Gregory IX appointed an Augustinian canon, Palmiero da Campagnola, to investigate. The commune, by what must have been more than a coincidence, chose this moment to attack the episcopal castles of Persiceto, Cento, Pieve, and others. Palmiero's report was, of course, unfavorable to the commune, which at

[9] *M.P.L.*, vol. 143, col. 809; vol. 200, cols. 504–505; Carlo Sigonio, *Historia de Rebus Bononiensibus Libri VIII* (Frankfort, 1604), p. 159.

[10] Alfred Hessel, *Geschichte der Stadt Bologna von 1116 bis 1280* (Berlin, 1910), p. 399.

once gave orders for the occupation of the castles and passed statutes forbidding laymen to act as the bishop's stewards in any of the castles and withdrawing communal support from the bishop's efforts to collect the tithe.[11] The bishop then went into voluntary exile, and Palmiero laid the city under an interdict. When the Pope, through his legates in Lombardy, exhorted the commune to restore the bishop's rights, the commune replied by an act of open defiance: it appointed praetors in all the castles and put an end to the last remnants of the bishop's temporal jurisdiction. The Pope then ordered three neighboring bishops to lay another interdict upon the commune and took the even more effective step of ordering the students to leave Bologna. The commune at last decided to come to terms with its bishop. It surrendered to the bishop the castles of Cento and Pieve in lieu of the tithe; and the bishop raised the interdict and returned to Bologna, where the citizens gave him an ovation. By this settlement, which was reached in 1233, the commune withdrew the civil sanction from the ecclesiastical tithe in Bologna. Many Bolognese citizens seem to have decided to give their tithes directly to the poor, obeying the Biblical precept in regard to the tithe but refusing to acknowledge any compulsive authority on the part of the Church.[12]

A violent contest with a similar outcome took place at Reggio, where, as at Bologna, power had passed to the bourgeoisie.[13] In 1280 a dispute arose between the bishop and the commune over the payment of tithes. The Captain of the Popolo,

[11] Sigonio, p. 160. References to this affair occur in Gaudenzi's account of the commune of Cento and the episcopal tithes, "Il monastero di Nonantola," *BISI*, xxxvi (1916), 222–254.

[12] The tithe owners tried to continue collecting their tithes by force. The statutes of 1288 commanded them not to seize the property of guild members or peasants under Bolognese jurisdiction but to submit their claims to the communal courts.

[13] The contemporary source for this is the chronicle of Alberto Miliolo, *Liber de Temporibus et Aetatibus, M.G.H., SS.,* xxi, 555–557. The incident is retold by Quintino Santoli, "Dego dei Cancellieri e una questione di decima a Reggio Emilia nell'anno 1280," *BSP*, xvi (1914), 113–183.

a certain Dego dei Cancellieri, and twenty-three officials called
Defenders of the Popolo enacted statutes forbidding laymen
to gather tithes for the clergy. When the bishop retaliated by
excommunicating the magistrates and communal council and
laying an interdict upon the city, the commune chose a special
committee of twenty-five which drew up stringent laws against
the clergy themselves. Citizens were forbidden to pay any tithes
to the Church at all and the clergy were subjected to a boycott.
While this was in effect, the clergy could not communicate in
any way with the laity and could not transact business, hire lay
servants, hold public office, get their grain ground at local mills,
or even use the services of the city barbers. The boycott lasted
about two months, during which the commune did a thriving
business in collecting fines from violators of its laws. At last a
compromise was reached: a new law declared that no one in
Reggio was to be compelled to pay tithe in the future except as
his conscience dictated. In this way the commune removed
from the tithe the prop of civil enforcement, refusing to support the Church in its efforts to collect the tithe by force while
at the same time recognizing the giving of tithes as a religious
duty. The point of view of the communal government comes out
very clearly in the statutes which were then passed:

(1) Tithes were henceforth to be collected only by members
of the clergy and to be paid according to conscience. No citizen
was to be cited before either an ecclesiastical or civil magistrate
because of difficulties encountered in the collection of tithes.

(2) Collectors of tithes must henceforth abstain from making threats.

(3) Ecclesiastics were permitted to solicit voluntary gifts
of tithes from laymen outside their parishes and might visit the
houses of such laymen for this purpose.

(4) Although tithes were now declared to be voluntary in
respect to the civil law, they were stated to be still binding upon
believers as part of the divine law.[14]

[14] Santoli, pp. 173–183.

The Emilian cities of Parma, Bologna, and Reggio illustrate the more violent aspects of the communal reaction against the tithe. A less spectacular but equally important conflict was in progress in the Lombard communes.

In Asti during the second half of the twelfth century the cathedral chapter was having trouble in collecting its tithes, especially from the tenants of the manor of Quarto, which was under the feudal jurisdiction of the chapter. By the early thirteenth century disputes had become so common that the chapter appointed a special procurator to handle lawsuits over the payment of tithes.[15] At the same time the commune of Asti declined to give support to enforcement of clerical claims. A law passed by the commune to this effect was quashed by Frederick II in 1220.[16]

At Tortona in the reign of Frederick I the consuls of the commune tried to force the Church to contribute to an imperial subsidy. The Emperor, to whom the clergy appealed, forbade the commune to force the clergy to contribute and commanded it to compel all its citizens to pay their tithes.[17] Towards the end of the twelfth century the commune forbade the citizens to pay tithes from their rents in kind when these consisted of a percentage of the produce. Celestine III demanded that this statute should be revoked; if the commune refused, its officers were to be excommunicated and the city laid under an interdict.[18] The dispute seems to have died down. Later documents show the consuls enforcing payment of the tithe.[19] Around the middle of the thirteenth century, however, further anticlerical legislation was passed, only to be suppressed in 1256 as part of the Guelf reaction which was taking place in the Piedmontese towns.[20]

[15] *ACA*, doc. 247.   [16] *Ibid.*, doc. 284.   [17] *ACT*, doc. 76.
[18] *Ibid.*, doc. 126.   [19] *Ibid.*, docs. 222, 573, 574.
[20] *Ibid.*, doc. 540. Turin experienced a similar reaction. Witness the repeal of a statute which had aimed at restricting the base of the tithe. *Le carte dell'archivio del Duomo di Torino*, ed. G. Borghezio and G. Fasoli, BSSS, cvi (Pinerolo, 1931), doc. 64.

The cases hitherto cited were open conflicts between the Church and the communes. At the same time the issue was joined, more quietly but even more drastically, between canon law and communal law. By the thirteenth century canon law had finally crystallized in the Decretals. The communes, equally under the influence of the study of Roman law, were actively scrutinizing, amending, and codifying their ancient customs. From each commune issued a stream of statutory law, much of it in affirmance of ancient custom, some of it new legislation. These two systems of law came into collision, and at no point did they conflict more vigorously than in the domain of the tithe. Canon law assigned the noval tithes to the parish priests; the customary law of the Lombard communes gave them to the bishops. Canon law condemned in principle the holding of tithes by laymen; customary law accepted the practice and protected laymen in their rights.[21] In the statutes passed by the communes from the thirteenth century on may be traced the slow victory of the communes over the ecclesiastical authorities. The intractability of the communes manifested itself especially in the whittling away of ecclesiastical jurisdiction over the tithe, which was drawn within the orbit of the civil courts.

From the large mass of communal legislation on the tithe we cite examples from six north Italian cities—Brescia, Bergamo, and Lodi, Padua, Vicenza, and Mantua. These may serve as samplings of a movement which was taking place throughout upper Italy.

Brescia.[22] (1) Secular judges were given competence in lawsuits over the tithes.

(2) Laymen could hold tithes if they held their titles from the Church or from other laymen legally possessing such titles; once invested with tithes, they could transfer them to other laymen without the consent of the original owner.

(3) No one in Brescia could receive tithes except in the

[21] See pp. 166 and 214, n. 17.
[22] *Statuta Civitatis Brixiae* (Brescia, 1557), p. 84.

presence or with the consent of the owner or the possessor.

(4) No resident of Brescia had the right to gather tithes unless he had held it for ten years. Nonresidents could not hold tithes in Brescia unless they had held their titles for twenty years.

Bergamo.[23] (1) A tithe owner wishing to sell his right to the tithes was obliged to give a written option to the owner of the land on which the tithe rested; the landowner had to reply within a few days in writing, saying whether or not he wished to buy the tithe and thus liberate his land from the burden.

(2) No one was to deny the competence of the podestà, judges, and consuls of Bergamo to decide cases involving the tithes owed to laymen or involving the *fructus decimarum* when this was due to ecclesiastics.[24] An exception would be made when the case involved the *jus decimandi.*

Lodi.[25] (1) Lay judges were to have the same competence as ecclesiastical judges to hear cases involving tithes and usury.

(2) No one was to contest the right of the podestà and his judges and consuls to render judgment in lawsuits over tithes.

(3) Citizens who had held tithes for forty years would be protected in their rights by the communal government.

Padua.[26] (1) The commune would protect the rights of anyone who had held tithes for thirty years.

(2) No layman was to collect the tithe within the city limits, under a penalty of a fine of forty *librae.* (This was interpreted to mean that laymen could not buy or rent the collectorship of the tithe in the future; but tithes might still be collected by lay tithe owners who had held them in the past.)

(3) The cultivator who tilled lands owned by another had to notify the owner of the tithe before gathering his crops in

---

[23] *Statuta Bergomi* (Bergamo, 1727), ii, 52, and iv, 33.

[24] This is the distinction between the usufruct of the tithe and the ownership of the tithe which had been established by the canonists.

[25] *Laudensium Statuta* (Lodi, 1586), nos. 36, 336, 337.

[26] *Statuti del comune di Padova dal secolo xii all'anno 1285,* ed. A. Gloria (Padua, 1873), pp. 216–217.

order that the owner or his agent might come to fetch the tithe.
If the owner did not have an agent in that village, the cultivator,
on gathering his crops, was obliged to summon two of his neighbors to act as witnesses of the amount of the tithe, then store it
away until it was collected. At the same time he had to segregate
and pay the parochial fourth, or *quartese*. Any violation of this
statute was subject to a fine of sixty shillings, of which half went
to the commune, half to the tithe owner.

Vicenza.[27] (1) Anyone who had paid tithe in the past but
now refused to pay it to the tithe owner was to be fined sixty
shillings and forced to pay the tithe.

(2) Those who had had peaceful possession of tithes or
other property for thirty years were not to be disturbed in their
possession.

(3) No sharecropper was to divide the produce of his land
or separate the tithe without notifying his landlord or the landlord's steward to come and take his part of the crops. The landlord
or his agent had to be present when his portion of the crops, i.e.,
the half, third, or fourth of the produce, was separated from the
total harvest. If the tithe owner wished to take his tithe in the
fields, this was permissible, and the cultivator had to carry the
tithe to the village, just as he did when the separation was performed there.[28]

Mantua.[29] (1) The podestà was charged with the duty of
enforcing the rule that peasants and cultivators and those who
owed the tithe or a portion of their produce should not harvest

[27] *Statuti del comune di Vicenza, 1264*, ed. F. Lampertico, *Monumenti
storici della R. Deput. Ven. st. pat.*, Second Series, i (1886), 98, 135–137.

[28] Occasionally a statute seems to envisage the case in which landlord
and tithe owner were the same person. As a result of sales and exchanges
of property, this condition had become common by the second half of the
twelfth century. Hence the leases illustrated in Chapter XII.

[29] Carlo d'Arco, *Studi intorno al municipio di Mantova dall'origini di
questo fino all'anno 1863* (Mantua, 1871–1874, 7 vols. in 3), ii, 177–179,
223. The regulations on the tithe occur in the codification of Mantuan
laws made in 1303 but incorporating earlier legislation. A critical edition
of these statutes is much needed.

their crops in the absence of the owners or their agents. Rents and tithes must be paid within fifteen days of the stipulated time or not less than eight days afterwards, except that a cultivator who had not paid tithe from his holding for thirty years should not be compelled to pay it.

(2) No one might hold by any title or acquire in any way from any ecclesiastical or secular person or corporation the spiritual tithe or right to such a tithe which was not in the possession of the individual or corporation at the time of the transaction and had not been so possessed for at least ten years.[30]

(3) No layman or cleric of the bishopric and jurisdiction of Mantua should acquire a tithe or right to the tithe in that bishopric from any lay or clerical person belonging to another bishopric or jurisdiction. The bishops of Mantua likewise should not give the tithe or the right to the tithe to anyone not of the bishopric or jurisdiction of Mantua.

It is impossible to generalize on the basis of this legislation, although certain patterns or trends do recur from one commune to another. An analysis of these statutes, the substance of which is repeated in the legislation of still other communes, points to the conclusion that the principal purpose of the north Italian communes in the thirteenth century was to bring the tithe under the jurisdiction of the communal courts. Many of the statutes were actually rather conservative in that they defended established rights and customs in regard to the tithe. However, those rights and customs were usually contrary to the new canon law. If the tithe remained under the jurisdiction of the church courts (an issue which seems not only to pervade the communal legislation but to underlie the disputes studied at the beginning of this chapter), those courts would enforce the provisions of canon law in regard to it. Hence the determination of the communal governments to bring the tithes under their own jurisdiction.

[30] For the phrase "spiritual tithe" and further comment on this statute, see pp. 218–219.

In each commune there had formed in regard to the tithe a body of secular custom, and this the communes sought to preserve or to revise as the interests of the ruling groups might dictate. Because of the shifting alignments of parties and groups in the communes, there were changing policies in respect to the tithe. Some communes refused to enforce the collection of tithes; others merely discouraged the further acquisition of this source of revenue; still others promoted the eventual extinction of the tithe as part of a general policy aiming at the transformation of feudal and other conditional tenures into allodial proprietorship. As policies differed, so was the outcome different in the various communes. In short, one cannot generalize about this question in default of detailed monographs dealing with the history of each commune. Provisionally it may be said that the general direction of communal policy in upper Italy during the thirteenth century was hostile to the tithe in the larger communes and the territories under their immediate jurisdiction; but large tracts of the countryside were comparatively untouched by the revolt against the tithe, especially in regions which remained under feudal influence. In upper Italy these areas were numerous and extensive.

After threading one's way through the mazes of communal policy, it is interesting to reconsider some of the reasons for the hostility towards the tithe manifested by most communes. Undoubtedly the heretical groups in the cities of northern Italy during the high Middle Ages spread a leaven of discontent among the orthodox as well by accenting abuses in the Church. In cities like Parma and Bologna the wealth of the cathedral chapters was much resented, especially since the opulent canons were believed to be neglecting their duties towards the poor. This point of view, regarded as a mark of sophistication distinguishing the burgher and educated man from the peasant, was expressed by the jurist, Odofredo of Bologna:

I shall now state to whom I ought to pay tithe. I do not want my tithes to go to the cathedral canons, for among them are many who gad about in the manner of laymen and who keep palfreys, falcons, and armed men. Moreover, these tithes ought to benefit the poor. . . . Men of gentle birth, and almost all the citizens of this commune, are of the opinion that it is better to pay one's tithes directly to the poor; peasants, on the other hand, believe that they should be paid to the clergy.[31]

In somewhat the same vein of thought, the fourteenth-century jurist, Pietro dei Boattieri, expressed the view that the wealth of the Church in modern times had made the tithe unnecessary: in the olden days the tithe was given to the Church because of its poverty and was divided into three portions, for the clergy, the fabric, and the poor respectively; but now the churches, although rich, gave so little to the poor that the tithe had lost its reason for existence.[32] At Reggio and Bologna the citizenry obviously subscribed to this idea.

But the animus of the communes was not only directed against the clergy who misused the tithes conferred upon them by divine law. The reaction against the tithe during the thirteenth century was to some extent but one facet of an antifeudal movement aimed both against the temporal jurisdiction of the bishops and against the magnates of the commune and its contado, who had translated their rights over the tithes into compulsive jurisdiction over the peasants who owed them.[33]

[31] Quoted by Gaudenzi, "Il monastero di Nonantola," *BISI*, xxxvi (1916), 236, and discussed by Nino Tamassia, "Odofredo," *AMR*, Third Series, xii (1894), 343.

[32] Gaudenzi, *op. cit.*, p. 237.

[33] The magnates were charged with this kind of usurpation by the compiler of the Milanese custumal of ca. 1216: "Sciendum tamen est, quod districtus et iurisdictio quasi synonima nomina sunt, licet ob pravam quorundam dominorum avaritiam, qui cum suis rusticis de parte bonorum et aliarum compositionum danda pepigerunt, districtuum potestas sit coarctata, sicut fere in omnibus locis iurisdictionis nostrae manifeste potest videri. . . ." Berlan, *LCM*, p. 52.

This factor emerges very clearly in the Bolognese statutes of 1288, which forbid the "magnates, nobles, or *potentes* of the city and county of Bologna, whether laymen or clergy, male or female," to seize or damage the property of members of the guilds of Bologna or of peasants under the jurisdiction of the commune on the pretense of collecting the tithe; such claims must be submitted to the communal courts.[34]

Nevertheless, the material effects of the communal revolt against the tithe should not be overestimated. In some instances restraining legislation resulted from a temporary gust of anti-clerical sentiment, fanned by struggles against the temporal jurisdiction of the bishops or the arrogance of the magnates. When the crisis died down, the laws against the tithe were relaxed. Furthermore, when the bourgeoisie or members of the town nobility of more recent origin themselves became owners of rural estates cultivated by dependents, the conservation rather than the abolition of the remaining tithes became an object of governmental solicitude. Indeed, in some regions a new kind of serfdom seems to have developed in the course of the thirteenth and fourteenth centuries, under which the tenants were shackled by obligations almost as restrictive as those of the old manorialism. Clan property in the Italian countryside dissolved; but individual properties were consolidated, as able and energetic individuals, some of noble stock, others of mer-cantile origin, invested their wealth in rural estates and laid the foundations of agrarian capitalism in Italy. The policies followed in regard to the tithe by the Italian communes and by the despotisms or republics which succeeded them reflect these changes in the distribution of rural property and in the structure of Italian society. It is impossible to trace those policies here, even in outline, because they are part of the social history of Italy in a period which has not been adequately explored, from this point of view, by historians. But we should beware of thinking that the ecclesiastical tithe in Italy was extirpated by

[34] *Statuti di Bologna dell'anno 1288*, pp. 202–203, 312–313.

the communal revolt. Many tithes were undoubtedly extinguished, particularly in the orbit of the greater communes. But such as survived the attack seem to have been salvaged in the years immediately following and to have been transmitted to posterity, partly in the form of the parochial *quartesi*, which had never been questioned even at the height of the communal reaction, partly as an ingredient in the seigniorial revenues of monasteries, bishops, and the lay aristocracy old and new.

Nor should it be supposed that the resistance of the Italian communes to the tithe was unique. Opposition to the tithe existed in feudal and Catholic France, where at the end of the high Middle Ages custom and not canon law was finally taken as the regulatory principle.[35] What was unique in Italy was the ease with which hostility could express itself in legislation and the rapidity with which the tithe was laicized. Not until the sixteenth and seventeenth centuries were the French kings able to treat the tithe as a purely seigniorial revenue and to regulate it through secular legislation.[36] The Italian communes anticipated this result by three centuries. This should not surprise us if we recall that secular civilization and the lay state were born in Italy.

It has not seemed necessary or feasible to discuss in this book the impact of the communal movement upon the parishes.[37] But it should be mentioned in concluding this chapter that many Italian communes in the later Middle Ages came to agreements with their clergies, whereby a fixed salary was substituted for the tithe. This was the origin of the "contractual tithes," the nature of which was debated in the nineteenth

[35] See Viard's admirable studies on the tithe in France, especially *Philippe le Bel et les dîmes insolites* (Dijon, 1911).

[36] Viard, *Histoire de la dîme ecclésiastique en France au xvie siècle* (Paris, 1914), pp. 138–139.

[37] There is an extensive literature on this subject in Italian. The various theories in regard to the rural communes are well summed up by G. P. Bognetti, *Sulle origini dei comuni rurali del medio evo* (Pavia, 1927).

century and later.[38] Thus the Venetian Republic late in the
fourteenth century ended a long-standing dispute with the
bishop of Castello over the distribution of tithes by agreeing to
pay him an annual subsidy in lieu of the personal tithes formerly
paid by the residents of Venice.[39] This practice was followed
by other cities and by some rural communes. But in the rural
districts which were less advanced economically or still under
feudal influences, the peasants continued to pay tithes, although
with a general tendency to commute the tithe into a money rent
or to substitute fixed payments in kind. Some rural communes
even purchased from the bishops or from lay tithe owners the
three-fourths of the tithe which had formerly been leased or
infeudated. In Olubra, near Piacenza, and in the Piedmontese
commune of Cannobbio, the *vicini*, or leading families who
constituted the commune, collected three-fourths of the tithes,
defending their rights against the claims of the parish churches.[40]
It would be hard to find a better illustration of the secularization of the tithe. Increasingly common, however, was the es-

[38] After 1887 some local courts maintained that these contractual
tithes had not been suppressed, since the communes, in assuming the
obligation of paying a salary to the parish priests, had exempted the people
from paying tithes. This view was opposed by Francesco Ruffini, "Della
novazione in materia di decime sacramentali," *Studi giuridici in onore di
Carlo Fadda* (Naples, 1906), iv, 227 ff., reprinted in *Scritti giuridici
minori*, i, 615–652. Ruffini reasoned that contractual tithes were in fulfillment of the ecclesiastical precept to pay tithes and that the communes,
by assuming this charge, had not changed the nature of the tithes. But in
1920 the Appellate Court of Venetia ruled that a tithe could change in
course of time from sacramental to dominical. *FV*, 1920, pp. 228–229.

[39] The dispute involved the so-called "tithes of the dead," levied by the
Church on the estates of Venetian residents after death. The Venetian government took the attitude that such tithes should be paid only when expressly willed to the Church by the testator. The agreement suppressed the
tithes of the dead but preserved the tithe on agriculture, obviously affecting only the rural properties of Venetian citizens. Cecchetti, *La repubblica
di Venezia e la corte di Roma*, i, 282, 289, and 123.

[40] F. Nasalli-Rocca, "Origine e primordi della pieve di Olubra," *ASPP*,
xxx (1930), 154–155; Campi, i, 124; Lattes, *Il diritto consuetudinario
delle città lombarde* (Milan, 1899), p. 325.

tablishment of a contractual relationship between commune and parish clergy, in which the latter received fixed salaries instead of the tithe. The lay domination of the parish which is implied in this arrangement involved, it is true, a subordination of the spiritual to the secular power, of Church to State; but the priest who received a salary from the commune and was appointed or dismissed by it at will was probably better off than the priest who had only the *quartese* or who received such a portion of the ecclesiastical tithe as was granted him by a clerical impropriator.[41]

[41] E. W. Watson reaches similar conclusions in "The Development of Ecclesiastical Organization and Its Financial Basis," *Cambridge Mediaeval History*, vi, 553.

CHAPTER XI

Gathering the Tithes

† INFORMATION as to the collection and administration of the tithes has to be gleaned piecemeal from hundreds of scattered documents. In this chapter we shall bring together some of the more significant or interesting details concerning the gathering of the tithe, the base of the tax, and the customs which grew up around it.

In Genoa during the twelfth century the archbishop's curia did not administer its tithes directly but leased them to laymen of the districts in which the tithes were raised.[1] The term of such concessions was short, usually from six to sixteen years, but even so these rights tended to become hereditary, and there were cases in which the tithe or a pension from it was leased to the heirs or the widows of former collectors.[2] Sometimes the lay collector gathered the rents (*introitus*) due to the curia as well as the tithes.[3] He then brought both rents and tithes to some central place, often to the market place of Rapallo, where he delivered them to the archbishop's agent, giving him at the same time a refection or its equivalent in money.[4] Occasionally

[1] Genoa, *Registro I*, pp. 11–14.
[2] Genoa, *Registro II*, App., docs. 30, 43, 76.
[3] Genoa, *Registro I*, docs. 49, 179, 204.
[4] *Ibid.*, docs. 123, 216.

the tithes of the curia were leased to the local clergy. Thus the archbishop's share of the tithe of oil paid by the inhabitants of Sori was leased to the archpriest of the local baptistery.[5] The archpriest and clergy of the baptistery of Lavagna likewise held a lease on the archbishop's portion, amounting to one half, of the tithes of some villages within the baptismal district (*plebegium*) as well as on all the lands of the curia within the district.[6]

In addition to the ordinary tithe, Genoa had a special variety of the tithe called the *decima maris*, or tithe of the sea. Since the resources of the Genoese consisted not so much in land as in ships and their cargoes, the communal government permitted the archbishop, by special arrangement, to collect a special tithe from the sailors on Genoese vessels, whether or not they were citizens of Genoa.[7] Every ship entering the port of Genoa had to pay tithe to the archbishop, the scale of payments varying according to the nature of the voyage and of the cargo. All ships from Alexandria, Constantinople (Romania), Africa, and Tunis had to pay twenty-two and a half shillings in lieu of the regular tithe, those from Sicily paid eleven shillings and three *denarii*, those from Sardinia eight shillings. If the cargo consisted mostly of grain, each sailor had to give one *mina* of grain to the archbishop, except when the ship came from Calabria or Provence, in which case each mariner paid a *quartinum* of grain instead.[8] The tithe of the sea was obviously a commutation of the ordinary tithe into money or fixed payments in grain made necessary by the peculiar economic circumstances of Genoa, if the local church was to share in the increasing wealth of the citizens. The Genoese regarded the tithe of the sea as a species of the ordinary

[5] *Ibid.*, pp. 14–15.

[6] *Ibid.*, p. 344. For examples of the leasing of the collectorship to the local priest, see *Registro II*, docs. 95, 146, 192, 200, 214.

[7] ". . . decimam super naves antiquitus ex consensu civium constitutam que de ianua exeuntes per pelagus ad negociationes vadunt." *Registro I*, p. 391. ". . . de foritanis hominibus qui navigabant cum hominibus nostre civitatis." *Ibid.*, p. 117.

[8] *Ibid.*, pp. 9–10.

tithe, and the local church applied to it all the rules governing the ordinary tithe. During the campaign against the lay tithe waged by Archbishop Siro and his successors, laymen were enjoined to restore any tithes of the sea which they had usurped.[9] The communal government during the twelfth century supported the archbishops in their claims, and the two archiepiscopal registers which have come down from this period contain several decisions of this nature in regard to the tithe of the sea rendered by the consuls of the commune in lawsuits over the tithe.[10]

Besides the tithe levied on the ships which came to the port of Genoa, the archbishop levied the tithe of the sea on ships which anchored in the maritime parishes of his diocese. The parish churches, it is interesting to observe, had no share in the tithe of the sea. These tithes were administered in the same way as the ordinary tithe, that is to say, they were farmed out to lay collectors by the archbishop's curia, sometimes to the same collectors who gathered the ordinary tithe.[11] The coastal territory subject to this tithe was carefully delimited. Like the ordinary tithe, the *decima maris* was occasionally usurped or evaded, and the archbishop had to make strenuous efforts to enforce payment.

The Genoese tithe on shipping illustrates how the principle of the ecclesiastical tithe might be adapted to local conditions. An equally unusual situation existed at Venice. Since the city of Venice did not yield the agricultural produce on which the

[9] Witness the action taken by the Archbishop after the Lateran Council of 1139: "In quo concilio placuit ei [Pope Innocent II] dare sententiam de laicis qui tenebant ecclesiarum dei decimas quod quicumque laicus decimas ecclesie tenuerit nisi ecclesie reddiderit sciat se sacrilegium crimen committere et periculum eterne damnationis incurrere. Quod preceptum cum dominus Archiepiscopus Syrus predicaret, alii ex illis qui tenebant decimas timore dei compuncti propter salutem animarum suarum decimas quas tenebant sive in mari sive in terra deo et domino Syro refutaverunt." *Ibid.*, p. 28. For the decree of 1139, see Mansi, *Concilia*, xxi, 528.

[10] *Ibid.*, pp. 57–59, 127–129, 389–396.

[11] Genoa, *Registro II*, docs. 54, 111, 140. Occasionally the tithe of the sea was leased to the local archpriest. *Registro I*, p. 384.

tithe was normally levied, the Church in Venice had recourse to what the canonists designated as the "personal tithe," that is, a tithe of the income gained in commerce or industry.[12] The personal tithe did not lend itself to collection on a seasonal basis, and so there grew up at some indeterminate time among the Venetians the practice of paying tithe only once, after death, as a kind of inheritance tax or death duty on the wealth accumulated during the individual's lifetime. Thus originated that curious institution, the "tithe of the dead," which won for the bishop of Castello the somewhat unenviable name of "the dead men's bishop." Such tithes were paid by the testamentary executors directly to the bishop. The Venetians resented the fact that, when the city was stricken by a plague or epidemic, a tithe might be collected several times from the same estate.[13]

Venetians who settled in the Latin Empire of Constantinople after the Fourth Crusade sometimes refused to pay tithe to the Latin Patriarch; instead, they returned to their native city to die and left their tithes to St. Mark's Cathedral. This practice was condemned by Innocent III, who ordained that Venetians living in the East must pay their tithes in the normal way, "notwithstanding the custom followed by the residents of Venice, of paying only at death a tithe on the gains of their lifetime." [14]

The more usual modes of collecting the tithes have already been analyzed for the bishopric of Turin.[15] Tithes not assigned

---

[12] Cardinal Roland, in his commentary on the *Decretum,* gives this Venetian custom as an example of the personal tithe: ". . . quod maxime in Venetiarum partibus cernitur custodiri, ubicumque enim quis lucratus fuerit, lucri decimam ecclesie suae tantum reddere compellitur." Thaner, *Die Summa Magistri Rolandi,* p. 41.

[13] Cecchetti, *La repubblica di Venezia e la corte di Roma,* i, 122–123. Some Venetian sources call these personal tithes "tithes of the clergy" to distinguish them from the income tax of a tenth which the Republic levied upon its citizens.

[14] ". . . non obstante consuetudine quam habitatores Venetiarum observant, ut videlicet in morte duntaxat deciment illa quae acquisierunt in vita." Quoted by Thomassin, *Ancienne et nouvelle discipline de l'église,* vi, 45.   [15] Chapter IX, pp. 173–176.

to the cathedral chapter, monasteries, or parishes, were in this diocese, as in Genoa, infeudated or leased to laymen. Usually the contract stated that the grantee should carry the tithes to a place designated by the bishop, where the division should be made in the presence of the bishop's agents. The bishop of Turin had special storehouses for this purpose. More often, however, the division of the tithes was made at the local parish church, and the parish priest acted as the bishop's agent or witness of the division. Sometimes the perishable products of the tithe were sold on the spot and the money remitted to the bishop.[16]

The cathedral chapters of Italy were large owners of tithes. So jealously did each chapter guard its right to tithe the lands immediately adjacent to the walls of the city that the urban parishes which grew up in the high Middle Ages had to struggle with the canons for a share of the tithes of their parishoners, in most cases having to admit the cathedral church as a benefi-ciary.[17] The cathedral chapters usually employed special offi-cials (*decimani* or *decimatores*) to collect their tithes; but when they also owned tithes in rural districts they often leased the collectorship to laymen.[18] The control exercised by the chapters over the tithes of impropriated parishes was usually very close.[19] Such a church might be committed to one of the canons, who

---

[16] *LI*, doc. 124; *Carte d'Ivrea*, doc. 294.

[17] The term "urban parish" as used here does not necessarily indicate the possession of a baptismal font, though some of these churches had the right to baptize, but the exercise of the parochial ministry.

The extensive holdings of tithes by the cathedral chapters are illustrated by numerous documents cited by Kehr, *IP*, *passim*. Padua, 1130: the chap-ter collected all the tithes of the city and of the impropriated parish of Pernumia. Gloria, *CDP*, ii, doc. 212. Piacenza, 1132: the chapter held the tithes of the city and those of eight baptismal churches and sixteen chapels. Campi, i, doc. 23. Cremona, ca. 1150: a papal legate decided that all the parishes of the city should divide their tithes into five parts, of which one should go to the chapter. Kehr, *IP*, vi, pt. 1, 277, no. 30.

[18] *ACN*, docs. 396, 574, 599. The statutes of the canons of Monza in 1237 permitted them to lease their tithes to laymen but prohibited the leasing of any other part of their prebends. Frisi, *Memorie di Monza*, ii, doc. 114.   [19] As in *ACT*, doc. 320.

either served the church personally, taking the tithes as his salary, or else appointed a stipendiary priest as vicar, to whom he granted the tithes from certain designated areas.[20] In the thirteenth century, when the property of most cathedral chapters was divided into prebends, the tithes were included in these individual allotments. In the cathedral of Turin this arrangement was initiated in 1213, when tithes were included in most of the canonical prebends then created and the tithes of the city were assigned to the prebends enjoyed by the bishop, the provost, and two canons.[21] When the tithes were divided into prebends in this way, part of the product was sometimes reserved for the common use of the chapter; this was called the *decima communis,* and occasionally a gift of tithes was made to the canons on condition that it should be included in this "common tithe." [22]

Parochial tithes were usually gathered by the local clergy, who might at the same time collect the bishop's share. Sometimes all the tithes of a parish were gathered by the laymen who held the larger part and who would then give the priest his share. A variety of usages in this respect prevailed in the Milanese parishes, where the greater part of the tithe was in the hands of the local *capitanei.* In some of the rural parishes of Milan the knights, or those to whom they had infeudated their tithes, collected all the tithes and gave the local clergy their fourth (Vigonzone). In others the clergy were assigned the total tithe of an area within the parish, the product of which was calculated as a fourth of the total tithe of the parish (Vimercate). In still others each cultivator paid a fourth of his tithe directly to the local church, the remainder to the lay tithe owners (San Donato, Biasca).[23]

[20] The technical term for the regime of impropriated churches described in the text is "vicarage system." R. A. R. Hartridge, *A History of Vicarages in the Middle Ages* (Cambridge, 1930), unfortunately for our purposes, excludes Italy from his discussion of this subject.

[21] *Carte del Duomo di Torino,* doc. 34.

[22] *Ibid.* [23] Bognetti, "Le pievi delle Valli di Blenio," pp. 48–49.

In some bishoprics within the archdiocese of Milan there existed in the thirteenth century a curious custom in regard to the tithes—the distribution of olive branches and wine to the tithe payers.[24] In Milan itself, on the morning of Palm Sunday, the archbishop was accustomed to distribute olive branches at the church of San Lorenzo to all who desired them.[25] In the rural districts of the diocese, all who held the tithes of a baptismal church from the archbishop had to distribute to the people on Palm Sunday the so-called palms or olive branches and on Easter Sunday were obliged to give these same people a feast of bread and wine after the general communion.[26] The right to bestow the olive branches, sometimes designated in the documents as *jus dandi olivas,* and to dispense the bread and wine was cited in lawsuits as proof that the donor owned the tithes of the district, and the church to which the tithes in question were attached was called the *caput decimae.*[27] Sometimes a baptismal church might acquire all the tithes itself. This happened in the case of the baptismal church of Vimercate, which by the early years of the thirteenth century had purchased all the tithes from the local *capitanei.* Two lawsuits occasioned by refusals to pay tithe to this church not only illustrate the custom of giving the olive branches to the tithe payers but also show that it was recognized by the commune of Milan. The baptismal church claimed to be the *caput decimae* of its district. It rested its claim both on the fact that it was the baptistery of the region and therefore entitled to the tithe *plebatu iure seu presumptione canonum* and on the right of purchase. It submitted as concrete evidence of its right the facts that it distributed olive branches to the burghers of Vimercate and that at each gate of the town

[24] G. Biscaro, "Di un'antica costumanza dell'archidiocesi milanese," *ASL,* xxxiv (1907), 538–542.

[25] *Beroldus sive Ecclesiae Ambrosianae Mediolanensis Kalendarium,* ed. Marco Magistretti (Milan, 1894), p. 96.

[26] Biscaro's documents illustrating this custom come from the years 1192–1271.

[27] *Atti del comune di Milano,* docs. 319, 336.

it maintained a collector who took the tithe of grain, vegetables, wine, and other produce as they were brought to market.[28] Somewhat earlier than this, the *capitanei* of Vigonzone had proved their right to take the tithe of Varia by showing that by local custom they distributed olive branches on Palm Sunday and wine at Easter. The wine and olive branches, we learn, were carried to the church on a cart, often making a heavy load; the bread and wine, which the people consumed on the spot, had to have a definite value in money.[29] This custom of distributing olive branches to the tithe payers was also practiced in the bishoprics of Novara and Tortona.[30] By the fourteenth century it seems to have died out.

At Padua the collection of the tithe was regulated by a statute passed sometime before 1236. The cultivator had to notify the tithe owner before gathering his crops. If the tithe owner did not have a collector in that district, the cultivator was to summon two neighbors as witnesses of the amount of the tithe, then gather his crops, and store the tithe for the owner or his agent. The *quartese,* or parochial fourth, he had to pay immediately to the parish priest.[31]

In Pirano the much-mooted tithe of oil was gathered by two collectors, a cleric appointed by the baptistery and a layman chosen by the citizens and their gastald.[32] Sometimes the people seem to have carried their oil directly to the church and delivered it to the official in charge of the candles, who in turn

[28] G. Barni, "Note su di una causa per decime riguardante la chiesa di Santo Stefano in Vimercate," *RSDI*, xiii (1940), 148 ff., believes that these documents in themselves do not prove conclusively that the tithes at dispute were sacramental in character. I agree with him that no single document or small group of documents can be regarded as decisive; the tithe has to be studied in its total evolution over an area wide enough to make it possible to apply comparative methods. On this basis it is difficult to deny the spiritual character of the tithes of Vimercate.

[29] Biscaro, "Di un'antica costumanza," pp. 540–541.

[30] *ACN*, doc. 548; *ACT*, docs. 113, 152, 302.

[31] *Statuti di Padova*, p. 217.

[32] *Chartularium Piranense*, doc. 22 (p. 30).

committed it to the sacristan for safekeeping. It was the sacristan's duty to divide the oil between the baptismal church and its chapels, where it helped to illuminate the altars.[33] Oil not needed for the candles was sold and the proceeds used to purchase service books and equipment for the church.[34]

Few products or occupations escaped the tithe. In Genoa, as we have seen, it was levied upon sea-borne commerce; in Venice upon the profits of industry and trade. In agricultural areas the tithe did not merely fall on the products of the soil and on the increase of livestock; in Padua, for example, fishermen had to pay a tithe of their fish. Mills also were tithed.[35] The fullest account of the base of the tithe, with many details as to the way in which it was gathered, is found in the *Liber Consuetudinum Mediolani,* the compilation of Milanese customs of the early thirteenth century already referred to on several occasions.

In the Milanese the base of the tithe was very broad, although some restrictions had been made by the moderating hand of custom. Hay, grass, and wood were exempt from tithe, as were garden fruits such as apples, figs, and plums, unless such fruits were sold, in which case a tithe of the selling price was due. Tithe was taken from all kinds of grain and vegetables and from nuts and chestnuts. Sheep and chicken escaped the tithe, but most animals and even some insects were affected. The tithe was levied on newborn animals and on bees. The Milanese custumal describes in minute detail the applications of the tithe to livestock. From his newborn lambs, goats, pigs, and male bees the cultivator had to give the tithe owner one of every ten; if he had less than ten, then a tenth of the selling price of those he did possess. He must keep his lambs, goats, and pigs for thirty days after their birth, unless they were born in Lent, when he had to keep them until Easter. If he paid tithes of wool, milk, or cheese from his animals, he was not obliged to give a tithe of the animals themselves. For horses, cattle, and asses another method of

---

[33] *Ibid.,* doc. 22 (pp. 24–25).   [34] *Ibid.,* doc. 58 (p. 76).
[35] *Statuti di Padova,* p. 216; Gloria, *CDP,* iii, doc. 743.

levying tithe prevailed, because it would rarely happen that ten of these animals would be born at the same time. From his bull-calves, colts, and asses, therefore, the tithe payer gave the tenth of its genus in order of birth. He was not obliged to give a tenth of his bees if he paid tithe from his wax or honey.

Besides defining the base of the tithe, the *Liber Consuetudinum* tells how the tithe was collected in the Milanese and shows that the commune enforced the rules formulated in the custumal. Prescription could not extinguish the tithe owner's right, even if the tithe was not paid for thirty or forty years; but if the tithe had been paid to another during that time, the two claimants might bring their case before the commune. If the tithe owner wished, he might take his tithe from the crops before they were harvested, with the proviso that, having elected this method, he must observe it through the whole year; after that he might wait and take his tithe after the crops had been gathered. Milanese customs in force at the beginning of the thirteenth century obviously favored the tithe owners.[36]

Enforcement of these customs by the consuls of Milan in the thirteenth century is illustrated by the records of various lawsuits over the tithes. Several documents of this period contain a formula, evidently drawn up to guide the judges, which sums up the customs described in the *Liber Consuetudinum*. Particularly interesting is the distinction which came to be made between allodial lands and those held by tenants. In tithing freehold property, the tithe owner had the option described in the preceding paragraph; but from leaseholds from which the rent consisted of a fractional part of the produce, that is, a third, fourth, or half, as the case might be, the tithe owner had to wait until the crops had been gathered and the rents had been paid. Thus the communal authorities enforced the principle of Lombard customary law that sharecroppers should pay tithe only on what was left of the harvest after they had paid their rents.[37]

[36] Berlan, *LCM*, pp. 58–59.
[37] *Atti del comune di Milano*, doc. 336. The provisions of the customary

We shall conclude by noting a few of the many anomalies
that pervaded the medieval tithe. Since the tithe was a well-nigh
universal income tax, resting on the productive resources of
Italy, sharing in any increase of prosperity and difficult for the
rural classes to evade, it came to be regarded as a sound investment, a desirable form of annuity, and excellent collateral for
loans. Mortgages were sometimes made with the tithe as security.
In order to garrison the fortress of Sant'Albano, the bishop of
Asti borrowed seventy Genoese *librae* from a private person,
presumably a banker, to whom he gave as security the episcopal
portion of the tithes of Sant'Albano, with the understanding that
if the tithe did not have an annual value of ten and a half *librae,*
he would make up the deficiency.[38] Unable to complete a church
in process of construction, the priory of Moncalieri raised funds
by mortgaging its tithes in Saluzzo and a nearby village to the
countess of Saluzzo for a period of ten years.[39] To cover the expenses of attending an imperial coronation in Rome, the bishop
of Arezzo mortgaged to a Sienese moneylender his share of the
tithes of two parishes.[40] Laymen mortgaged their tithes in the
same way.[41] Pensions were sold or given from the tithes.[42] To
show how the tithe was denatured by these practices, we may
cite instances where laymen collected tithes from priests and

law in regard to this point are so important in connection with the problem of the tithes that I cite them in full: "Quod rusticus sive colonus qui
nomine alieno terram colit, non nisi de sua parte fructuum decimam per-
solvere tenetur nisi speciali consuetudine vel pacto in quibusdam terris
sive locis obtineat si ut de super toto decima detur, et hoc ea consideratione
introductum est, ut detracta portione dominorum, coloni de sua parte
duntaxat decimam solvant, quia domini in civitate vel in aliis locis plerun-
que habitant, et spiritualia ibi non recipiunt ubi decimae solvuntur et
ideo de sua parte fructuum decimas dare non tenentur." Berlan, p. 58.
Canon law, to the contrary, insisted that the tithe should be levied on the
gross product.   [38] *ACA,* doc. 396.
 [39] *Cartario della chiesa di Santa Maria di Testona (1194–1300),* ed.
Vittore Ansaldo, BSSS, xliii (Pinerolo, 1911), doc. 46.
 [40] Pasqui, *Documenti di Arezzo,* ii, doc. 500.
 [41] Gloria, *CDP,* ii, doc. 430.   [42] *ACA,* doc. 87.

even appointed priests to collect their tithes.[43] These anomalies are not inexplicable when we realize that the tithe had long since been deflected from an exclusively spiritual purpose and with the exception of the portion set apart for the parochial clergy, had come to be regarded as a profitable source of revenue in which all the property-owning classes shared.

[43] In *ACN*, doc. 426, a priest pays tithe to the cathedral chapter of Novara.

CHAPTER XII

Tithes and Rents
in Agrarian Contracts

✝ AS WE approach the end of this study, it is well to pause and ask whether this account of the ecclesiastical tithe has thrown any light upon the problem of the tithes in modern times. Whatever its positive contribution to the solution of that problem, the preceding narrative has revealed that the ecclesiastical tithe in Italy during the Middle Ages, far from being exceptional or occasional, was one of the most characteristic institutions of that period. Its widespread extension is a self-evident fact to anyone who will take the pains to examine a representative medieval cartulary. Is this also true of the dominical tithe?

According to some historians and lawyers, the dominical tithe was a rent consisting of a fixed proportion of the produce. The fraction, one historian tells us, was not necessarily a tenth, but the term *decima* was used even when the measure was larger or smaller.[1] The dominical tithe, under this definition, was a contractual obligation in private law, while the sacramental tithe

[1] Salvioli, *Trattato di diritto italiano* (6th ed., 1908), p. 541. This view is obviously related to the broad extension given to the term "dominical tithe" in the parliamentary debates of 1887. See p. 11, n. 25. It became widely current among legal writers.

had a semipublic character. These distinctions in the manuals of ecclesiastical law have a logical clarity which is positively enchanting; but they have been created by modern jurisprudence after centuries of schooling in Roman law. A retrospective survey of the ecclesiastical tithe in the medieval period shows that it was freely bequeathed, mortgaged, infeudated, or divided on a territorial basis among churchmen and laymen indiscriminately, and collected by laymen from the clergy, sometimes by priests acting as the laymen's agents. Furthermore, with the exception of some "personal" tithes, exemplified by the "tithes of the dead" at Venice and the "tithe of the sea" at Genoa, the tithe rested upon the land and was very remotely connected with the sacraments. Consideration of these facts tends to awaken skepticism as to the possibility of applying modern categories to an institution so deeply involved in medieval habits and customs. But let us bear these categories in mind as we analyze a specific group of documents, chosen from as wide an area as possible. These documents are agrarian contracts, in which cartularies of the high Middle Ages abound.

A contract which has been cited as an example of the dominical or feudal tithe appears in a document of 1215 in which the bishop of Mantua invests the commune of Campitello, an episcopal seigniory, with some uncultivated lands belonging to the bishopric in that district. The feudal investiture includes common lands, waste, and woodland and stipulates that each of the thirty-three men receiving investiture in the name of the commune shall pay from his share of the land a tithe of all the products except wood.[2] The commune paid the bishop four hundred

---

[2] ". . . reddendo tamen quilibet de parte sibi contingenti episcopatui Mantue ad voluntatem domini episcopi de omnibus proventibus decimarum, excepto de lignamine." Giuseppe Bonollo, "Su di una investitura del vescovo di Mantova, Enrico II," *ASL,* ii (1875), 8. Torelli notes that feudal investitures made by the bishop in Campitello and some other places of which he was seignior require only a *decima* and that only in the case of newly cultivated lands. *Un comune cittadino in territorio ad economia agricola* (Mantua, 1930), pp. 166–169, 198, n. 1.

Mantuan *librae* with which to discharge his debts, gave him some other land in exchange for this concession, and pledged him fidelity. A close examination of this document leads to the conclusion that it is a concealed alienation of church property. A comparison with a similar concession of common lands made in 1230 to the rural commune of Volta and with an earlier contract made with some knights of Mantua indicates that the financial straits of the see of Mantua were forcing its bishops to concede episcopal lands to rural communes or to knights in return for cash payments and an oath of fidelity, without imposing any rent but merely reserving the right to the noval tithes from lands not yet reduced to cultivation. The concession to the commune of Volta, made by the bishop and cathedral chapter as joint seigniors of Volta, also brought a price of four hundred *librae* and carried the provision that the commune should pay a tithe of all the products of the land except from trees and their fruits and from the grass and hay grown in the meadows.[3] These exceptions are in themselves an indication that we are here dealing with the ordinary tithe, because the contemporaneous Milanese *Book of Customs* discloses that in the archbishopric of Milan, whose customs were widely imitated, wood, hay, and grass were exempt from the ecclesiastical tithe.

We shall next consider some typical agrarian contracts relevant to this problem, arranging them according to regions.

Throughout northern and central Italy, during the twelfth and thirteenth centuries, the churches followed the custom of leasing their lands in *colonia parziaria,* i.e., for a rent consisting of a fraction or various fractions of the produce, sometimes accompanied by a money rent as well. For the first type of rent a generic term was available in the word *terraticum,* and the universal use of this term would have prevented much later ambiguity. However, this term was generally used only in the

---

[3] Torelli, *ACM*, doc. 89. By the contract made with the knights in 1204 the bishop ceded an island with the episcopal tithes and all his temporal rights over the island for 5,600 *librae*. Torelli, *Un comune cittadino,* pp. 197–198.

Roman law territories, Emilia and the South, with an occasional borrowing by the notaries of other regions.[4] In Ravenna *terraticum* was used quite consistently in agrarian contracts, the precise fraction of the product being fixed by local custom. The most common fractions were a third, fourth, fifth, or seventh of the yield of the land; occasionally a ninth, but never a tenth. The use of a tenth would obviously have led to confusion with the tithe. In none of the documents composing the register of the archiepiscopal church of Ravenna is it possible to mistake the *terraticum* for other than it was.[5]

The persistence of Roman law in Emilia probably contributed to greater clarity of definition. In the region of the Lombard law the terminology was less distinct, but the contracts themselves are quite unambiguous in the great majority of cases.

On the lands owned by the cathedral chapter of Asti the *colonia parziaria* was common, the tenant most often giving a third of his harvest to the chapter. On the estate of Quarto, manorial custom required the payment of a third by the tenants.[6] Some documents speak of a fourth (*quartum*), occasionally joined with a *decima;* others, of land in *mezzadria,* or *métayage,* from some of which a *decima* accompanied the half of the crops destined to the landlord.[7] In these cases it is impossible to avoid

[4] *Chartularium Imolense,* docs. 483, 752; *Chronicon Vulturnensis del monaco Giovanni,* ed. V. Federici (Rome, 1925, 2 vols.), ii, doc. 158, pp. 289–290; *Cod. Dip. Cavensis,* doc. 187. Its use in Pistoia ca. 1132 was exceptional: ". . . habemus afficctum et terraticum de quibusdam terris mediam partem, de quibusdam terciam, de quibusdam quartam. . . ." Caggese, "Note e documenti del vescovado di Pistoia," p. 179.

[5] Ravenna, 1220: ". . . et de omni alia terra terraticum de grano et sicalle, faba et trisico, lino et vino septimam partem secundum usum mase." *Regesto di Ravenna,* i, doc. 203. Ravenna, 1230: "de primo recoltu nichil Raven. ecclesie dare debeatis, postea dare debeatis terraticum, scilicet nonam partem de omnibus fructibus quos inde perceperitis." *Ibid.,* doc. 293. This cartulary also contains documents recording the infeudation of the ecclesiastical tithe by the archbishops. *Ibid.,* i, docs. 32, 489; ii, doc. 571.

[6] *ACA,* docs. 128, 131, 365, 368, 395.

[7] One contract notes that the canons are to take half of the harvest and the cultivators the other half, while the canons are to take the tithes at

the conclusion that the *decima* referred to was the ecclesiastical tithe, which was written into the lease.

Analogous practices were followed in the neighboring Piedmontese bishopric of Tortona. Here every variety of fraction occurs in the cartularies of clerical landowners—the *tertium, quartum, nona, medietas*—and *decima.*[8] In some of the documents mentioning the *decima,* it is impossible to be sure of its nature; but in most cases it appears to be the ecclesiastical tithe, which the cultivators promise to pay together with their rents.[9] Obviously this method of enforcing payment of the tithe was available to those clerical landowners who were at the same time tithe owners.

In the *Libro delle investiture,* chiefly valuable as a record of the ecclesiastical tithe in the bishopric of Turin, a few contracts between the bishop and the tenants of episcopal lands are included, but in no case do they refer to a rent of a tenth; the word *decima* in these documents clearly refers to the ecclesiastical tithe.[10] In the marquisate of Saluzzo, in the southern part of the diocese, the fifth (*quintum*) seems to have been the normal fraction paid by the tenant from the eleventh through the thirteenth century. Some tenants of the nunnery of Rifreddo and of the neighboring priory of Revello paid a fifth of their produce. Occasionally a *decima* was paid, together with a money rent.[11]

---

will: "Et ipsi canonici debent percipere decimas ad eorum voluntatem." *Ibid.,* doc. 329.

[8] *ACT,* doc. 62, 172 (*tertium*); 50, 81 (*quartum*); 104 (*nona*); 70, 143 (*decima*).

[9] The lease of a vineyard by the cathedral chapter in return for half the wine, a money rent, and two capons, contains the additional clause ". . . et debet dare decimam cum medietate in caneva." *Ibid.,* doc. 231.

[10] In the thirteenth century the bishop of Turin sometimes wrote the ecclesiastical tithe into a lease; a contract of 1201 requires a *quintum et decima. Le carte dell'archivio arcivescovile di Torino fino al 1310,* ed. F. Gabotto and G. B. Berberis, *BSSS,* xxxvi (Pinerolo, 1906), doc. 119.

[11] In 1245 Rifreddo leased six *giornatae* of land in return for a money rent and *decimam omnium fructuum qui in dicta terra nasceretur. CR,* doc. 83. Doc. 143: . . . *ad fictum reddendum denarii vii . . . et decimam vini.*

Since we know from other documents that the nunnery owned two-thirds of the ecclesiastical tithes in this region and the priory had also bought up rights in the tithes, the presumption is that the word *decima* in these contracts refers to the ecclesiastical tithe. A few contracts in the bulky cartulary of the Cistercian abbey of Staffarda are more enigmatical. Five concessions made between 1290 and 1294 of uncultivated land to be converted to vineyards within five years, require a money rent and one-fifteenth of the fruits. Three of them state that the fifteenth of the fruits is paid "instead of the tithe" (*pro decima*).[12] Gabotto classifies this as a dominical tithe, stating that the tenant was also subject in addition to the ordinary ecclesiastical tithe.[13] Another interpretation, however, is suggested by a slightly earlier contract, in which the tenant promises to pay a money rent for his vineyard and a tenth of the wine *if Staffarda could obtain this from the parish priest of Saluzzo*.[14] Since this precedes the first of the other contracts by only a few weeks, it may be supposed that Staffarda had made an agreement with the parish priest in regard to the tithe.

Most of the documents hitherto cited come from the archives of bishoprics, cathedral chapters, or monasteries. An interesting variation is provided by the agrarian arrangements of the baptismal church of Voghera. This church had the usual parochial fourth of the ecclesiastical tithe of its district, which in 1259 it leased to the local commune.[15] From the tenants of its own lands it customarily took a fourth of the produce; but a lease given by the archpriest in 1282 required a fourth and a tithe of

---

[12] *CS*, docs. 618, 619, 623, 626, 628.

[13] F. Gabotto "L'agricoltura nella regione saluzzese dal xi al xv secolo," *Miscellanea saluzzese*, BSSS, xv (Pinerolo, 1902), xxi.

[14] *CS*, doc. 617: ". . . decimam vero si monasterium posset eam obtinere cum plebano Saluciarum."

[15] *Documenti degli archivi Tortonesi relativi alla storia di Voghera*, ed. V. Legè and F. Gabotto, BSSS, xxxix (Pinerolo, 1908), docs. 116, 85, 102, 109; *Le carte dell'archivio della cattedrale di Voghera*, ed. V. Legè, *ibid.*, docs. 10, 13. In 1282 the baptistery demanded a fourth of the noval tithes from a hospice, clearly the ecclesiastical tithe.

all the produce,[16] an indication that when parish churches acquired land subject to the tithe, in this case probably outside the *decimaria,* or tithing, regularly assigned to the church, they followed the example of other tithe owners by including their rights to the tithe in their leases.

Lombard agrarian customs are described in great detail by the Milanese *Liber Consuetudinum.* Here the word *decima* refers exclusively and explicitly to the ecclesiastical tithe, implying that the jurisconsult who compiled the custumal around 1216 knew of no other kind of tithe.[17] After defining the tithe in St. Augustine's words as the *tributa egentium animarum* and noting the discrepancy between canon law and custom in regard to lay ownership of tithes, the compiler describes the Milanese customs in regard to the collection and base of the tithe and outlines the procedural rules for claiming tithes in the communal courts in terms which might serve as a résumé of the communal legislation of north Italy on the subject. Most of the statutes which were discussed in Chapter X of this book might, indeed, be used as illustrative footnotes to the general rules regulating the tithe set forth in the *Book of Customs.* Most of the deviations which occur in the statutes are purely minor and local.

Lombard agrarian leases and practices are almost identical with those in Piedmont. A series of documents from Como shows how the ownership of the land and that of the tithe resting on the land could be vested in two different persons or institutions

---

[16] *Le carte dell'archivio della cattedrale di Voghera,* doc. 14.

[17] "Videamus ergo quid sit decima et qualiter per nostram consuetudinem et de quibus rebus decimae danter. Decimae sunt tributa egentium animarum ut in decretis causa XXI [XVI] eo quod egenis et pauperibus idest filiis Levi, qui nullam partem suppresserant dabantur, licet hodie per consuetudinem generalem obtineat quod non solum filiis Levi solvantur, verum etiam Laicis diversis de causis praestantur. Et ideo si per feudum vel alio titulo aliquis laicus decimam acquisierit licet iure canonum a Laicis possideri non debeant, per generalem tamen consuetudinem est obtentum, ut laici petere possint et exigere decimas in effectu." Berlan, *LCM,* pp. 57–58.

without necessarily causing confusion.[18] The archives of Lodi
as published by Vignati contain few leases but further the solution of our problem by giving detailed information in regard to
the subdivision of the ecclesiastical tithe among laymen. So
minute was the fragmentation of the ecclesiastical tithe that
some episcopal infeudations to laymen specify the plots of land
subject to the tithe and define their boundaries in minute detail.[19]

Mantua alone, among the north Italian bishoprics, exhibits
peculiarities demanding an explanation. Mantuan agrarian contracts have survived in large numbers from the twelfth and
thirteenth centuries and have been analyzed and tabulated by
Torelli.[20] These documents make it evident that the ecclesiastical
institutions of Mantua and its countryside during the twelfth
and first half of the thirteenth centuries followed very extensively
the custom of ceding their lands to cultivators in return for a
fourth or third of the produce, frequently augmented by a
decima. Very common was the requirement of a *quartum et
decima* from arable land, a *tercium et decima* from vineyards.
Sometimes in leases of land to be reduced to cultivation only a
decima was imposed. Leases of lands to be converted to vine-

[18] *Cartario di Chiavenna, PC,* xxiii (1918), doc. 150 (p. 59).

[19] Vignati, ii, doc. 104.

[20] *Un comune cittadino.* Torelli does not mention the ecclesiastical
tithe in his otherwise exhaustive account of agrarian customs, nor does
he discuss the nature of the tithes in Mantua, all of which he assumes to
be secular in nature (*Un comune cittadino,* p. 212, n. 2). I am unable to
agree with him in this conclusion, although it seems probable that some
secular tithes are here intermingled with those of ecclesiastical origin.
The mention of the *quartese* in some documents (Torelli, *ACM,* doc. 34,
p. 52, and doc. 42), allusions to the fourfold division of the tithes (*Un
comune cittadino,* p. 175, n. 2) and to the infeudated tithes (*Regesto di
Mantova,* docs. 592–593, 605, 612, 676), as well as the statutes of Mantua
(see above, pp. 188–189) suffice to prove the existence of the ecclesiastical
tithe in Mantua apart from all other evidence. A definitive solution of
this problem must, however, wait upon a more thorough study of agrarian
tenures in the high Middle Ages than exists at present.

yards granted by the cathedral chapter resemble the leases by
Staffarda already described above. In a contract of 1224 the
tenant promises to pay a money rent (*fictum*) and a tithe for
three years; after the vines have been raised, he will give a
fixed amount of wine each year instead of the tithe (*pro
decima*).[21] A contract of 1197 is typical of the tenurial arrangements set up in new colonies of peasants. Some tenants who
agree to form a new settlement in territory owned by the monastery of San Benedetto of Polirone promise that from the arable
land they will render a fourth and a tithe of the produce; from
their vineyards a third and a tithe; from land newly reduced to
tillage only a tithe for six years, then a third and a tithe; on
woodland cleared by the tenants only a tithe for two years, then
a fourth and a tithe.[22] The preoccupation of the ecclesiastical

[21] Torelli, *ACM*, doc. 69.

[22] *Regesto di Mantova,* doc. 580. For other characteristic examples of
a *decima* combined with some other fraction of the produce, see Torelli,
ACM, docs. 30, 31, 60, 87, 103, 324; *Regesto di Mantova,* docs. 600, 603.
A document of 1297, cited by Torelli, *Un comune cittadino,* p. 168, suggests that on one monastic estate it was customary for tenants to pay a
tenth from some products, a fifth from others. The hypothesis that the
decima in such cases is merely a constituent part of the rent is so obvious
that the present writer considered it carefully in examining the agrarian
contracts cited in this chapter, only to discard it in favor of the interpretation given in the body of the text, for reasons derived in part from a
previous study of the ecclesiastical tithe but reinforced by other considerations. The hypothesis that the *decima* is merely a rent is contradicted by
similar contracts from other regions, many of which state or imply that the
decima is superimposed upon the proportional rents in kind, in short, that
it is *sui generis.* Most conclusive is the evidence of the communal statutes
regulating the tithe during the very period in which these contracts were
drawn up. The statutes of the north Italian communes, with the single
exception of Mantua so far as the writer is aware, know only one *decima,*
the ecclesiastical tithe.

Moreover, the laws of expropriation and allodiation in some of the
north Italian communes clearly recognize the *decima* as a distinct category of charge, distinguished from all other burdens resting upon the
land. Thus the laws of Parma, in requiring owners of rural lands under
communal jurisdiction to cede their properties to others under certain
conditions in return for lands of equal value, provided that all charges

landlord seems to have been to establish immediate title to the noval tithe in the case of new lands. The fact that the tithe continued to be paid after the third or fourth was levied indicates that those who made the agreement recognized it as being distinct from the fourth or third.

Such concessions were practiced especially by ecclesiastical institutions in Mantua; but laymen also used this type of contract. In some cases the imposition of a *decima*, in addition to the fourth or third and the other charges upon the land, was made by a layman whom we know to have held concessions of the ecclesiastical tithe directly or mediately from the bishop of Mantua. But it is not always possible to establish any connection with the ecclesiastical tithe. Some documents suggest the hypothesis that the imposition of a tithe, together with other charges, had become customary in Mantua, although certainly not all peasant cultivators paid a *decima* to their landlords. The explanation which the present writer would suggest for the very perplexing agrarian contracts from this bishopric is that Mantua presents an extreme example, unique among the Italian bishop-

---

resting upon one piece of land should pass over to the land received in exchange. Excepted from this requirement, however, was the *decima*, which inhered in the soil and passed to the charge of the new owner. Some exchanges of this nature, authorized by the official assessor (*ingrossator*) of Parma, therefore contain the significant clause, "excepta decima que transeat cum terra," or "excepta decima quam non removeo que transeat cum terra." See Alessandro Lattes, "Le ingrossazioni nei documenti Parmensi," *ASPP*, New Series, xiv (1914), 207–233, especially pp. 216, 231, 232 and Nino Tamassia, "Il diritto di prelazione e l'espropriazione forzata negli statuti dei comuni italiani," *Archivio giuridico*, 1885, pp. 282–294. A study of the laws of expropriation, which originated in the twelfth century and were still enforced in the eighteenth century in Italy, might, in the opinion of the present writer, demonstrate that the term *terra decimalis*, mentioned in medieval Italian documents, designates land subject to this special charge, of ecclesiastical origin, and not simply land from which the tenant owes a rent in kind consisting of a tenth of the harvest; e.g., "feudi, allodi, terre emphiteotice vel fictalicie vel decimales aut conditionales," in the Mantuan statute, "De ingrosationibus," quoted by Torelli, *Un comune cittadino*, p. 244.

rics studied, of the early assimilation of the ecclesiastical tithe
to other seigniorial dues. The monasteries, which exercised
seigniorial powers over numerous rural communities, and the
bishop of Mantua, two-thirds of whose property in the high
Middle Ages was feudal, may have set the precedent of levying
tithes upon their tenants in written contracts, together with
other charges upon the land. So long as this practice was confined to ecclesiastical institutions, the ecclesiastical tithe was
recognizable as such, no matter how far removed from any
connection with the sacraments. But when laymen became large
owners of tithes—and it will be recalled that three-fourths of
the tithes in many places were in the hands of laymen—and
when such tithes were minutely subdivided and dispersed
through sales, exchanges, and other transfers of property, the
ecclesiastical tithe tended to be transformed into a form of
secular property, no different in incidence or purpose from a
rent.

This process seems to have been under way in Mantua by
the end of the twelfth century and to have been consummated
when the commune of Mantua enacted a statute ordaining that
peasants living in the bishopric or jurisdiction of Mantua who
kept small animals (e.g., pigs, goats, or sheep) in their cottages
must give each year a tithe of those animals to the owner of
the cottage unless they paid him a money rent. Those who try
to evade this law, the statute continues, by keeping their animals
on other lands of theirs from which no tithe is due, must pay the
tithe of new-born animals to the owner of the cottage where they
live with their families.[23] This *decima nascentium,* or *decima
casamenti,* while it may have been modeled upon the ecclesiastical tithe or upon customs followed on the estates of ecclesiastical landowners, was evidently not the ecclesiastical tithe, for
it affected all owners of cottages. Moreover, the second paragraph of the statute referring to this cottage tithe goes on to
state that "the spiritual tithe or right to such tithe" cannot be

[23] Arco, *Studi intorno al municipio di Mantova,* ii, 179.

transferred without proof of ten years' possession. This use of the term "spiritual tithe," the only one which I have encountered in a medieval Italian source, implies that in Mantua there were tithes which were *not* spiritual; and given the context we may probably assume that the allusion is to the cottage tithe itself. Probably the term "spiritual tithe" distinguishes the ecclesiastical tithe in all its forms from the secular *decima* which the commune had just created or the existence of which in local custom it had just affirmed.

In summary, the nature of the *decima* referred to in many of the agrarian contracts of Mantua should be regarded as an open question. But the documents themselves, studied in their total context, suggest that the communal government, made up in the twelfth and early thirteenth centuries of episcopal vassals, accepted and generalized customs which had grown up around the ecclesiastical tithe on the estates of the Church and had been so widely imitated by laymen, whether or not holders of ecclesiastical tithes themselves, as actually to bring into existence tithes of a purely secular nature, resting upon a secular sanction. But Mantua seems to have been exceptional in this respect; nothing like this "cottage tithe" at Mantua appears in the voluminous cartularies of the Piedmontese bishoprics, in Milan and its neighboring dioceses, in Verona, Vicenza, or Ravenna, to mention only a few bishoprics which have been most closely studied. Furthermore, as the thirteenth century progressed, the tendency in Mantua was in the direction of money rents. By the sixteenth century the *decima* had become more especially characteristic of the ecclesiastical estates.[24]

[24] *Ibid.*, iv, 156. The abbey of San Benedetto of Polirone levied a *decima* on 3,802 *bibulcae* of land in seven villages. It is perhaps significant that almost half of this land lay in the village adjacent to the monastery itself, where the inhabitants probably attended the monastic church.

A single instance of a *decima nascentium* is to be reported for Parma in 1182, in this case, however, susceptible of interpretation as the ecclesiastical tithe. The cathedral chapter invests a tenant with land for his cottage, stipulating the payment of a money rent, fixed dues in kind, and

The practice of writing the ecclesiastical tithe into agrarian contracts which assumed such magnitude in Mantua, existed everywhere, although in varying degrees, in upper Italy. An enumeration of such contracts, bishopric by bishopric, would be monotonously repetitive. We shall cite only a few more examples to support those already given.

In a Paduan document of 1182 a lease of land owned collectively by the parochial clergy of the city contains the clause that the tenants shall pay an annual rent (*affictum*) of a third of the produce together with the totality of the tithe (*cum integritate decime*).[25] A contemporaneous statute of Padua no doubt refers to this custom when, in fixing the rate of the tithe, it states that the customs governing the *terraticum* shall not be affected.[26] The statutes of Vicenza in 1264 distinguish clearly between tithing the land and taking the landlord's share of the crops.[27]

In the Emilian bishopric of Imola the tithe was likewise coupled with the *terraticum* in leases, the fraction of the latter being carefully defined for each product.[28] In Gubbio a lease given by the archpriest of a baptismal church, after enumerating the rents and services owed by the tenant, added that the tithe of the land should be paid to the church.[29]

---

decimam omnium que ibi nascentur. From the rest of the land the tenant must pay a third of all his produce and a tithe and in addition must plant vines from which a third and a tithe of the wine will be due. *Carte di Parma*, App., doc. 44. Cf. *ACN*, doc. 394, clearly the spiritual tithe.

[25] Gloria, *CDP*, iii, doc. 1434.

[26] ". . . salvo eo quod propter hoc statutum ius terratici non aufferatur, vel qui consueverunt habere terraticum." *Statuti di Padova*, p. 216.

[27] One statute forbids the division or tithing of the crops in the absence of the landlord or his steward: "Et quod absente domino, vel eius nuncio, vel non requisito, non deciment vel parciantur. . . ." The same provision holds for the tenant of land "de qua reddat partem, scilicet medium, tercium, vel quartum." *Statuti di Vicenza, 1264*, pp. 135–136.

[28] ". . . ita ut omni anno inferatis nobis terraticum de labore maiore septimo, de minuto octavo, de lino et caneva nona de vino anforam quartam, si vineam ibi pretineveritis, et decimationem fideliter." *Chartularium Imolense*, doc. 752.   [29] *Carte di Gubbio*, doc. 461.

Documents in the cartulary of the abbey of Bobbio distinguish between *fictum, reditus,* and *decima*.[30] Four brothers, in donating land to the abbey, except the tithe which they hold as a fief and cannot alienate.[31] An investiture of land states that the rent shall be paid to the abbey's agent, the tithe to its owner, who is unnamed.[32]

Twelfth-century documents from Parma show that there existed in this bishopric a tenure in villeinage under which the cultivator usually paid his landlord a third from some of the products of his holding and a fourth from others. In some contracts a *decima* is joined with the third or fourth or with both, usually in such a way as to prove that the *decima* does not rest upon a different group of products but to the contrary is an additional charge upon the same products which pay the third or fourth. Thus some tenants have to pay a third or a fourth and a *decima* of their grain and a third and a *decima* from their fruit trees, while others give a third of all their products and a *decima* (*tercium omnium usufructuum et decimam*).[33]

These contracts from the archives of Parma and hundreds like them from other regions state very explicitly the precise fractions of the various products to be paid by the tenants. Docu-

---

[30] Investitures of land in return for *fictum* and *decima* combined. *Cod. dip. di Bobbio,* ii, docs. 200, 210, 239, 247, 255, 305. Investiture in return for *fictum* and *decima* and *tertiam partem unius panerii uvarum. Ibid.,* doc. 293. A list of tenants with their obligations shows that some owed *redditum et decimam* or *medietatem et decimam,* one owed *medietatem redditi et decimam totam. Ibid.,* ii, doc. 271 (p. 277).

[31] ". . . preter decimam ipsius alodii, quam per feudum tenemus et quam dare non possumus." *Ibid.,* ii, doc. 153 (p. 25).

[32] *Ibid.,* ii, doc. 253.

[33] *Carte di Parma,* doc. 841 (*tercium et decimam blavis et tercium et decimam arborum*) and App., doc. 44. Cf. doc. 379.

The word "villeinage" used in the text, while not entirely satisfactory, is the closest English equivalent to the Latin phrases *ad villanaticum, ad manentaticum,* etc., which seem to describe a transitional tenure between early medieval serfdom and the later *métayage.* Cf. docs. 469, 562. A similar tenure and similar agrarian customs existed in Cremona, Piacenza, and Fidenza. *Ibid.,* 349, 673, 693, 695.

ments of the high Middle Ages provide no justification for the opinion, cited earlier in this chapter, that the word *decima* in medieval contracts, while designating primarily a tenth, was sometimes applied to rents consisting of other fractions of the produce. It is of course true that the ecclesiastical tithe could be levied at a rate other than a tenth or even commuted into a money rent or fixed payments in kind without losing its identity as the tithe. But in the precise context of a medieval agrarian contract (and actually this is true of modern contracts also) the *decima* could not be a generic term for all proportional rents in kind. It obviously indicated either the ecclesiastical tithe or a rent literally of a tenth. Most of the evidence seems to favor the first hypothesis.

It may be alleged that when the terms *quartum, tertium,* and *decima* appear together in an agrarian contract, the notary and his clients made no distinction between the legal nature of these dues. This opinion is not tenable. The documents cited in the previous paragraphs prove that distinctions did exist in people's minds and that tenants knew whether they were paying rents or tithes. There was indeed a good reason why they should. Canon law, as set forth by the Fourth Lateran Council in 1215, prescribed that tenants should pay tithe on the entire product of their holdings before giving the landlord his rents in kind. The customary law of northern Italy, reaffirmed in communal statutes, insisted quite as emphatically that the landlord's share of the harvest should be paid first and that the tenant should pay his tithe only on what remained.[34] Consequently the landlord first received his fourth, or third, or fifth, as the case might

[34] The canonical point of view was expressed by Innocent III, *Decretales Gregorii IX,* III, xxx, "De decimis," 13, 26. Just as imperative on the other side was the *Liber Consuetudinum Mediolani,* c. 25. The same struggle was enacted in France. Witness the decree of a French council: "We strictly command that tithes and first-fruits shall be paid in full to the parish churches . . . and they shall be paid immediately when the crops are gathered and before the rents (*census vel tributa seu tasquae*), that is the fifth or the fourth, are separated from them." Martène and Durand, iv, 737.

be; then the tenant paid his tithe to the church, to a lay tithe owner, or to both when the tithe was owned in severalty. Landlords and tenants had to keep these distinctions in mind, and there is considerable evidence that they did so. Numerous communal statutes safeguard the landlord's right by providing that he or his steward must be present when the crops are gathered; and some of these statutes distinguish very clearly between the landlord's share (*terraticum* or *pars*) and the *decima*, or tithe. Particularly interesting in respect to this distinction is a statute of 1295 from the small commune of Bassano stating that if the cultivator has to gather his crops in the absence of landowner or tithe owner, his oath shall suffice as to the amount of the tithe; but the landlord's portion must be gathered and set aside in the presence of a witness of good repute.[35]

Sometimes, of course, landowner and tithe owner might be the same person; but when they were distinct (even though the word *dominus* or owner was applied indiscriminately to both in the documents), there was no confusion. A lawsuit of 1197 between the bishop of Gubbio (in Umbria) and the cathedral chapter over the tithes of a manor distinguishes clearly between ownership of the manor (*proprietas*), which was vested in the bishop,

---

[35] *Statuti del comune di Bassano dell'anno 1259 e dell'anno 1295* (ed. Gina Fasoli, Venice, 1940), pp. 275–276: "Item quod quilibet cui debetur decima vel pars alicuius vinee vel terreni, sive sit sacerdos sive laicus, non accipiet ipsam decimam vel partem nisi prius per unam diem ante quam denunciet laboratori diem in quo vult eam recipere." Similarly, if the cultivator wishes to gather his crops or tithes, he must notify their owners. "Et facta denunciacione laborator possit fruges colligere et de decima credatur suo sacramento, partem vero domini colligere et servare in presencia unius testis bone opinionis." Cf. the statute of 1259 requiring the tithe owner who wishes to gather his tithes to notify both the landowner (*illi cuius fuerit terra vel vinea*) and the cultivator (*qui ipsam laboraverit*). *Ibid.*, p. 68. The statutes of Bassano are particularly full with regard to the tithe, three-fourths of which had been infeudated to local nobles by the bishop of Vicenza. The revolt of this commune against the infeudated tithes and its subsequent acquisition of them by purchase are described by Gina Fasoli, "Un comune veneto nel duecento: Bassano," *AV*, Fifth Series, xv (1934), 23–24.

and ownership of the tithes of the estate, which was shared by the bishop and his vassals, the local church, and the cathedral chapter.[36] Most conclusive in this connection is a richly documented Veronese lawsuit of 1219 from the unpublished archives of San Giorgio in Braida. In the village of Trebenciolo, the church of San Giorgio leased lands to tenants in return for rents consisting of a third of the wine and a fourth or fifth of the rest of the produce. The tithes of the village were shared by a layman named Faccioli and the local church in the customary proportions, the church collecting the *quartese* and the layman the remaining three-fourths. According to Italian custom, the tenants gave their fourths or fifths to San Giorgio, then from what was left of the produce paid their tithes to Faccioli and the parish priest. The lawsuit was provoked by Faccioli's attempt to collect the tithes on the fourths or fifths due to San Giorgio, that is, to tithe the total product of the land and not merely the part which remained after the rent was paid. In this instance the ownership of the land was vested in a church while the greater part of the tithe belonged to a layman. As confusing as this situation seems at first glance, the testimony of the witnesses in the case proves that these Veronese rustics distinguished clearly between their tithes and their rents.[37] In reading their testimony, one is struck by the contrast between the directness and simplicity of their thinking and the confusion which some modern students of the tithe have introduced into the subject.

Some years ago a study of agrarian contracts in the cartularies of Piedmont led the writer to the conclusion that the word

[36] *Chartularium Imolense,* doc. 452 (p. 577). Cf. docs. 451, 453.

[37] ACNV, San Giorgio in Braida, especially nos. 6864–6873. "Ego scio quod ego do illis dominis de sancto Georgio cintas et quartas de illis terris quas ego laboro in palude pro illis de sancto Georgio et postea do de mea parte decimam domino Fazolo que mihi remanet, datis cintis et quartis illis de sancto Georgio . . . (No. 6864). ". . . et datis cintis et quartis et tercio illis de ecclesia sancti Georgii, postea dabam de mea parte que mihi remanebat decimam domino Fagolo et presbiteris Trevezole et non dedi umquam decimam domino Fagolo de cintis neque de quartis neque de tercio de racione illorum de sancto Georgio . . . (No. 6866).

decima in such documents of the twelfth and thirteenth centuries refers to the ecclesiastical tithe, which received the additional guarantee of being written into a lease. This conclusion, reached independently and later reinforced by an analysis of documents from areas other than Piedmont, was in accord with views expressed earlier by Gaudenzi for Bologna and Scaduto for the Sicilian bishopric of Catania. Gaudenzi pointed out that, when the bishop of Bologna leased land in his seigniory of Cento, the tenant had to pay both a rent and the tithe, which was declared to be an ancient custom.[38] Scaduto showed that for Catania there were numerous leases of land in return for a money rent and the *decima solita;* when, however, the bishops of Catania ceded lands outside their diocese, the contract did not mention the tithe, an omission which indicates that the bishop collected the tithe in his ecclesiastical capacity and not as a landlord.[39]

It is interesting to speculate upon the reasons which led tithe owners to include their tithes whenever possible in their leases. The abuses which had grown up around the tithe, its minute subdivision in many cases among several owners, created ambiguities concerning it and lay at the root of the multitudinous lawsuits over it which fill the cartularies of medieval churches. The inclusion of the tithe in a lease gave definiteness and certainty to the tithe owner's right in the impost. Moreover, in Italy a special factor was operating to make tithe owners seek this guarantee. Some communes in the thirteenth century removed the civil sanction entirely from the tithe; the communal governments in these cases refused to enforce the tithe, which they declared to be binding upon the conscience but not in secular law. Other communes refused to enforce rights in the tithe except when thirty or forty years' possession could be proved by the claimant. Under these circumstances ecclesiastical tithe owners who were at the same time proprietors of the

[38] "Sulle enfiteusi e sulle decime vescovili," p. 247.
[39] "Decime regie, specie siciliane," pp. 559–561.

lands from which they claimed the tithe found it to their advantage to include the tithe in the leases they gave their tenants.
Writing the tithe into a contract which could be enforced in
secular law was in many cases their only way of securing themselves in possession of their tithes. The Fourth Lateran Council,
held in 1215, was fully aware of these practices. In harmony
with Innocent III's policy of protecting the rights of parish
churches in the tithe, the Council decreed:

Several members of the regular and secular clergy, so we have
learned, in letting out houses or conceding fiefs, put into their contracts the additional clause, detrimental to the parish churches, that
the renters and feudatories shall pay tithes to them and elect to be
buried in their churches. Since this practice is rooted in greed, we
invalidate such agreements, ordaining that any tithes gathered as a
result of them shall be restored to the parish churches to which they
belong.[40]

This decree reminds us that some of the bishops, cathedral chapters, and monasteries who issued the contracts studied in this
chapter also had churches to which they sought to deflect parochial tithes; and this may have prompted them in some cases to
include the tithe in their leases to tenants.

From the point of view of the problem to which we have
addressed ourselves in this book, it should be observed that the
writing of the ecclesiastical tithe into a lease gave it the character
of a patrimonial due resting upon the land; or, in other words, it
transformed the tithe into a rent. This deterioration from the
original nature of the tithe also occurred in France, where it has
been described with typical French clarity by Paul Viard. "From
a charge upon the land, the tithe became very quickly the price
for the concession of the land; it was a second *champart*. This
transformation is already visible in some documents of the
twelfth and thirteenth centuries." [41] Sometimes in thirteenth-

---

[40] Mansi, xxii, 1043 (c. 56).

[41] "L'évolution de la dîme ecclésiastique en France aux xive et xv^e
siècles," *ZSSR*, xxxiv (1913), *Kan. Abt.*, iii, 128. Viard tells us that the re-

century France the tithe even replaced the *champart*, or *terrage*, the French equivalent of the fourths, fifths, or thirds of the produce which have been noted for Italy. In France as in Italy lands were conceded in return for a money rent, the tithe, and the *terrage*. Bishops and abbots in France as in Italy regarded the tithe not as an ecclesiastical tax but as a seigniorial due.[42] As late as the sixteenth century ecclesiastical tithe owners were still including the tithe in their concessions of land or demanding it by virtue of their temporal lordship. Lay and ecclesiastical tithe owners alike believed firmly that the relations between tithe payers and tithe owners were identical with those between landlords and tenants.[43] And Viard concludes his narrative by pointing out that the tithe was abolished in France, not as a result of the confiscation of ecclesiastical property by the National Assembly, but as a part of the remnants of the feudal and manorial regimes which were swept away by the legislation that followed the night of August 4, 1789.[44]

---

gional custom of Normandy was that the *terrages* (corresponding to the *terraticum* of Italian documents) should be paid before the ecclesiastical tithe. *Histoire de la dîme ecclésiastique dans le royaume de France*, p. 13. This was precisely the custom established throughout northern Italy.

[42] *Ibid.*, pp. 176–177, 194–195.

[43] *Histoire de la dîme ecclésiastique en France au xvie siècle* (Paris, 1914), pp. 27–28, 138–139. This, of course, was not the view officially held by the Church. Canon law always maintained that the nature of the tithe could not be changed and that it remained the ecclesiastical or spiritual tithe, whether written into a lease, superseded by a contract between priest and people, or infeudated to a layman.

[44] A study of the abolition of tithes in France has been made by Henri Marion, *La dîme ecclésiastique en France au xviiie siècle et sa suppression* (Bordeaux, 1912). The Revolutionary legislation of 1789 distinguished between ecclesiastical tithes, collected by the churches, and infeudated tithes, held by laymen as fiefs, decreeing the suppression of the first class of tithes but making the second class subject to commutation. Later laws, passed between 1790 and 1793, swept away all classes of tithes without distinction.

CHAPTER XIII

Sicily and the South

† OMITTED from this account of the ecclesiastical tithe, save for a few incidental references, has been the realm over which the sacramentalists and dominicalists fought their most bitter duel—Sicily. Some of the reasons for omitting Sicily and the South were stated in the Preface. Others may be added here. The Lombard conquest in the early Middle Ages bisected the Italian peninsula into two halves, whose history and institutions thenceforth diverged. This difference was accentuated by the Frankish conquest, which did not extend to the South. Consequently, after the eighth century North and South followed two distinct legal systems; the North, except for Emilia and an intermediate zone along the Po, adhered to the Lombard law; the South, except for its Lombard enclaves, continued to follow Roman law.[1] Ecclesiastical institutions in the North were affected by the reforming movement launched in the Frankish dominions; in the South they evolved independently of Frankish

---

[1] P. S. Leicht, *Diritto privato pre-irneriano* (Bologna, 1933), distinguishes three zones of law in Italy prior to the twelfth century: the Lombardo-Tuscan territory, which followed Lombard law; the Romano-Ravennate region, an area of Roman law; and the South, which also adhered to Roman law. In the twelfth century the legal unification of Italy was accomplished by the triumph of Roman law in all parts of the peninsula.

legislation. Then, in the eleventh century, the Normans added their customs and traditions to the already complex amalgam of Lombard, Byzantine, and Arab influences in the South. An adequate study of the tithe in this region would properly form a separate task in itself.

The ecclesiastical tithe in Italy, whatever its more remote origins, was definitely established as a compulsory tax by the Frankish sovereigns of the Carolingian dynasty in the provinces known to them as Longobardia and Tuscia,[2] where it became part of the Lombard law in the later sense of the word.[3] Soon it penetrated also to Emilia, a sphere of Roman law, and to Venetia.[4] The history of the tithe in Italy to the close of the eleventh century is necessarily the history of its evolution in those regions, to which this book has been restricted. But since a full understanding of the tithe in medieval Italy requires at least a mention of its introduction into Sicily and the South, the present chapter is appended to the history of the institution in the North and Center.[5]

[2] In Carolingian times northern Italy formed one large province, Longobardia, or Italia, which did not include Tuscany (Tuscia). The later *regnum italicum* as an administrative division was equivalent to the old Longobardia and likewise did not include Tuscany, although both the *regnum* and Tuscany followed the Lombard law. Solmi, *L'amministrazione finanziaria del regno italico nell'alto medio evo*, pp. 172–173.

[3] The Lombard law originally consisted of the edicts of the Lombard kings. The Frankish conquerors of Italy took over the Lombard law, adding their own capitularies to the royal edicts. Edicts and capitularies together constituted Lombard law in the later sense.

[4] The reaction against the tithe in the Emilian communes may have been partly due to the fact that the civil enforcement of the tithe rested upon the Lombard law, which was not accepted in Emilia.

[5] Abundant material for the agrarian history of southern Italy exists in the published cartularies of that region, notably the *Codice diplomatico barese*, *Codex Diplomaticus Cavensis*, and *Codice diplomatico amalfitano*, as well as in numerous articles and documents in historical periodicals. An excellent beginning for the history of the private church and related subjects in this region has been made by H. E. Feine, "Studien," ii, "Die Eigenkirchenwesen in Unteritalien, inbesondere Kirchgründung und Kirchfreiung nach südlangobardischem Recht," ZSSR, lxii (1942), *Kan. Abt.*, xxxii, 1–105.

So far as the author is aware, practically nothing is known of the ecclesiastical tithe in the South before the coming of the Normans. If the institution existed, it must have been on the same basis as in the Lombard period in the North, that is, it was given without compulsion in obedience to the Biblical precepts. Greek influence in the South would in itself have tended to discourage the imposition of a compulsory tithe, which was not a Byzantine institution. A little indirect evidence concerning the status of the tithe in the South comes from a canonical collection of the early tenth century in the Beneventan script. Of this collection Fournier significantly remarks: "On the tithe, which the Carolingian dynasty had generalized in the West, it omits the classical texts of the capitularies and the councils in order to give only a few fragments from the Irish collections." [6] It appears, therefore, that at a time when the tithe was well established in northern Italy, it still had no effective legal basis in the South. At the close of the eleventh century, however, the Norman dynasty, in the person of Count Roger I, introduced the compulsory tithe into its newly conquered dominions.

Any interpretation of Roger's policy in regard to the tithe hinges to some extent upon the authenticity of a group of documents purporting to be the foundation charters granted by Roger to the Sicilian bishoprics. These charters, each of which contains a delimitation of diocesan boundaries and a concession of tithes, were published by Pirro in his *Sicilia Sacra* and ever since his time have occasioned much controversy. Some historians of the late nineteenth century impugned their authenticity on the grounds that the originals of the charters had been lost and that Pirro had used late copies.[7] Others, while accepting the

[6] "Un groupe de recueils canoniques italiens des xe et xie siècles," *MAIB*, xl (1917), 67.

[7] R. Starabba, "Contribuito allo studio della diplomatica siciliana dei tempi Normanni. Diplomi di fondazione delle chiese episcopali di Sicilia," *ASS*, New Series, xviii (1893), 30–135, denied the authenticity of the diplomas but maintained that the tithes to which they referred were sacramental.

substance of the charters as genuine, invented various explana-
tions of the tithes ceded by the Norman conqueror, suggesting
every possible origin from a Roman derivation to the transformation of the tribute paid by the Sicilian Christians to the
Arabs. Still others claimed that the tithes were ecclesiastical
tithes infeudated by the papacy to the conquerors of the island.[8]
Probably the most intelligent comment on the charters was
that made by Erich Caspar in his monograph on Roger II.[9]
Caspar maintained that purely textual criticism of the documents
should be supplemented by a study of their historical background, pointing out that the substance of the charters harmo-
nizes with the undoubtedly genuine papal bulls confirming the
foundation of the Sicilian bishoprics and with the narrative in
contemporary chronicles; moreover, in their dating and sequence
they accord with the ecclesiastical policy of Count Roger and
with the order of events in the conquest of the island and the
consolidation of the new realm; they should not be rejected
merely because they have survived in late copies. The same type
of historical criticism might very profitably be applied to the
phrases in the charters referring to the tithes; and on this point
it may be observed in advance that a reading of these documents
in the light of a previous study of the tithe leaves no doubt in
the mind that the documents refer to the ecclesiastical tithe. It
is significant, moreover, that the dominicalist historian, Salvioli,
conceded that the tithes of Girgenti were probably sacramental.[10]

Count Roger came from a French province where the tithe
had been established for centuries and formed part of the local
customary law. To the tithe was applied in Normandy the tripartition enjoined by the French and Spanish councils of the
sixth century and practiced by the Normans in respect to mov-

[8] Scaduto, "Decime regie, specie siciliane," pp. 555 ff., gives an account
of some of these theories.

[9] *Roger II (1101–1154) und die Gründung der normannischen-
sicilianischen Monarchie* (Innsbruck, 1904), pp. 583–631.

[10] *Le decime di Sicilia, specialmente di Girgenti* (Palermo, 1901).

able property as well.[11] By Roger's time both tithes and churches alike in Normandy had been engulfed in the proprietary system against which the French reforming councils were inveighing. In the very years when Roger was organizing the Church in his new dominions, three Norman councils sanctioned the tripartite division of the tithe and set aside a third of the product for the parochial clergy, not to be invaded by the laymen who by implication held the other two-thirds as fiefs from the bishops.[12]

Immediately after the capture of Palermo in 1072 the Count began his organization of the Sicilian Church. Palermo was made the seat of an archbishopric, while the bishoprics of Troina, Syracuse, Catania, Girgenti, and Mazzara were erected in rapid succession. From the point of view of Catholic Christianity, Sicily was then colonial territory, to be organized *de novo;* and the Sicilian Church was for some time a mission church in which it was possible to apply principles obscured in more settled regions by an overgrowth of customs. To each of the Sicilian bishoprics were assigned definite boundaries within which the bishops were to collect the tithes, a policy, be it noted, entirely consonant with the principle of episcopal jurisdiction over the tithe so much stressed by the Gregorian reformers. The right to collect the tithe, stated in general terms in the foundation charters and confirmed by the papacy, was further defined by Roger in 1097 in connection with a dispute between the bishops and the Norman barons to whom a large part of the conquered realm had been enfeoffed:

A lawsuit and dispute over the tithes arose between the Sicilian bishops and the barons. . . . Count Roger granted to the bishops his tithes, which at that time he was keeping in his own hands, with the understanding that the bishops were to use these tithes to provide suitably for the churches in the Count's cities and castles; and Count

---

[11] See Jean Yver, "La tripartizione dei beni mobili nell'antico diritto francese," *RSDI,* xii (1939), 38–56.

[12] See p. 116.

Roger also gave the bishops the tithes of his barons to hold and administer. The bishops at the same time conceded a third of the tithes to the chapels in the barons' castles, on the understanding that the priests of these chapels should hold the third part of the tithes from the bishops, should recognize their authority, come to their synods, and if they sinned, should be punished according to the episcopal customs and pay whatever was just to the bishops. If a baron wished to appoint as his chaplain a priest, known or unknown, from another place, this priest must first be presented to the bishop.[13]

Thus all the soil of Sicily was made subject to the tithe, the royal demesne as well as the baronial lands; the bishops were to be the recipients and administrators of the impost but were to assign a third of the tithes of the baronial estates to the chaplains of the baronial castles, who might be appointed by the barons but must acknowledge the bishops' spiritual jurisdiction.[14] This arrangement was confirmed by Roger II in 1142, when he commanded his barons to pay all their tithes to the bishops unless they had castles, in which case they might retain a third for the service of the local church.[15] Thus the Sicilian Church, modeled on that of eleventh-century Normandy, was organized under the proprietary system, subject to the safeguards and reservations which the Gregorian reformers were wresting from the lay aristocracy.

Soon after his organization of the Sicilian Church, Roger I ordained similar arrangements for his dominions in Calabria, commanding the bishops of that region so to divide the tithes from the baronial lands that two-thirds would benefit the cathedral while the remaining third would be reserved for the priests

---

[13] Pirro, *Sicilia Sacra,* i, 696. The charter of Girgenti appears on p. 695. In translating the document cited in my text I have corrected an error in Pirro's edition by substituting "tertiam" (third) for "etiam," which did not make sense. This change is justified in the light of some of Pirro's later documents which clearly say "tertiam."

[14] This was clearly an application of Norman church law, which required that a third of the tithes should go to the local priest.

[15] Pirro, i, 698.

of the castles.[16] These measures embody the same principles as
the Norman legislation of the same period, except that in Normandy the reforming councils strove to protect the parochial
third from lay encroachment; in Sicily and southern Italy, where
the churches were newly organized and the lay aristocracy less
strongly entrenched, it was the bishops who had to promise that
the local clergy should be guaranteed their third.

Since the papacy sanctioned the erection of the Sicilian
bishoprics, it seems likely that it approved these arrangements.
Moreover, the recognition of episcopal jurisdiction over the
tithes, subject to the reservation of a fourth for the parochial
clergy, was canonical in that period. That the Norman rulers of
the South practiced the tripartition instead of the quadripartition of the tithe did not destroy the principle of the reform and
was a concession to regional custom such as the papacy has
always sanctioned when it has been to the advantage of the local
churches.

A detailed account of the evolution of the tithe in southern
Italy is beyond the purpose of this book. But to understand the
tithe as a European institution it is important to note the in-
tensive development in the Norman kingdom of a special variety
of the ecclesiastical tithe, the tithe of the regalia, which also
existed in Germany but can best be illustrated by documents
from the Norman kingdom.[17]

Grants of tithes from the royal demesne and the baronial
fiefs by the Norman conquerors of the South did not exhaust the
royal generosity toward the Church. In Sicily and southern Italy
the Normans found a pre-existing system of public revenues,
including customs duties, harbor dues, tolls, and market and

[16] F. Ughelli, *Italia Sacra* (2nd ed., Venice, 1717–1722, 10 vols.), viii,
426–427.

[17] The documents cited in the following sections are taken from J. L. A.
Huillard-Bréholles, *Historia Diplomatica Friderici Secundi*, (Paris, 1852–
1861, 6 vols. in 12), and *Codice diplomatico salernitano del secolo xiii*,
i (1201–1281), ed. Carlo Carucci (Subiaco, 1931).

fishing taxes, which they adopted and expanded; and from these revenues they also granted tithes to the Church. This type of concession may properly be called the tithe of the regalia, for it was derived from state revenues, not from land, and was usually paid in money. It differed from the ordinary ecclesiastical tithe in incidence and mode of collection, usually being gathered by the royal officials and by them transmitted to the ecclesiastical authorities. Such grants were made by the Norman sovereigns throughout the twelfth century, reaching their climax under Empress Constance. As a result of this lavishness on the part of the Norman dynasty, the Church in the Norman kingdom by the opening of the thirteenth century was not only richly endowed with the usual tithes from agriculture and livestock on the royal demesne and from the baronial lands, it enjoyed in addition extensive revenues from taxes and monopolies. In some cases it exercised the monopoly itself. Thus in 1211 the archbishop of Palermo held the Jew-monopoly of that city, the Jews being serfs of his church and answerable only to its courts; he controlled two public monopolies, the dyeworks and the warehouse of Palermo with the financial prerogatives attached thereto; and he received the tithe from the royal fisheries, which by a special concession was no longer to be paid in money as previously, but was to be collected in kind by special officials appointed by the Church.[18] The archbishop of Messina received a tithe of all the harbor dues and customs duties of that city, while the bishop of Girgenti held the tithe of all royal revenues in the lands under his jurisdiction.[19] The bishoprics and monasteries on the mainland were similarly endowed. The archbishop of Salerno, already the recipient of the tithe from all the revenues of the royal demesne in Salerno, was further enriched by Constance with the tithe of the markets, dyeworks, and silk

[18] Huillard-Bréholles, i, pt. 1, 182–183, 187.

[19] ". . . decimas portus et omnium gabellarum civitatis Messane" (*ibid.*, p. 186); "Ecclesia Agrigentina semper consuevit percipere et habere decimas omnium regalium proventuum terrae Agrigentinae . . ." (*ibid.*, pp. 419–420, n. 3).

manufactories of Eboli as well as the tithe of livestock there.[20] Other bishoprics collected tithes from such royal revenues as the fees from lawsuits, the public baths, market taxes, and import and export duties. The abbey of La Cava also held various regalia, notably market rights and harbor dues, and towards the middle of the thirteenth century challenged the right of the archbishop of Salerno to collect the tithes of the market taxes in his city.[21]

In the early part of his reign Frederick II confirmed the concessions made by his predecessors. But when, after his crusade, he set up his celebrated system of state monopolies, he was careful to make no new grants and limited the rights of the churches to such tithes and regalia as they could prove to have been in their possession in the reign of King William II. An announcement of this policy was made in the Constitutions of Melfi (1231), under the heading "De decimis exhibendis," in which the Emperor, by confirming to the churches in his realm all tithes which they had held in the time of King William, by implication forbade new concessions.[22] At the same time he was

[20] ". . . decimas de omnibus redditibus demaniorum nostrorum civitatis nostre Salernitae . . . et decimas de redditibus platearum, plancarum, tincte et celendra terre nostre Eboli et de omni nutrimine animaliorum . . . totum Judeum ipsius civitatis Salerni . . . exceptis illis qui de terris que sub demanio nostro sunt venerint ad eandem . . . necnon et tinctam . . . que vulgo cabella dicitur cum celendra nostra et cum omnibus appenditiis, domo et aliis ad eamdem tinctam et celendram pertinentibus. . . ." *Ibid.*, ii, pt. 1, 112. The slaughterhouse of Salerno was also an archiepiscopal monopoly.

[21] ". . . decimam omnium reddituum portus, decimam etiam de judiciis, de balneis, de omnibus solidis et pecuniis que provenerint tam de christianis quam de hebreis, de plateatico et de omnibus introitus tam in auro quam in argento et omnibus legitimis reddibus. . . ." Frederick II to the bishop of Otranto, *ibid.*, i, pt. 2, 639–640. Cf. the grants to the archbishop of Cosenza, *ibid.*, ii, pt. 1, 388–392 and to the bishop of Ascoli, *ibid.*, ii, pt. 2, 701–702. The position of La Cava in respect to the regalia appears *ibid.*, ii, pt. 1, 121. For the dispute with the archbishop of Salerno, see *Codice diplomatico salernitano*, doc. 125. It is clear from these documents that the royal officials paid the tithes of the regalia directly to the Church.

[22] ". . . attendentes quod solutio decimarum, quarum debitum ex

creating new taxes and monopolies from which no tithes were given to the Church, a policy resented by the Emperor's critics as an innovation.[23] It may be assumed that the rights of the Church to the tithes of the regalia in Sicily and the South, while never formally withdrawn by Frederick II, were actually curtailed by the erection of state monopolies and new taxes which quietly drained away the income of the older system. Nevertheless, the extensive privileges of the Church could not be destroyed in one reign. The tithes of the regalia persisted far into the thirteenth century, some of them being confirmed by Charles of Anjou after the French conquest.[24]

In the seventeenth century, when the confusion between spiritual and temporal tithes was beginning to trouble the canonists, De Luca noted that temporal tithes were particularly common in the Kingdom of Naples. "The term 'tithes,'" he observed, "is ambiguous, for it is equally applicable to spiritual and temporal revenues. This is especially true in the Kingdom of Naples, where those dues customarily paid to the owners of land, and more frequently still to the barons, consist of a certain quota of the produce."[25] This comment raises the question of the dominical tithe in the South, where the term actually originated in the Bourbon legislation of the eighteenth century suppressing parochial tithes.

A backward glance at De Luca's own discussion of the tithes

---

utriusque tabulis Testamenti confirmatur . . . officialibus nostris . . . mandamus, ut decimas integre, prout regis Giullelmi tempore consobrini et predecessoris nostri, ab antecessoribus officialibus et baiulis exsolute fuerunt, locorum prelatis exsolvere absque omni difficultate procurent . . . Subjectis nostris etiam indicimus ut decimas, quas de feudis et bonis suis antecessores eorum predicti regis Giullelmi tempore prestituerunt, venerabilibus locis, quibus decime ipse debentur, cum integritate persolvant." Huillard-Bréholles, iv, pt. 1, 11–12.

[23] *Ibid.*, Introduction, pp. 419–420, and iv, pt. 1, 250. Frederick's policy is discussed by Ernst Kantorowicz, *Frederick II* (New York, 1931), pp. 282–283.

[24] *Codice diplomatico salernitano*, docs. 190, 225, 236.

[25] *Theatrum Veritatis et Iustitiae*, xiv, pt. 3, 41.

and at the contents of the Neapolitan legislation quickly reveals the fallacies underlying the thinking of the seventeenth- and eighteenth-century jurists. They were of the opinion that episcopal tithes must be *ipso facto* derived from property rights, since the tithe according to canon law was a parochial revenue.[26] They did not realize, of course, that the ecclesiastical tithe in the South from its very inception was assigned to the bishops.

More enlightening than any general remarks, however, is an examination of the cartularies of southern Italy. Since the ecclesiastical tithe was established relatively late in Sicily and the South, it was likely to conflict with established agrarian customs.

Agrarian tenures of the pre-Norman period have been studied by Lizier, who attempted a statistical analysis of his findings.[27] He reported that rents consisting of a fraction of the produce were very common in southern Italy, especially in the Neapolitan region, but that generally speaking the most common measure of the *terraticum,* as this kind of payment was usually called, was one-third, sometimes rising to one-half, sometimes falling to a fourth or fifth, only in one or two cases in the documents sinking to a tenth.[28] On consulting Lizier's documents, particularly those in the *Codex Diplomaticus Cavensis,* one does indeed find a few concessions of land in *parziaria* stipulating that the rent shall consist of one-tenth of some of the products of the holding. Such contracts may be accepted as examples of the dominical tithe, with the important reservation that they do not use the word *decima.* Thus one contract of 992 states that the abbey of La Cava shall receive from the grain raised by the tenant a *terraticum* consisting of one measure of grain out of every ten (*de decem modia unum*).[29] Another contract requires from the tenant a third of the wine produced on his holding but of the onions "*de decem combinas uno pro*

[26] See pp. 6, 7.

[27] Augusto Lizier, *L'economia rurale dell'età prenormanna nell'Italia meridionale* (Palermo, 1907).

[28] *Ibid.,* pp. 92–96.

[29] *Cod. Dip. Cavensis,* ii, doc. 448.

terraticum." [30] Such contracts, with their clear designation of the rent as *terraticum*, cannot possibly have caused any confusion with the ecclesiastical tithe when the latter made its appearance. However, the fraction of a tenth in such contracts was very rare.

If from pre-Norman times we pass into the Norman period, it is possible to uncover a few examples of what seems to be the dominical tithe. I cite two examples:

(1) A sale of land at Aquinum, near Naples, in the twelfth century, makes the following reservation:

Nor have we reserved anything thereof to us, to our heirs, or to any man, nor do we claim that anything is to be kept back, except that we should have the usufruct of the lands as long as we live. And we shall give to the said church to which the sale has been made a tithe of the fruits (*decimas de frugum*) which shall come from the lands every year.[31]

The meaning of this document is somewhat obscure; but it would seem that the owners of the land are surrendering their title to the monastery, at the same time promising to pay the nominal rent of one-tenth of the fruits of the land for the privilege of occupying it as usufructuaries.

(2) In 1196 the abbot of Santa Maria de Valle Giosafat made an agreement with some Calabrian colonists for the settlement of some of the abbey's lands in Paterno, Sicily. The contract, the essential parts of which are freely translated below, is believed to reflect Calabrian agrarian customs.

Be it known that I, Amatus, . . . together with all my convent have made this pact and agreement with the men who have gone from Calabria to Sicily to build a settlement on our land in the place called Mesep in Paterno. In the first place we have given them enough land in the aforesaid place to build dwellings for them. To each man we

[30] *Ibid.,* iv, doc. 542 (an. 1002).

[31] Herbert H. Coulson, "Twelfth-Century Land Transfers in the Saracen Quarter of Aquinum," *Speculum,* viii (1933), 488, n. 3. Another similar reservation is noted on the same page.

have given eight *psalmatae* of arable land, from which they are to give to our church *only a tenth of the fruits*. . . . We have granted them also three pieces of vineyard and land toward Paterno, whence they are to pay our church each year both *from the trees and the vines a tenth of the produce*. Of an olive grove also we have given them a portion in order that they may cultivate it and improve it, and *from the yield of this also they are to give a tenth to our church*. They shall render us transport service on one day of each week. . . .[32]

This document seems to record a clear case of the dominical tithe, in which a nominal rent of one-tenth is exacted in order to encourage and reward colonization and the cultivation of new land.

Simultaneously with contracts of this kind where the term *decima* seems to indicate a rent consisting of a tenth of the produce, we note the survival of the older and less ambiguous type of contract in which the rent in kind is designated as *terraticum;* i.e., a lease granted in Salerno in 1212, which requires the tenant to pay *pro terratico* a tenth of the produce of his holding (*de decem partibus unum*).[33]

These scattered examples gleaned from south Italian cartularies are by no means conclusive. Such rents of only a tenth of the produce were not common. However, the very existence of such contracts indicates that the South diverged considerably from the North in its agrarian customs, just as it deviated in respect to the ecclesiastical tithe. One suspects that the ecclesiastical tithe was more easily and more justifiably confused with ground rents in this region than in the North, where the cartularies are so barren of even the scattered and ambiguous examples of the dominical tithe yielded by a perusal of similar documents from the South.

[32] Raffaele Corso, "Consuetudini giuridici calabresi in un documento del xii secolo," *Archivio storico per la Calabria e la Lucania,* vi (1936), 203–204, n. 1.

[33] *Codice diplomatico salernitano,* doc. 7.

CHAPTER XIV

Conclusion:

The Nature of the Tithes

† THE IMPLICATIONS of the present study for the problem of the tithes in modern Italy may be briefly summarized as follows. Prolonged and careful research in medieval Italian documents has yielded very little evidence of the existence of dominical tithes in northern and central Italy in any historical sense of the word *decima*. On the other hand, it has resulted in very positive proof of the sacramental nature of the *quartese*. The writer's considered opinion is that the historical records refute conclusively any presumption in favor of the dominical nature of such tithes as survived into modern times.

In any subject as controversial as this, there is always danger that results achieved by scientific research may be seized upon and misinterpreted in a partisan spirit. Lest the conclusions reached by this study should have such a fate, it seems desirable to restate as clearly as possible the objectives of this investigation as well as the methodological limitations under which it was conducted.

In the first place, this was primarily an investigation of the development of the ecclesiastical tithe; any light thrown upon

agrarian tenures or other types of tithes was purely incidental to the main problem.

In the second place, the research has been carried on within definite chronological and geographical limits. Generally speaking, the end of the thirteenth century was taken as the terminal point of the investigation, although a few later documents have been cited. Similarly, the detailed documentation has been drawn from five major areas—Piedmont, Lombardy, Venetia, Tuscany, and Emilia—supplemented by a sampling of documents from Sicily and the South.

The conclusion in which this study terminates is neither more nor less than that in the period and in the areas covered by this investigation, namely in northern and central Italy in the early and high Middle Ages, the ecclesiastical tithe was the general rule, the dominical tithe the exception. Since southern Italy and Sicily have not been studied with the same thoroughness as the North and Center, any conclusion in regard to them would be premature. Such evidence as has been uncovered concerning the ecclesiastical tithe and agrarian tenures in those areas during the same period points substantially in the same direction as the results achieved for the North, although it is less conclusive.

It is not the intention of the writer to state dogmatically that dominical tithes did not exist in medieval Italy. Actually it has been hard to find indisputable examples of dominical tithes in northern Italy, an experience which has been shared by a number of reputable Italian historians who have professed themselves unable to find any dominical tithes in local documents.[1]

---

[1] G. P. Bognetti stated that he had found no trace of tithes other than the ecclesiastical in Lombard agrarian documents from the eleventh century on. An example of a "civil" (i.e., dominical) tithe cited by him for the early Middle Ages proves upon examination to be a donation of tithes by a Lombard noble in 745 (Porro-Lambertenghi, *CDL*, doc. 11), similar to those cited on pp. 34–35 of this book. "Le pievi delle Valli di Blenio. La presunta pieve di Faido," *Archivio storico della Svizzera italiana*, i (1926), 46–47.

Similar views were expressed by Gaudenzi for Bologna. Existing legislation, in his opinion, was incomprehensible except on the theory that

However, the historian would be most incautious who relied wholly upon the argument *ex silentio*. For one Italian bishopric, namely Mantua, there is some indication of the existence of dominical or secular tithes intermingled with the ecclesiastical tithes. How numerous such tithes were or how long they survived the triumph of a money economy we can only surmise. As long as a single document existed in which the word *decima* was susceptible of interpretation as a dominical tithe, no honest historian could deny that the dominical tithe existed, even if he suspected that most of the doubtful cases were actually ecclesiastical tithes assimilated to seigniorial revenues or to ordinary rents.

In southern Italy this possibility is especially admissible, and indeed it seems probable that dominical tithes did exist in this region during the high Middle Ages, partly as a survival of pre-Norman tenures, partly as a result of economic conditions conducive to lower rents. It would be accurate to sum up the results of this book by saying that such possible examples of the dominical tithe as appear before the close of the thirteenth century in documents of the northern half of the peninsula are exceedingly rare, isolated, and usually susceptible of interpretation as ecclesiastical tithes in the process of being written into agrarian contracts. In short, most of the northern examples are dubious. In the South, on the other hand, concessions of land for a tenth of the produce clearly existed in the pre-Norman period before the introduction of the ecclesiastical tithe, and later documents show the survival of this practice, although some ecclesiastical tithe owners, notably in Sicily, followed the practice current in the North in the same period of writing the tithe into their leases as an additional guarantee of payment. In any case, when any of the concessions, either the dubious ones from the North or the relatively certain ones from the South, are

Church and State in Italy were interested in maintaining a distinction between the two kinds of tithes which was historically untenable. "Il monastero di Nonantola," *BISI*, xxxvi (1916), 222–239. See also *Sulle decime di Cento dalle origini all'anno 1598* (Bologna, 1899).

restored to their contexts in the cartularies, they support the presumption in favor of the sacramental tithe, for they are exceptional rather than normal in relation to the total agrarian milieu from which they have been detached.

The writer would be the last to claim that all *decimae* mentioned in medieval Italian documents are either sacramental or dominical tithes. Secular impositions of various kinds called *decimae* occur sporadically. Forest tithes, tithes of pigs, and similar exactions were characteristic of primitive Germanic law and appeared wherever Germanic influence was strong. Tolls called *decimae* were certainly collected along the northern frontier of Italy in the early Middle Ages; the contents of some royal diplomas of the tenth century suggest that some internal tolls may have borne the same name.[2] Clerical income taxes called tenths or tithes and the tenths imposed by the Florentine and Venetian governments have already been discussed.[3] There is little likelihood of confusing them with the ecclesiastical tithe.

At this point an imperative question arises. Granting that the dominical tithe was rare or nonexistent, according to the region, in the centuries between the introduction of the compulsory ecclesiastical tithe and the end of the thirteenth century, should we not consider the possibility that such a tenure became more widespread in the later Middle Ages and the early modern period? Since the writer's research has dealt with the earlier period, it is not possible to answer this question entirely at first hand. It is possible, however, to point to certain facts which affected the situation.

Italian agrarian history of the fourteenth and fifteenth cen-

[2] See, for example, the concession by Berengar I to a favored monastery: ". . . de theloneis vero mercatorum et pontum et decimas ad portam monasterii dari iubemus." *I diplomi di Berengario I*, ed. Luigi Schiaparelli (Rome, 1903), doc. 124. Ambiguous also is the phrase *omnia decima, frea et iudiciaria* or *omnia frea et iudiciaria vel decimas* which occurs in several diplomas of the same period. *I diplomi di Ugo e di Lotario*, ed. Schiaparelli (Rome, 1924), doc. 145; *I diplomi di Guido e di Lamberto*, ed. Schiaparelli (Rome, 19–6), doc. 18.

[3] Pp. 2, 3.

turies has not been studied with sufficient thoroughness to make generalization possible. However, some good work of a regional character has been done by Italian historians, and its results have been summarized by two acknowledged masters of Italian economic history, Alfred Doren and P. S. Leicht. Doren points out two coexisting tendencies in Italian agriculture of the later Middle Ages: In regions where the trading and industrial cities imposed their supremacy upon the surrounding countryside, the latter was given over to capitalistic agriculture by the urban bourgeoisie, and *métayage,* or equal division of the crops, became the dominant tenure; in the regions not affected by urban influences the feudal forms of landholding persisted with but little change.[4] If we consider the economic aspect of this problem, it is obvious that few capitalistic proprietors would be satisfied with a tenth as their share of the produce, except on land to be brought under cultivation or on products from which they could not expect a higher rent. As for the feudal landowners, any changes in tenures on their estates took the form of increased burdens for the peasantry. A rent of a tenth of the produce would be imposed only upon wasteland, marsh, or forest in order to get it reduced to tillage or pasturage, or upon newly constructed vineyards during the first years of the tenure; then, as the land became productive, the fraction of the produce would almost certainly be increased by the landowner. It is conceivable and even probable that some dominical tithes were created in this way; but it does not seem likely that this tenure could have become common under the economic conditions existing in the greater part of upper Italy.

Doren's general conclusions are accepted and amplified by P. S. Leicht, who has added an excellent summary of the changes which occurred in Italian agrarian tenures during the Renaissance.[5] During the fifteenth and sixteenth centuries many varieties of tenures existed in the northern half of the peninsula, none

---

[4] *Storia economica dell'Italia nel medio evo, pp.* 215–222.

[5] *Operai, artigiani, agricoltori in Italia dal secolo vi al xvi* (Milan, 1946), pp. 149–152, 178–182.

of them, however, conducive to the growth of the dominical tithe. In Tuscany, *métayage,* or equal division of the produce between landlord and tenant, continued to be common; in some regions further north, especially in the provinces of Padua and Verona, *métayage* in this period yielded to fixed rents. In the South conditions were so diverse as to forbid any scientific generalization. In some areas perpetual *enfiteusi* was practiced. Contracts of *parziaria,* whereby landlord and tenant shared the products of the land in varying proportions, were very common. Widespread also in the South was the contract known as *pastinato,* whereby new land was given to a tenant to be brought under cultivation, for a rent consisting of a fraction of the produce, the percentage gradually being increased as the land became productive. The poverty of the soil in some regions and the existence of large tracts of uncultivated land multiplied these contracts of *pastinato* and were certainly favorable to the concession of land for low and even nominal rents; in this respect conditions in some parts of the South were conducive to the development of dominical tithes. Any final solution to this problem, however, must wait upon further detailed research in local documents.

In considering the problem of the tithes, one does not have to rely upon the evidence of agrarian contracts alone. The continued existence of the ecclesiastical tithe in the forms which it had assumed by the close of the thirteenth century is certified by numerous documents from later periods, and in itself must have militated against the growth of the dominical tithe as an agrarian practice. Apart from the economic reasons against a rent in kind so small as to be almost nominal, the imposition of a dominical tithe upon land or produce already subject to the ecclesiastical tithe would have meant that two tithes rested upon the same land—an obvious contradiction in terms. Land burdened with the ecclesiastical tithe could not pay, in the literal sense, another tithe; the fraction had to be larger or smaller. In short, the existence of the ecclesiastical tithe was

in itself unfavorable to the extension of the dominical tithe.

On the other hand, it must be conceded that the ecclesiastical tithe had in many instances assumed the character of a patrimonial due resting upon the land, and this may well have eventually created confusion in the minds of landowners and renters as to its nature and origin. It must for a long time have been evident to the patient reader of this book that much of the modern difficulty in determining the nature of the tithes has been caused by a misconception of the character and history of the ecclesiastical tithe itself. At no time during the Middle Ages in Italy did the larger part of the tithe belong to the parish churches or have even a remote connection with the sacraments. From at least as early as the time of Gratian to the close of the Middle Ages, it was essentially and primarily a charge upon the land. In the course of the high Middle Ages part of the tithe was transformed from a charge upon the land to the price for the concession of the land. The writer hazards the conjecture that the confusion in regard to spiritual and temporal tithes which perplexed the canonists in De Luca's time probably originated in the later Middle Ages as a result of the gradual assimilation of many ecclesiastical tithes to obligations difficult to distinguish from rents, since they were actually written into agrarian contracts. It would seem likely, therefore, that some of the tithes which seemed to De Luca and his contemporaries to be most indisputably temporal in their nature, were spiritual, i.e., ecclesiastical tithes in their origin. That the *quartese,* as distinct from the integral tithe of which it originally formed a part, retained on the whole its ecclesiastical character, preserved its identity.

It would be both ungracious and misleading to refrain from mentioning the contributions of Italian scholars to this subject. While the controversy over the tithes was raging in the late nineteenth century, historians of the caliber of Pertile and Gloria never questioned the sacramental nature of the *quartese.*[6]

[6] Pertile, *Storia del diritto italiano* (2nd ed., 1893), iv, 445, wrote that the *quartesi* of the parishes, which had survived the *decima,* were de-

Among the contributions of those who studied the problem locally during the nineteenth century, one should especially recommend Todeschini's work on the tithes of Vicenza, Gaudenzi's documented studies of the tithes of Cento in Bologna, and Scaduto's work on the Sicilian tithes. Some reference should also be made in this connection to Carlo Bertagnolli, an early pioneer in the study of Italian agricultural history.[7] The later contributions of Ruffini, Jemolo, and Falco have already been noted. In 1936 and 1937, when Jemolo and Falco first published their opinions on the nature of the tithes, the preliminary work on this book had already been incorporated into a doctoral dissertation, which was completed in 1934.[8] The ensuing years of research and reflection have enriched the documentation of the present book, thrown light upon the legal aspects of the problem, and made the writer more aware of its ramifications; but they have effected little essential change in the point of view. The task of putting the details together and relating them to the total structure of Italian medieval institutions has been arduous. Many details have been omitted for lack of space, and some of the technicalities have been softened down in the interests

---

rived from the fourth which the bishop or cathedral chapter left to the parish priests in regions where they exceptionally gathered the tithes. In his *Statuti di Padova* (1873), p. 217, Gloria noted that the *quartese* belonged to the parish priests throughout the diocese. In *CDP*, i (1877), pp. lxiii–lxxv, he declared himself to be in favor of the abolition of all tithes, except the *quartese*, with compensation to the owners.

[7] Reference has already been made *passim* to the works of Todeschini, Gaudenzi, and Scaduto. Bertagnolli wrote two studies of Italian agriculture which have been superseded by later research but are historically interesting: *La colonia parzionaria* (Rome, 1877), a monograph on an agrarian tenure peculiarly relevant to the problem of the tithes, and *Delle vicende dell'agricoltura in Italia* (Florence, 1881). In a short pamphlet, *Politica agraria e politica ecclesiastica nella questione della decima* (Rome, 1887), he reports that his research in medieval agrarian contracts has not yielded a single example of the dominical tithe.

[8] Radcliffe College, Graduate School of Arts and Sciences, *Summaries of Theses Accepted in Partial Fulfilment of the Requirements for the Degree of Doctor of Philosophy, 1931–34* (Cambridge, Mass., 1935), pp. 138–141.

of a lucid presentation. It is hoped that this work will satisfy the need voiced by an Italian legal journal in 1935 for "a historical study which goes to the roots of the question." Whatever its shortcomings and possible errors of detail, this book ought at least to demonstrate that the study of medieval institutions may have a vital relevance to problems of the present. In a civilization as venerable as that of Italy, past and present form part of the continuous tissue which we call history, no portion of which can be torn away without mutilation of the whole.

Epilogue

† THE YEAR 1942, when the Italian Supreme Court rendered its last important decision in regard to the tithes, was taken as the terminal point of the narrative in Chapter I, partly in order to maintain historical perspective, partly because no important change in the status of tithes in Italy occurred between 1942 and the completion of the present book towards the end of 1950. Recent developments which may prove fertile in consequences should, however, be reported. In October and December of 1950, the Appellate Court of Venetia reversed its former stand on the question of the tithes, rejecting all the old presumptions and rendering decisions favorable to the sacramental nature of the tithes in dispute.[1]

At the moment this book goes to press, the ultimate fate of these two decisions and their practical effects remain to be seen. The Appellate Court has shown remarkable courage and freedom from prejudice in breaking away from norms consistently followed since 1895. The burden of proving the dominical nature of the tithes has definitely been thrown upon the tithe owners of Venetia. More tithe payers may be expected to revolt against the continued payment of a burden which has always impeded the progress of land reclamation in Venetia. But the

---

[1] Reported in *DE*, Jan.–March, 1951, pp. 110–140. One of these cases was later carried on appeal to the Rome Court of Cassation.

Court of Cassation has not yet spoken; the decisions of 1941 and 1942 in support of the old doctrine still stand. The immediate future will no doubt show whether or not this national Court will also register a new orientation.

It is of considerable interest to the historian to observe that both the Venetian decisions of 1950 show a refreshing awareness of historical factors in the development of the tithe and a careful study on the part of the Court of the medieval documents involved in the two cases. But it is also evident that the judges, while well versed in history, lacked some of the keys to the interpretation of those documents which could be furnished only by a historical account of the tithe in Italy. This legal revolution in Venetia therefore, greeted by a new generation of lawyers as the triumph of reason and justice over legal conservatism, makes even more imperative a fully documented study of the medieval origins and development of the ecclesiastical tithe and a more complete reconstruction of the rural folkways of medieval Italy with which the tithe was closely interwoven. In this respect as in many others Italy's road to freedom points back to the Middle Ages, the truly glorious period in her history when Italian jurists, businessmen, thinkers, and artisans laid so many of the foundations of modern Western civilization.

The Literature of
the Private Church

THE PRIVATE CHURCH as an institution was virtually discovered by Ulrich Stutz, who elaborated this fertile concept both in his seminar at Berlin and in a series of works, now classical, which have left an indelible impress upon European scholarship. Of his numerous books and articles on this subject, the following are the most important: *Die Eigenkirche als Element des mittelalterlich-germanischen Kirchenrechts* (Berlin, 1895), trans. by Geoffrey Barraclough, *Mediaeval Germany, 911–1215* (Oxford, 1938, 2 vols.), i, 35–70; *Geschichte des kirchlichen Benefizialwesens von seinen Anfängen bis auf des Zeit Alexanders III* (Berlin, 1895, one vol. published); art. "Pfarre, Pfarrer," in Hauck, *Realencyklopädie für protestantische Theologie und Kirche*, xv (1904), 239–252, and art. "Eigenkirche, Eigenkloster," *ibid.*, xxiii (1913), 364–377; "Das Eigenkirchenvermögen," *Festgabe zu Otto Gierke siebzigstem Geburtstag* (Weimar, 1911), 1187 ff.; "Gratian und die Eigenkirchen," ZSSR, xxxii (1911), *Kan. Abt.*, i, 1 ff.; art. "Kirchenrecht," in F. Holtzendorff, *Encyklopädie der Rechtswissenschaft* (7th ed., Leipzig, 1914), v; "Papst Alexander III gegen der

Freiung langobardischer Eigenkirchen," *Abhandlungen der preussische Akademie der Wissenschaften,* 1936, Hist.-phil. Klasse, no. 6; "Ausgewählte Kapitel aus der Geschichte der Eigenkirche und ihres Rechts," *ZSSR,* lvii, *Kan. Abt.,* xxvi (Weimar, 1937), 1–85.

Stutz's reconstruction of the history of the proprietary church and his appraisal of its influence on the ecclesiastical law of the Middle Ages are unlikely to be superseded or overthrown in essentials. But later scholarship has modified or amplified some of his conclusions, particularly those regarding the exclusively Germanic origin of the proprietary church, so that they are no longer tenable in the extreme form in which they were first stated. Among the critics of Stutz's theories should be mentioned Paul Fournier, "La propriété des églises dans les premiers siècles du moyen âge," *NRHDFE,* xxi (1897), 486–506, especially pp. 505–506; R. Génestal, "Les origines du droit ecclésiastique franc," *ibid.,* xxxviii (1914–1915), 524–551; Arnold Pöschl, *Bischofsgut und Mensa Episcopalis* (Bonn, 1908–1913, 3 vols.), i, pt. 2, *passim,* and iii, pt. 1, 105, n. 5. Paul Thomas, *Le droit de propriété des laiques sur les églises* (Paris, 1906) took an independent approach to the problem. Heinrich Böhmer studied its English aspects in "Das Eigenkirchenwesen in England," *Festgabe für Felix Liebermann* (Halle, 1921), 301–353. The history of the private church in Spain has been analyzed by M. Torres, *El origen del sistema de iglesias propias* (Madrid, 1929) and P. Ramon Bidagor, *La iglesia propia in Espana,* Analecta Gregoriana iv (Rome, 1933). Andrea Galante traced the origins of the private church in Italy in *La condizione giuridica delle cose sacre* (Turin, 1903), ch. 5. More recently the history of the proprietary church in Italy has been reviewed, with impressive wealth of documentation, by H. E. Feine, "Studien zum langobardisch-italischen Eigenkirchenrecht," *ZSSR,* lxi (1941), 1–95; lxii (1942), 1–105; lxiii (1943), 64–190 (*Kan. Abt.,* xxx–xxxii). Gerd Tellenbach, *Church, State, and Christian Society at the Time of the Investiture Contest* (trans. R. F. Bennett, Oxford, 1940), dis-

cusses the relations between the proprietary church and the Gregorian Reform.

Very little has been written on the subject of the *Eigenkirche* in English. Dom David Knowles, *The Monastic Order in England* (Cambridge, 1940), pp. 562–568, especially p. 562, n. 1, calls attention to its importance.

APPENDIX II

Tenth-Century Leases of Parish Churches in Lucca

A. *Leases of Parochial Property and Tithes by Parish Priests*

Church	Object of Concession	Rent [1]	Date	Document (*MD*, v, pt. 3)
Marlia	Various fractions of property and tithes	Varied	938	1261, 1262, 1266, 1267
San Genesio in Vico Vallari	All property of church	20 *sol.*	943	1300
Santa Cristina of Massa Pisana	All property of church	10 *sol.*	943	1304
Tranaldo	All the tithes	2 *sol.*, 12 *den.*	944	1308
San Cassiano in Barginne	All the property and the tithes of 35 villages	15 *sol.*	952	1350
Tripallo	All the property	2 *sol.*	954	1360
Massa di Burra	Half the landed property and all the tithes of 16 villages	2 *sol.*, 10 *den.*	979	1497

[1] The *solidus*, or shilling, contained twelve *denarii*, or pennies. It is impossible to give modern monetary equivalents.

Church	Object of Concession	Rent	Date	Document
Decimo	All the property and tithes	(Omitted)	979	1499
Arriana	All property	23 *sol.*	980	1503
San Ginese	All property and tithes	22 *sol.*	980	1506
Arliano	Half the property and tithes	1 *sol.*, 20 *den.*	980	1509
Casabasciana	(1) One *casa massaricia* [2] and one-twelfth of the tithe	1 *sol.*	985	1602
	(2) Same	21 *den.*		1603
	(3) All property and tithes not previously leased	20 *den.*		1604

B. *Leases of Parish Churches and Their Property by the Bishops of Lucca*

Date	Church	Object of Concession	Rent	Document [3]
970	Flesso	All lands and tithes of *pieve* and its chapels Tithes were drawn from 11 villages	15 *sol.*	1420
973	Massa Pisana	Two *cas. mass.;* tithes of oil, wine, and grain from 8 villages	20 *sol.*	1446
974	Fabbrica	All lands and tithes	22 *sol.*	1448
979	Cellari	Three-fourths of lands and tithes	8 *sol.*	1501
980	San Gervasio	Half of 6 *cas. mass;* half the tithes of 34 villages; half of the bishop's castle and demesne	15 *sol.*	iv, pt. 2, doc. 74
	Flesso	Half the property; half the tithes of 10 villages	7 *sol.*, 6 *den.*	1515
	Suvigliano	15 *cas. mass.;* tithes of 36 villages	30 *sol.*	1517

[2] A *casa massaricia* was the typical holding of a peasant family.

[3] Unless otherwise indicated, all the documents are taken from *MD*, v, pt. 3.

Date	Church	Object of Concession	Rent	Document
980	San Gennaro	3 *cas. mass.*; tithes of 19 villages	12 *sol.*	1518
983	Loppia	*Casa et curtis domnicata;* 10 *cas. mass.*; tithes of 28 villages	20 *sol.*	1538
	Marlia	Various fractions of lands and tithes	3 *sol.*	1541–44, 1547–48
	Pescia Maggiore	All lands and tithes	20 *sol.*	1555
	Vajano	All lands and tithes	15 *sol.*	1556
	Sesto	Tithes of 3 villages	5 *sol.*	1557
	Massa Pisana	Half the tithes of 6 villages; half of 2 *cas. mass.*	10 *sol.*	1558
	Massa di Burra	Two *cas. mass.*; all the tithes of 7 villages	20 *sol.*	1560
	Villora	All landed property; tithes of 12 villages	20 *sol.*	1561
	Flesso	Half of landed property; tithes of 7 villages	7 *sol.*	1563
	Atriana	Church, land, and tithes of 11 villages	7½ *sol.*	1564
	Marlia	One-fourth of lands	3 *sol.*	1565
	Quaratiana	Church, land, and tithes of 39 villages	20 *sol.*	1568
	Santa Maria a Monte	Some land and the tithes of 24 men	8 *sol.*	1571
	Granajolo	Three-fourths of 6 *cas. mass.*, of the tithes of 24 villages and of 2 chapels	30 *sol.*	1572
984	Camajore	Half of lands and tithes	67 *den.*	1582–83, 1586–87
	Marlia	One-fourth of landed property; tithes of 13 villages	4 *sol.*	1593
	Ilice	All tithes of 14 villages	4 *sol.*	1596
986	San Gervasio	Various lands	4 *sol.*	1606

Date	Church	Object of Concession	Rent	Document
988	Sesto	Four pieces of land; tithes of 9 villages	60 *den.*	1628
	Sesto	Tithes of 3 villages; oblations of 1 chapel	60 *den.*	1631
	Sugrominio	All tithes of 33 villages	15 *sol.*	1634
	Fabbrica	Church, all property and all tithes	Omitted	1635
	San Paolo in Gurgite	Church, all property, tithes of 10 villages	8 *sol.*	1636
	San Tommaso in Arriana	Church, all property, tithes of 33 villages	45 *sol.*	1639
989	Lammari	All property and tithes	8 *sol.*	1643
	Santa Reparata	All property and tithes	20 *sol.*	1644
	Camajore	One-fourth of lands and tithes	67 *den.*	1646
991	San Giusto di Padule	All property and tithes	6 *sol.*	1653
	Santa Maria di Pescia	Church, property, all tithes	20 *sol.*	1658
	Flesso	Church, all property and tithes	14 *sol.*	1662
	Massa Pisana	Half of the church; 2 *cas. mass.;* all the tithes	10 *sol.*	1664
	Granajolo	Three-fourths of church and property; tithes of 24 villages; 2 *cas. mass.;* 2 chapels	30 *sol.*	1665
	Marlia	Half of church	3 *sol.*	1667
	Cellari	Half of church, property, and tithes	4 *sol.*	1669
	San Genesio	All land, tithe of 27 villages	22 *sol.*	1672
	Atriana	Half of lands and tithes	4 *sol.*	1676

Date	Church	Object of Concession	Rent	Document
991	Massa di Burra	Half of landed property; tithes of 21 villages	5 *sol.*	1682
	Camajore	One-fourth of church, lands, and tithes	67 *den.*	1683
	Ducenta	Half of church, lands, and tithes of 8 villages	42 *den.*	1692
		Two grants of one-fourth of church, land, and tithes	42 *den.*	1693–94
994	Loppia	*Casa et curtis dominicata;* 10 *cas. mass.;* tithes	21 *den.*	1697
995	Barginne	Tithes of 2 villas; half the tithes of one village	28 *den.*	1699
	Rogiano	Tithes of 3 villages	5 *sol.*	1700
997	Gallicano	Half of church, lands, and tithes	30 *den.*	iv, pt. 2, App., 72
998	San Gervasio	Half the tithes paid by the men of one village; half the tithe from a *vinea dominicata*	6 *den.*	1734
	Arriana	Church, property, and tithes of 32 villages	30 *sol.*	1737

Parochial Tithes in
the Archbishopric of Genoa

OF THE twenty-eight known parishes of Genoa, twenty-one are included in the list compiled by order of Archbishop Siro ca. 1143. The contents of the survey may be summarized as follows:

1. San Martino "de Hirchis": Here the tithes were divided into four parts, of which one belonged to the baptistery, while the remaining three were divided equally among laymen. One fourth was held as a fief.

2. San Siro of Nervi: The tithes were likewise divided into four parts, one to the baptistery. Half of the other three-fourths belonged to the archbishopric, while the other half was apportioned between a layman and his relatives.

3. San Michele of Sori: The baptistery had a fourth of the tithe, a group of laymen held the rest.

4. SS. Gervasio and Protasio of Rapallo: Here the territory of the baptistery had itself been divided into four parts, each equal in value to a fourth of the tithe. Each of these territorial divisions was called a *quarterium* [*quartesium?*]. In one the tithes had been broken up into twelve parts, of which the arch-

bishop held two, while the baptistery of Rapallo shared one with the counts of Lavagna. The three remaining *quarteria* were apportioned among laymen.

5. Santo Stefano of Lavagna: The situation in this parish was hopelessly confused. The inventory simply gives a list of laymen who held tithes in the district. There is no mention of the usual fourth of the baptistery.

6. Santo Stefano of Sestri: The fourth of the baptistery has been omitted from the document. Three-fourths of the tithe belong to laymen.

7. San Giovanni Battista of Varese: The baptistery had the usual fourth; the counts of Lavagna held another fourth; and two groups of laymen held one fourth each.

8. Santa Croce of Moneglia: The baptistery had a fourth; the remainder was divided into three equal fourths, each in the hands of laymen.

9. *Pieve* of Plicano: The situation here was extremely confused. The tithes were held by a large number of people. The serfs of the local marquis had a fourth of the tithes of this parish, which they had purchased from the heir of a layman who had held them *pro libellaria.*

10. Santa Maria of Bargagli: The baptistery had the usual fourth, a group of laymen held another fourth, while the archbishop's curia had the rest.

11. San Siro of Molaciana: The baptistery and the curia shared a fourth of the tithe; the other three-fourths were in the possession of laymen.

12. *Pieve* of Bavari: The baptistery had a fourth, here called a *quarterium;* laymen had most of the remaining tithes. The curia held a few tithes which laymen had surrendered.

13. Sant'Ursicino: The baptistery had a fourth; the rest of the tithes were minutely subdivided, some belonging to the curia.

14. San Piero of Arena: The baptistery had the usual fourth. The remaining three-fourths were divided into four parts, two

of which belonged to the curia and had been infeudated by it to laymen, while the other two belonged to laymen.

15. Santo Stefano of Borzoli: The baptistery had the usual fourth. The remainder was divided into two parts, one of which belonged to the cathedral chapter. The curia held the tithes from one village.

16. Santa Maria of Rivarolo: Here we meet with an interesting distinction between the parish and the baptismal district. The baptistery had the entire tithe of its own parish (*parrochia*) in lieu of the fourth from the baptismal district (*plebeium*). The curia held half of the tithe of wine and pigs from the village of Begali.

17. San Cipriano of Polcevera: The baptistery had a fourth; laymen held the rest.

18. Sant'Olcese of Castiglione: The baptistery had a fourth. One-fourth of the remaining three-fourths belonged to the curia, the rest to laymen.

19. Santa Maria of Ceranese: The baptistery had a fourth; laymen held the rest.

20. Santo Stefano of Lagnasco: All tithes seem to be in the hands of laymen. The fourth of the baptistery is not mentioned.

21. San Giovanni Battista of Caragno: The baptistery had its fourth, and a group of laymen held another fourth. The remaining fourths were divided between the archbishop and the sons of the cleric Adaldo.

APPENDIX IV

Monasteries and Tithes

THE RELATIONS between the monasteries and the ecclesiastical tithe in Italy centered around two problems: the monastic exemption from payment of tithes and monastic ownership of churches endowed with tithes.

The papal curia in the twelfth century exempted regulars from the tithe on lands which they cultivated themselves.[1] Since most of the Benedictine abbeys let out their lands to serfs and free tenants, this exemption had very little significance for them. Cluny set the example of paying tithe to the legal tithe owners, whether priests or laymen. Peter the Venerable, in a letter to St. Bernard of Clairvaux, defended the right of monasteries to receive and to pay tithes by appealing to episcopal concessions; the bishop, he argued, has a right to bestow his share of the tithe upon any church and is not forbidden to give away the whole tithe.[2] In still another letter the Abbot stood forth as the champion of the existing order in regard to the tithe, pointing out that in olden days tithes were paid not only by laymen to the Church, but by one church to another, by one monastery

[1] The fullest treatment of the monastic exemption is that given by Georg Schreiber, *Kurie und Kloster im 12. Jahrhundert* (Stuttgart, 1910, 2 vols.).

[2] *M.P.L.*, vol. 189, cols. 140–141.

practice that a baptismal church impropriated to a monastery
should give the monastery half the tithes.[11] As the chapels gained
the right to share in the tithes, breaking the monopoly formerly
exercised by the baptisteries, monastic churches in this category
collected the tithes of their parishioners but paid half of these
tithes to the monasteries.[12] When the monastery was the builder
of the tithe-owning church, the monastic share of the tithes
might be higher.[13]

The possession of tithes by monasteries brought the monks
into numerous conflicts with parish churches. A fully documented conflict was the lawsuit between the parish church of
Revello and the nunnery of Rifreddo (diocese of Turin), which
by gift and purchase from the local nobility had acquired two-
thirds of the ancient and noval tithes of Revello.[14] Another case
was that of the Paduan nunnery of Santo Stefano, which held
two-thirds of the tithes of Este, both ancient and noval, by episcopal concession, to the detriment of the local baptistery.[15] Still
another instance was the conflict between the baptistery of Sant'-
Abbondio di Bonifacio and the monastery of Villanova, which
by the end of the twelfth century had acquired three-fourths
of the tithes of San Bonifacio and Villanova. Monastic control
of the tithe was challenged by the archpriest of the baptistery,
who was supported by his parishioners. The archpriest was at
first excommunicated by the bishop of Reggio, temporary administrator of the diocese of Verona, but finally forced the abbot
to concede him half of the monastic tithes.[16]

[11] Romani-Feliciangeli, doc. 20; *Chartularium Imolense*, doc. 371.

[12] Romani-Feliciangeli, doc. 5.

[13] Gloria, *CDP*, iii, doc. 33.

[14] Boyd, *A Cistercian Nunnery*, chs. 3 and 7.

[15] Gloria, *CDP*, ii, docs. 240, 422; iii, doc. 743.

[16] This information was taken from original documents in the Antichi
Archivi Veronesi, furnished through the courtesy of the late Professor
Gino Sandri.

Abbreviated Titles

Abbreviations have been used to designate well-known collections of sources and serial publications and a few secondary works to which several nonconsecutive references have been made. Otherwise full bibliographical information has been given in the notes for all works actually cited.

ACA— *Le carte dell'archivio capitolare di Asti (830–1237)*, ed. F. Gabotto and N. Gabbiano, *BSSS*, xxxvii (Pinerolo, 1907).

ACN— *Le carte dell'archivio capitolare di Santa Maria di Novara*, ed. F. Gabotto, A. Lizier, and others, *BSSS*, lxxviii–lxxx (Pinerolo, 1913, 1915, 1924).

ACNV— Archivio della Cancelleria della Nunziatura Veneta. Vatican Archives. These manuscripts include the archives of San Giorgio in Braida.

ACT— *Le carte dell'archivio capitolare di Tortona (sec. ix–1313)*, ed. F. Gabotto and others, *BSSS*, xxix–xxx (Pinerolo, 1905–1907).

AKK— *Archiv für katholischen Kirchenrecht.*

AMM— *Atti e memorie della Reale Deputazione di storia patria per le provincie delle Marche.*

AMR— *Atti e memorie della Reale Deputazione di storia patria per le provincie di Romagna.*

Antiche carte di Asti—*Le carte più antiche dell'archivio capitolare di Asti*, ed. F. Gabotto, *BSSS*, xxviii (Pinerolo, 1904).

ASI— *Archivio storico italiano.*

ASL— *Archivio storico lombardo.*

ASLSP—*Atti della società ligure di storia patria.*

ASPP— *Archivio storico per le provincie parmensi.*

ASS— *Archivio storico siciliano;* or *Archivio storico per la Sicilia.*

Atti del comune di Milano—Gli atti del comune di Milano fino all'anno MCCXVI, ed. Carlo Manaresi (Milan, 1919).

AV— *Archivio veneto.*

Barsocchini, *Dissertazioni*—Domenico Barsocchini, *Dissertazioni sopra la storia ecclesiastica di Lucca, MD,* v, pt. 1 (Lucca, 1844).

Berlan, *LCM*—F. Berlan, *Liber Consuetudinum Mediolani Anni 1216* (Milan, 1866).

BISI— *Bullettino dell'istituto storico italiano.*

BSP— *Bullettino storico pistoiese.*

BSSS— *Biblioteca della società storica subalpina.*

Campi— Pietro Maria Campi, *Dell'historia ecclesiastica di Piacenza* (Piacenza, 1651–1662, 3 vols.).

Cartario di Chiavenna—Cartario pagense di Chiavenna, ed. A. Ceruti, *PC,* xxi (1914), 7–42, 129–159, 230–246; xxii (1915), 37–60, 153–236; xxiii (1918), 37–72; xxiv (1921), 72–92, 123–130; xxv (1924), 48–54.

Cartario di Pinerolo—Cartario dell'abazia di Pinerolo fino all'anno 1300, ed. F. Gabotto, *BSSS,* ii (Pinerolo, 1899).

Carte di Gozzano—Le carte del capitolo di Gozzano, ed. Mario Bori, *BSSS,* lxxvii, pt. 3 (Pinerolo, 1916).

Carte di Gubbio—Carte e diplomi di Gubbio dall'anno 900 al 1200, ed. P. Cenci (Perugia, 1915).

Carte d'Ivrea—Le carte dell'archivio capitolare d'Ivrea fino al 1230 con una scelta delle più notevoli dal 1230 al 1313, ed. E. Durando, *BSSS,* ix (Pinerolo, 1902).

Carte d'Oulx—Le carte della prevostura d'Oulx fino al 1300, ed. Giovanni Collino, *BSSS,* xlv (Pinerolo, 1908).

Carte di Parma—Le carte degli archivi parmensi del secolo xii, vol. iii, ed. Giovanni Drei (Parma, 1950).

Carte di Tiglieto—Le carte inedite e sparse del monastero di Tiglieto, ed. F. Guasco, F. Gabotto, and A. Pesce, *BSSS,* lxix (Turin, 1912–1923), 215–426.

CCF— *Le carte della canonica della cattedrale di Firenze (723–1149),* ed. R. Piattoli (Rome, 1938). [*RCI,* xxiii.]

Cod. dip. barese—Codice diplomatico barese, ed. Fr. Nitti di Vito and others (Bari, 1897–1936, 13 vols.).

Cod. Dip. Cavensis—Codex Diplomaticus Cavensis, ed. M. Morcaldi, M. Schiavi, S. de Stephano, and others (Naples, 1873–1893, 8 vols.).

Cod. dip. della Rezia—*Codice diplomatico della Rezia,* ed. F. Fossati, *PC,* iii (1883), 9–80, 173–220, 279–298; iv (1884), 33–60, 267–300; v (1885), 388–404; vi (1888), 91–122.

Cod. dip. di Bobbio—*Codice diplomatico del monastero di San Columbano di Bobbio fino all'anno 1208,* ed. Carlo Cipolla and G. Buzzi (Rome, 1918, 3 vols.). [*FSI,* lii–liv.]

Cod. dip. veronese—*Codice diplomatico veronese. Dalla caduta dell'Impero romano alla fine del periodo carolingio,* ed. V. Fainelli (Verona, 1940). Deputazione di storia patria per le Venezie, Monumenti storici, New Series, i.

CR— *Cartario dell'abazia di Rifreddo fino all'anno 1300,* ed. Silvio Pivano, *BSSS,* xiii (Pinerolo, 1902).

CS— *Cartario dell'abazia di Staffarda fino all'anno 1300,* ed. F. Gabotto and others, *BSSS,* xi–xii (Pinerolo, 1901–02).

DE— *Il diritto ecclesiastico e rassegna di diritto matrimoniale.* Formerly published as *Rivista di diritto ecclesiastico* and as *Il diritto ecclesiastico italiano.*

Dillay, "Régime de l'église privée"—Madeleine Dillay, "Le régime de l'église privée du xie au xiiie siècle dans l'Anjou, le Maine, la Touraine. Les restitutions des églises par les laïques," *RHDFE,* Fourth Series, iv (1925), 253–294.

Feine, "Studien"—H. E. Feine, "Studien zum langobardisch-italischen Eigenkirchenrecht," *ZSSR,* lxi (1941), 1–95; lxii (1942), 1–105; lxiii (1943), 64–190. [Kanonistische Abteilung, xxx–xxxii.]

Fliche, *HE*—Augustin Fliche and Victor Martin, *Histoire de l'église* (Paris, 1934 ff.).

Frisi, *Memorie di Monza*—Antonio Francesco Frisi, *Memorie storiche di Monza e sua corte* (Milan, 1794, 3 vols.).

FSI— *Fonti per la storia d'Italia dell'istituto storico italiano.*

FV— *Il foro veneto* (continued as *Il foro delle Venezie*).

Gaudenzi, "Il monastero di Nonantola"—Augusto Gaudenzi, "Il monastero di Nonantola, il ducato di Persiceto e la chiesa di Bologna," *BISI,* i, xxii (1901), 77–214; xxxvi (1916), 7–312.

This study includes several important sections on the tithes of Bologna: "La controversia tra il vescovo di Bologna e il monastero di Nonantola per le decime e le falsificazioni che vi si collegano," *BISI,* xxii, 144–158; "Sulla più antica storia di Cento," *ibid.,* xxxvi, 222–239; "Sulle enfiteusi e sulle decime vescovili," *ibid.,* 239–254.

Genoa, *Registro*—I. *Il registro della curia arcivescovile di Genova*, ed. L. T. Belgrano, *ASLSP*, ii, pt. 2 (1862). II. *Il secondo registro della curia arcivescovile di Genova, ibid.*, xviii (1887).

Giulini, *Memorie di Milano*—Giorgio Giulini, *Memorie spettanti alla storia, al governo ed alla descrizione della città e della campagna di Milano ne' secoli bassi* (Milan, 1854–1857, 7 vols.). A modern edition of a work published in 1760–1774 in twelve volumes.

Gloria, *CDP*—Andrea Gloria, ed., *Codice diplomatico padovano* (Venice, 1877–1881, 3 vols.). Reale Deputazione di storia patria per le Venezie, Monumenti storici, First Series, i–iii.

Hefele-Leclercq, *Histoire des conciles*—C. J. von Hefele, *Histoire des conciles d'après les documents originaux*, trans. from the German by Henri Leclercq and others (Paris, 1907–1938, 10 vols.).

Imbart de la Tour, *Origines religieuses*—Pierre Imbart de la Tour, *Les origines religieuses de la France* (Paris, 1900).

Kehr, *IP*—Paul Kehr, *Italia Pontificia* (Berlin, 1906–1935, 8 vols.).

Lesne, *Propriété ecclésiastique*—Emile Lesne, *Histoire de la propriété ecclésiastique en France* (Lille and Paris, 1910–1939, 5 vols.).

LI— *Il "libro delle investiture" di Goffredo di Montanaro, vescovo di Torino (1264–1294)*, ed. F. Guasco di Bisio, *BSSS*, lxvii (Pinerolo, 1913).

Lupi, *CDB*—Mario Lupi, *Codex Diplomaticus Civitatis et Ecclesiae Bergomatis* (Bergamo, 1784–1799, 2 vols.).

Lupi, *De Parochiis*—Mario Lupi, *De Parochiis ante Annum Millesimum Dissertationes Tres* (Bergamo, 1788).

MAIB— *Mélanges de l'académie des inscriptions et de belles-lettres.*

Manaresi, *Regesto di Monte Velate*—Carlo Manaresi, ed., *Il regesto di Santa Maria di Monte Velate sino all'anno 1200* (Rome, 1937).

Mansi, *Concilia*—J. D. Mansi, ed., *Sacrorum Conciliorum Nova et Amplissima Collectio* (Florence and Venice, 1759–1798, 31 vols.).

Martène and Durand—E. Martène and U. Durand, *Thesaurus Novus Anecdotorum* (Paris, 1717, 5 vols.).

MD— *Memorie e documenti per servire alla storia di Lucca.* Reale Accademia di Scienze, Lettere ed Arti (Lucca, 1813–1914, 15 vols.). The title of this collection has been changed several times.

Mengozzi, *Città italiana*—Guido Mengozzi, *La città italiana nel alto medio evo* (2nd ed., Florence, 1931).

M.G.H.—*Monumenta Germaniae Historica* (*AA.*—*Auctores Antiquissimi; Cap.*—*Capitularia Regum Francorum; SS.*—*Scriptores*).

M.H.P.—*Monumenta Historiae Patriae, Edita Jussu Regis Caroli Alberti* (Turin, 1836–1901, 21 vols.).

M.P.L.—J. P. Migne, *Patrologiae Cursus Completus, Series Latina* (Paris, 1844–1864, 221 vols.).

Muratori, *Antiquitates*—L. A. Muratori, *Antiquitates Italicae Medii Aevi* (Milan, 1723–1751, 6 vols.).

NAV— *Nuovo archivio veneto.*

NRHDFE—*Nouvelle revue historique de droit français et étranger.*

Oderici, *Storie bresciane*—F. Oderici, *Storie bresciane dai primi tempi sino all'età nostra* (Brescia, 1853–1865, 11 vols.).

Pasqui, *Documenti di Arezzo*—Ubaldo Pasqui, ed., *Documenti per la storia della città di Arezzo nel medio evo. Codice diplomatico, 650?–1337* (Florence, 1889–1896, 2 vols.). Documenti di storia italiana della R. Deputazione di storia patria toscana, xi, xiv.

PC— *Periodico della società storica per la provincia e antica diocesi di Como.*

Porro-Lambertenghi, *CDL*—G. Porro-Lambertenghi, *Codex Diplomaticus Langobardiae, M.H.P.,* xiii (1873).

RCI— *Regesta Chartarum Italiae.* Rome, Istituto Storico Italiano, 1907 ff.

Regesto di Mantova—*Regesto Mantovano,* ed. Pietro Torelli (Rome, 1914). [*RCI,* xii.]

Regesto di Modena—*Il regesto della chiesa cattedrale di Modena,* ed. E. P. Vicini (Rome, 1931). [*RCI,* xvi.]

Regesto di Pisa—*Il regesto della chiesa di Pisa,* ed. Natale Caturegli (Rome, 1938). [*RCI,* xxiv.]

Regesto di Ravenna—*Il regesto della chiesa di Ravenna,* ed. V. Federici and G. Buzzi (Rome, 1911, 1931, 2 vols.). [*RCI,* vii, xv.]

RHDFE—*Revue historique de droit français et étranger.*

RHE— *Revue d'histoire ecclésiastique.*

Romani-Feliciangeli—B. Romani and R. Feliciangeli, "Di alcune chiese rurali della diocesi di Camerino," *AMM,* New Series, iv (1907), 241–320.

Römische Quartalschrift—*Römische Quartalschrift für christliche Alterthumskunde und für Kirchengeschichte.*

RSDI— *Rivista di storia del diritto italiano.*

Schiaparelli, *CDL*—Luigi Schiaparelli, ed., *Codice diplomatico longobardo* (Rome, 1929–1933, 2 vols.). [*FSI,* lxii–lxiii.]

SM— Studien und Mitteilungen aus der Geschichte des Benediktinerordens und seiner Zweige.

Statuti di Padova—Statuti del comune di Padova dal secolo xii all'anno 1285, ed. A. Gloria (Padua, 1873).

Stutz, *Benefizialwesen*—Ulrich Stutz, *Geschichte des kirchlichen Benefizialwesens von seinen Anfängen bis auf des Zeit Alexanders III* (one volume published, Berlin, 1895).

Thiel, *Epistolae Pontificum Romanorum*—Andreas Thiel, *Epistolae Pontificum Romanorum Genuinae et quae ad eos scriptae sunt a S. Hilario usque ad Pelagium II.* Vol. i (461–523) (Brunsberg, 1866).

Thomassin, *Ancienne et nouvelle discipline de l'église*—Louis Thomassin, *Ancienne et nouvelle discipline de l'église touchant les bénéfices et les bénéficiers* (Paris, 1779, 3 vols.). References in this book are to the modern reprint, Bar-le-Duc, 1864–1867, 7 vols.

Tiraboschi, *Memorie modenesi*—Girolamo Tiraboschi, *Memorie storiche modenesi col codice diplomatico* (Modena, 1793–1794, 5 vols.).

Torelli, *ACM*—P. Torelli, ed., *L'archivio capitolare della cattedrale di Mantova fino alla caduta dei Bonacolsi* (Verona, 1924). Accademia Virgiliana di Mantova, First Series, Monumenta, iii.

Viard, *Dîme avant Gratien*—Paul Viard, *Histoire de la dîme ecclésiastique, principalement en France, jusqu'au décret de Gratien* (Dijon, 1909).

Vignati—Cesare Vignati, ed., *Codice diplomatico laudense* (Milan, 1879–1885, 2 vols. in 3). [Biblioteca storica lombarda, ii–iv.]

VSW— Vierteljahrschrift für Sozial-und Wirtschaftsgeschichte.

ZSSR— Zeitschrift der Savigny-Stiftung für Rechtsgeschichte. Since 1911 this has been published in three separate sequences, devoted to German law, Roman law, and canon law respectively.

Index

Acqui, bishopric, 137
Adelaide, countess of Turin, 104, 125
Adversus Simoniacos, 112, 113
Advowson, 154, 173
Africa (North), 50, 197
Agno, *pieve*, 160
Agrarian contracts, 69, 70, 71; in the high Middle Ages, 209-226; in southern Italy, 238-240
Agrarian tenures, 69-72, 238; in the later Middle Ages, 244-245; in the Renaissance, 245-246
Aistulf, king of the Lombards, 56
Aix, *see* Aix-la-Chapelle
Aix-la-Chapelle: council of, 63, 84; diet of, 42
Alexander II, Pope, 113-114, 117, 124
Alexander III, Pope, 142, 143, 144, 162, 163, 264
Alexandria, 197
Allodiation, 216
Amann, Emile, 63
Amiterna, 34
Ancient tithes, 143-144, 145, 170, 171, 175, 177
Anselm I, bishop of Lucca, 104
Anselm II, bishop of Lucca, 124
Anselmo da Baggio, 113, *see also* Anselm I
Antapodosis, 88
Anzola, 99
Apostolic movement, 129
Appellate Court of Venetia, 15, 19, 194, 250, 251

Aquileia, 159
Aquinum, 239
Aquitaine, 82
Archipresbyterate, *see* Archpriest
Archpriest, office of, 59-62, 156, 159
Arezzo, 54, 103, 126, 206
Ariald, 108, 110
Aribert, Cardinal, 144
Arliano, 81
Arnulf, chronicler, 99, 117
Ascoli, 236
Asti, 110, 145, 185, 206, 211
Atriana, 72
Avranches, council of, 116

Baptismal churches, *see* Baptisteries
Baptismal font, 50, 51, 81, 158
Baptisteries, 50-55, 155-164; acquisition of tithe by, 43-45, 74; election of priests in, 54, 61; financial prerogatives of, 160-161; organization of clergy in, 51-52, 59-64, 158-159; *see also* Rural parishes
Bartholomew of Brescia, 138
Basel, bishopric, 43, 174
Basilicae, 53
Bassano, 223
Beatrice, countess of Tuscany, 108
Beauvais, bishopric, 145
Benedictine Rule, 63
Berengar I, king of Italy, 65, 83, 244
Bergamo, 137, 179, 186, 187
Bernhard, king of Italy, 42
Bertagnolli, Carlo, 101

Biasca, 201
Biscaro, Girolamo, 101
Bobbio, abbey, 221
Bognetti, G. P., 242
Boniface, cardinal of Sant'Albano, 108
Boniface, marquis of Tuscany, 104, 125
Bonizo, bishop of Sutri, 123
Book of Customs, 201, 214; see also
　Liber Consuetudinum Mediolani
Boretius, Alfred, 37, 42
Bourges, council of, 116
Brescia, 137, 144, 166, 186, 187
Britain, 33
Bugey, 174
Burchard of Worms, 121, 122

Cadalus of Parma, 114
Caesarius of Arles, 27, 28
Calabria, 197, 233, 239
Calixtus II, Pope, 127, 130
Camaldoli, monks of, 126
Camerino, 161
Campitello, 209
Cannobbio, 194
Canon law, 5, 121-125, 166, 186, 189,
　222, 227; *see also* Code of Canon
　Law, *Corpus Juris Canonici*
Canonical life, *see* Canonical move-
　ment, Common life
Canonical movement, 109-112
Canonries, 110
Canosa, 99
Capannule, 94
Capella, 60-61; *see also* Chapels
Capitanei, 98, 100-102, 113
Capitularies, 37, 124, 125, 229; *de
　villis,* 4, 82; Heristal, 37-41, 42;
　Mantua, 42, 43-45, 78; of Lambert,
　74, 81, 90; Olonna, 45, 65, 80;
　Pavia, 67; Pitres, 85
Capodistria, 152
Cappiano, 95
Caput decimae, 202
Caput plebis, 102
Cardinal Damiani, *see* Peter Damiani
Carolingians: encouragement of ca-
　nonical reform by, 62-64; establish-
　ment of compulsory tithe by, 36-
　38, 42-46; policy of, towards parish
　churches, 43-44, 58; secularization
　of church property by, 38-40, 64
Casa Massaricia, 72, 256
Caserta, 6
Caspar, Erich, 231
Castello (Venice), bishopric, 194, 199

Catania, 225
Cathedrals, 52, 53, 84-86, 110, 200,
　201
Cattanei, 98
Celestine III, Pope, 184
Cento, 182, 183, 225, 248
Cerbaria, 91
Cervasca, 175, 176
Cesena, 125
Châlons, council of, 43
Champart (campi pars), 226-227
Chapels, 156, 164; see also *Capella,*
　Oratories, *Tituli*
Charlemagne, 37, 38, 40, 41, 42, 65,
　82
Charles Martel, 38, 64
Charles of Anjou, 237
Charles the Great, *see* Charlemagne
Chiavenna, commune, 166; *see also*
　San Lorenzo
Chiusi, 124
Christianity, 47, 48
Chrodegang, bishop of Metz, 63
Cisalpine Republic, 7
Cistercian monasticism, *see* Cister-
　cians
Cistercians, 126, 129, 264-266
Civitas, civitates, 49
Cluny, order of, 263
Code of Canon Law, 17, 158
Codex Diplomaticus Cavensis, 238
Collatio, see *Collectio*
Collectio: at Genoa, 30, 31, 34; at
　Rome, 29-31
Collegiate organization of clergy, 52,
　61, 158, 159
Colonia parziaria, 210, 211
Comacchio, 3
Common life, 61-64, 84, 109; *see also*
　Canonical movement
Communes, 154, 166, 178-195; hostil-
　ity to tithe, 178, 179, 190, 191; rela-
　tion to parishes, 193-195; statutes
　of, 181, 184, 186-189
Commutation of tithes, 9, 10, 11, 14,
　197, 227
Como, 160, 214
Concordat of 1929, 17
Concordat of Worms, 127
Concordia, 148, 161
Conforti bill, 9
Congrua, 7, 17, 18
Conrad II, Emperor, 102
Constance, Empress, 235
Constantinople, 30, 197, 199

Constitutio de Feudis, 102
Constitutions of Melfi, 236
Consuetudines Feudorum, 100, 101
Contractual tithes, 193-194
Convention of Sutri, 130
Corpus Juris Canonici, 5, 139; *see also* Gratian, Decretals
Corvaresi, lords of, 97
Cosenza, 139, 236
Cottage tithe, 218, 219
Court of Cassation (Rome), 22, 23, 24, 25, 250, 251
Cremona, 125, 144, 200, 221
Creti, 103
Cunibert, king of the Lombards, 34
Customary law, 166, 175, 205
Custos, custodes, 59

Damiani, *see* Peter Damiani
Decima, meaning of: in agrarian contracts, 209-226; in canon law, 5, 6; in medieval documents, 1-4, 244; *see also* Tithes
Decima antiqua, 143
Decima casamenti, 218
Decima communis, 201
Decima et nona, 38, 40; *see also* Double tithe
Decima maris, see Tithe of the sea
Decima nascentium, 218, 219
Decima novalium, 143
Decima porcorum, 4
Decima scalata, 3
Decima solita, 225
Decime dominicali, 7
Decimino testatico, 3
Decretals, 124, 138, 143, 146, 186
Decretals of Gregory IX, 138, 145, 169
Decretists, 5, 138, 140, 141
Decretum, 138, 139, 140, 141, 142, 152
Dego dei Cancellieri, 184
De Luca, Giambattista, 5, 6, 7, 139, 237, 247
Diritto (Il) ecclesiastico italiano, 23
Dominical tithe, 2, 5, 7, 9, 10, 11, 242, 243, 244, 245, 246, 247, 248; in agrarian contracts, 208, 209, 211; in southern Italy, 237-240
Dominicality, presumptions of, 16, 17, 21, 22
Donizo, 103
Doren, Alfred, 245
Double tithe, 38, 39, 41; see also *Decima et nona*

Eastern Empire, 30
Eboli, 236
Ecclesiae cardinales, 53
Ecclesiae decumanae, 53
Ecclesiae propriae, 56, 71; *see also* Proprietary churches
Ecclesiae sedales, 53
Ecclesiastical tithe: abolition of, 7, 8-11, 227; among the Lombards, 33-36; assigned to parish churches, 43-44, 142, 145; base of, 204-205; becomes compulsory, 36-38, 41, 44-45; collection of, 196-201, 203, 204; distribution of, in twelfth century, 132-153; episcopal control over, 135; episcopal surveys of, 132-135; in agrarian contracts, 210-217, 220-226; in Britain, 32, 33; in France, 7, 120, 143, 144, 193, 226, 227; in Gaul, 28; in Gregorian program, 115, 117, 118-125; in southern Italy, 230-237; leasing of, 91-95; redemption of, 167, 168; remoter origins of, 27-33; restitutions of, 125, 126; *see also* Episcopal tithes, Infeudated tithes, Lay tithe, Parochial tithes, Personal tithes, Predial tithes, *Quartese,* Sacramental tithe, Tithe of regalia, and *Decima* and its variants
Edict of Rotari, 4
Eigenkirche, Eigenkirchen, 55-57, 79, 118; *see also* Proprietary churches
Eigenkirchentum, 85
Einhard, 42
Emilia, 211, 228, 229; *see also* Bologna, Ferrara, Imola, Modena, Parma, Piacenza, Ravenna, Reggio
Enfiteusi (emphyteusis), 71, 106, 246
Enrico da Fratta, bishop of Bologna, 182
Episcopal tithes, 6, 7, 238
Este, 266
Eugippius, 31
Euphrasius, bishop of Parenzo, 34
Expropriation, laws of, 216, 217

Faccioli, 224
Fagiuoli bill, 9-11
Faido, 158
Falco, Mario, 20, 23, 248
Farfa, abbey, 34
Farming of tithes, 172-175
Ferraboschi, Mario, 23
Ferrara, 8, 14, 15, 131, 137, 151, 153

Feudalism, 87, 88, 89, 96, 97, 98, 100-102
Fidenza, 221
Fief of the tithe, 100
Flesso, 95
Fliche, Augustin, 109
Florence, 111, 124
Florentine Republic, 3
Fondo per il Culto, 10, 13, 14, 18
Forchielli, Giuseppe, 52, 158
Fournier, Paul, 230
Fourth Lateran Council, 222, 226, 264; *see also* Lateran councils
France, 7, 107, 120, 143, 144, 193, 222, 226, 227
Frankish conquest, 228
Franks, 4; *see also* Carolingians
Frederick I, Emperor, 185
Frederick II, Emperor, 180, 182, 185, 236-237
Friuli, council of, 36; province of, 14, 159
Fructus decimae, 172, 187

Gabotto, Ferdinando, 213
Gaudenzi, Augusto, 225, 242, 243, 248
Gaul, 33, 50, 60, 62
Gelasius I, Pope, 51, 56, 75, 76
Genoa, 30, 31, 131, 134, 135, 156, 167, 179, 196-198, 200, 209, 260-262
Gerard, bishop of Florence, 111, 124; *see also* Nicholas II
Gerard, bishop of Parma, 182
Germanic law, 4, 54, 57, 76, 121, 122, 244
Germany, 11, 33, 48, 77, 107, 144, 234
Gerona, synod of, 118
Girgenti (Agrigento), 13, 14, 231, 232, 235
Gloria, Andrea, 247, 248
Godfrey of Lorraine, 107
Goffredo di Montanaro, bishop of Turin, 172-175
Gratian, 5, 138-141, 152, 156, 247
Grazia, bishop of Parma, 181
Gregorian Reform, 107-128, 129, 132, 137, 139
Gregory I, the Great, Pope, 30, 32, 51, 76
Gregory II, Pope, 76
Gregory VII, Pope, 108, 111, 116, 121
Gregory IX, Pope, 139, 181, 182, 183
Grimizzo, bishop of Lucca, 103
Gubbio, 146, 220, 223
Gurgite, 91

Hatto, bishop of Basel, 43
Henry III, Emperor, 107
Henry IV, Emperor, 107, 116
Henry V, Emperor, 130
Heredity of fiefs, 102
Herlembald, 114
Hildebrand, 108, 111; *see also* Gregory VII
Hildebrand, bishop of Pistoia, 132-134
Honorantiae Civitatis Papie, 3
Honorius III, Pope, 180
House of Canossa, 125
House of Savoy, 8
Huguccio of Pisa, 138, 141, 142, 162
Humbert of Moyenmoutier, cardinal of Silva Candida, 105, 107, 108, 112, 113, 121

Imola, 220
Impropriation, 155, 265
Incorporation, 155
Indominicatum, 38, 83
Infeudated tithes, 166, 173, 176, 223, 227; *see also* Lay tithe
Innocent II, Pope, 130
Innocent III, Pope, 138, 139, 141, 142, 145, 146, 153, 162, 169-171, 175, 199, 226
Investiture contest, 178
Irish collections, 33, 230
Irenaeus, 26
Istria, 151
Ivrea, 137

Jemolo, Arturo Carlo, 20, 21, 22, 24, 25, 248
Jewish tithe, 26
Jew-monopoly, 235
Johannes Teutonicus, 138
John II, bishop of Lucca, 110
Jurisdictio, 79
Justinian, code of, 152
Jus adulterii, 159
Jus commune, 139, 150
Jus dandi olivas, 202
Jus decimae, 172

Kandler, Pietro, 34

La Cava, abbey, 236
Lambert, Emperor, 73, 74
Landulf, leader of Pataria, 108
Landulf of Carcano, archbishop of Milan, 99
Landulf the Elder, chronicler, 99, 100

Lateran Accords, 17
Lateran councils: (1059), 107-109, 115; (1078), 117; (1080), 117; (1123), 126, 130, 265; (1139), 130, 198; (1179), 143; (1215), 162, 169, 171, 222, 226, 264
Lateran synods, *see* Lateran councils
Latin Empire of Constantinople, 199
Latium, 49
Lavagna, 197
Law of 1887, 10, 11, 14, 15-16, 17, 18, 24
Lay investiture, 113, 127
Lay tithe, 11, 165, 166, 167, 168; campaign against, 130, 131; condemned by Church, 117, 143; origin of, 91-102; policy of Innocent III towards, 169-171; transformation of, in thirteenth century, 172-177
Leicht, P. S., 245
Lemonta, 82
Leo I, the Great, Pope, 29
Leo IV, Pope, 78, 141, 152
Leo IX, Pope, 107, 108, 109
Lewis I, the Pious, Emperor, 63, 80, 82
Lewis II, Emperor, 80
Liber Consuetudinum Mediolani, 204, 205, 214; see also *Book of Customs*
Liber de Vita Christiana, 123
Liber Papiensis, 40
Libro delle investiture, 172-176, 212
Libri Feudorum, 101; see also *Consuetudines Feudorum*
Lillebonne, council of, 116
Liutprand, bishop of Cremona, 88
Liutprand, king of the Lombards, 3, 69
Livellario (libellario) nomine, 69, 71, 91, 106; see also *Livello*
Livello, 69-71, 92, 99
Lizier, Augusto, 238
Lodi, 137, 146, 167, 187, 215
Lombard conquest, 228
Lombard law, 4, 96, 211, 228, 229
Lombardo-Tuscan territory, 98, 99, 228
Lombardo-Venetian theory, 15, 20
Lombards, 4, 30, 33, 35, 37, 57
Lombardy, 60, 83, 90, 99, 114, 115, 144, 173, 175, 183; *see also* Bergamo, Brescia, Como, Cremona, Lodi, Mantua, Milan
Longobardia, 229

Lonigo, 159
Lothair I, Emperor, 45, 65, 80
Lucca, 34, 35, 54, 56, 66, 68-73, 74, 81, 82, 90, 92, 93, 99, 104, 110, 113, 114, 120, 124, 135, 154, 255-259
Lupi, Mario, 53

Macerata, 120
Mâcon, council of, 28
Malandriano, 119
Mantua, 125, 149, 188-189, 209-210, 215-219, 220, 243
Marches, the, 8
Martinengo family, 166
Matilda of Tuscany, 103
Mazzara, 232
Mellegrano, 166
Mengozzi, Guido, 31, 52
Mensa, 84, 173
Messina, 235
Métayage, 69, 221, 245, 246
Mezzadria, 211
Milan, 59, 99, 105, 108, 110, 113, 115, 116, 145, 154, 201, 202-204, 210, 219; customs of, 166, 202, 204-205, 214; synod of, 66, 67
Milanese, 34, 204, 205; *see also* Milan
Militia of St. Ambrose, 88
Milites, 73, 88-90, 96, 178
Minella, Giuseppe, 15
Ministry of Agriculture, 11
Ministry of Finance, 18
Ministry of Justice, 10, 11
Minores tituli, 59
Modena, 61
Monasteries, 126-127, 263-266
Moncalieri, 206
Monopolies, 236-237
Monselice, 147
Monte Velate, 168
Montechiari, 144
Montemagno clan, 97
Monza, 34, 159, 200
Mulazzano, 167
Muratori, L. M., 131

Naples, Kingdom of, 6, 7, 11, 237
Nervi, 136
Nicholas II, Pope, 108, 109, 113
Norman Kingdom, 234, 235
Normandy, 116, 227, 231, 233, 234
Normans, 120, 229, 230
Norway, 54
Noval tithes, 143, 145, 170, 175, 210, 265

Novalia, 143, 264
Novara, 99, 137, 203

Odofredo of Bologna, 190
Olubra, 194
Oratories, 51, 55
Orleans, councils of, 77
Otranto, 236
Otto I, Emperor, 87
Otto III, Emperor, 99
Oulx, priory, 125

Padua, 7, 20, 119, 120, 147, 148, 152, 187-188, 200, 203, 204, 220
Pagus, 49, 51
Palermo, 13, 232, 235
Palmiero da Campagnola, 182, 183
Parenzo, 34, 168, 169
Paris, council of, 79
Parishes: *see* Baptisteries, Chapels, Parochial system in Italy, Rural parishes, Urban parishes
Parma, 119, 149, 180, 181, 182, 185, 190, 216, 217, 219, 221
Parochia, 50, 156
Parochial system in Italy, 47-74, 154-164
Parochial tithes, 7, 124, 125, 131, 132, 133, 134, 201, 260-262
Pars, 246; see also *Champart*
Parziaria, 246; see also *Colonia parziaria*
Paschal II, Pope, 130
Pastinato, 246
Pataria, 108, 113, 114
Paterno, 239
Patronage, 154
Pavia, 3; council of (1022), 108; synod of (ca. 850), 45, 58-61, 67, 80-81; synod of (876), 46, 63
Peace of Constance, 180
Penitential of Theodore, 32
Pepin, king of Italy, 41, 42, 58, 63
Pepin the Short, king of the Franks, 37, 38
Pernumia, 119, 200
Persiceto, 182
Personal tithes, 5, 6, 140, 209
Pertile, Antonio, 12, 34, 247
Pertualdo, 34
Peter Damiani, 105, 106, 108, 111
Peter II, bishop of Lucca, 73, 91
Peter the Venerable, abbot of Cluny, 126, 263
Philagrius, 30, 32

Piacenza, 85, 120, 158, 194, 200, 221
Piedmont, 60, 83, 173, 175, 214, 224, 225; *see also* Acqui, Asti, Novara, Saluzzo, Tortona, Turin, Vercelli
Pietro dei Boattieri, 191
Pieve, castle of, 182, 183
Pieve, 101, 155; see also *Plebs*
Pirano, 151-153, 203
Pirro, Roccho, 13, 230, 233
Pisa, 98, 99
Pistoia, 132, 133, 135
Placita christianitatis, 159
Plebania, 159
Plebanus, 60, 159, 160, 161
Plebegium, 197
Plebeium, 156
Plebs, plebes, 50, 101, 155, 156
Plebs urbana, 52
"Polycarpus," 157
Pomerius of Arles, 27
Popolo, 178, 182, 183, 184
Pordenone, 22
Port' Albera, 120
Portio congrua, 116, 162
Pöschl, Arnold, 76, 77
Predial tithes, 5, 6, 140
Priest's fief, 116
Private churches, 57, 67, 252-254; *see also* Proprietary churches, Proprietary system
"Prohibemus," 143, 165
Proprietary churches, 55-57, 79-81, 127, 252-254
Proprietary system, 79-81, 85, 86, 127, 128, 154, 155; attitude of Gregorian reformers towards, 112-118, 127
Provence, 27, 197

Quadripartition, rule of, 75-76, 86, 120, 122, 124, 146
Quaraitiana, 72
Quarteria, quarterium, 180, 260, 261
Quartese, 4, 21, 24, 119, 132, 135, 138, 152, 153, 158, 165, 180, 181, 188, 193, 195, 224, 241, 247, 248; in Venetia, 147-149; origin of, 119-125; survival of, 149-151
Quartesi del Veneto, 15
Quartesium, quartisium, 119, 147, 148
Quarto, 185, 211

Rapallo, 196
Rathier, bishop of Verona, 88, 105
Rationes Decimarum Italiae, 2
Ratold, bishop of Verona, 86

Ravenna, 211, 219
Reggio (Emilia), 104, 180, 183-185, 191
Register of Gregory VII, 117
Regnum italicum, 229
Reims, synod of, 127, 130
Revello, 137, 212, 266
Richelda, 125
Rifreddo, nunnery of, 137, 212, 266
Ripafratta, lords of, 97
Roger I, count of Sicily, 4, 13, 75, 76, 77, 230, 232, 233
Roger II, king of Sicily, 231, 233
Roland, Cardinal, 142, 199; *see also* Alexander III
Rolandinghi clan, 94
Romania, 197
Roman law, 79, 140, 186, 209, 211, 228
Roman synod (826), 58, 63, 66, 79, 80
Rome, city of, 8, 29, 30, 31
Rome, province of, 8
Rota, Sacred Roman, 5, 20, 24, 151
Rouen, council of, 116
Ruffini, Francesco, 15, 20, 24, 194, 248
Rule of St. Augustine, 212
Rural communes, 157, 194
Rural parishes: abuses in, denounced by reformers, 105-107; administration of property by, 54-55, 78; assignment of tithes to, 43-44; condition of, on eve of Gregorian Reform, 103-105; economic aspects of, 68-74; feudalization of, 90-95; growth of abuses in, 64-68; internal organization of, in high Middle Ages, 158-160; relation to tithes in high Middle Ages, 145, 146, 161-163; two kinds of parish, from twelfth century, 156-158; *see also* Baptisteries, Chapels, Parochial System in Italy, *Quartese*

Sacramental tithe, 2, 5, 9, 11
St. Ambrose, 27, 59
St. Augustine, 27, 214
St. Bernard of Clairvaux, 263
St. Boniface, 36, 76
St. Cyprian, 27
St. Jerome, 27
St. Leo, 29, 30; *see also* Leo I
St. Romuald, 110
St. Severinus, 31
Saladin tithe, 2

Salerno, 234, 236, 240
Salian dynasty, 107
Saluzzo, 175, 206, 212, 213
Salvioli, Giuseppe, 12, 13, 231
San Benedetto of Polirone, 216, 219
San Donato, 201
San Frediano, 34
San Giorgio in Braida, 158, 224
San Giorgio of Valpolicella, 59
San Giovanni in Revello, 158, 159
San Giovanni of Monza, 55, 159
San Lorenzo of Chiavenna, 158, 159
San Macario, 81
San Michele Archangelo, 34
San Pantaleone, 95
San Pietro in Somaldi, 56
San Vitale, 35
Sant' Albano, 206
Santa Maria a Monte, 110
Santa Menna, commune, 6
Sardinia, 8, 197
Sardinian clergy, 18
Scaduto, Francesco, 225, 248
Schreiber, Georg, 76
Second Lateran Council, 134; *see also* Lateran councils
Secundi milites, 115
Seigniorial regime, 57, 64, 74
Serfdom, 192, 221
Sesto, 67
Sicilia Sacra, 230
Sicily, 13, 228, 229, 230-233, 234, 235, 239, 243
Siena, 54
Simony, 44, 104, 106, 112, 128
Siro, archbishop of Genoa, 131, 134, 135, 198, 260
Sori, 135, 197
Spiritual tithe, 2, 5, 189, 220; *see also* Ecclesiastical tithe
Spoleto, 34, 146
Staffarda, 213, 216
Stephen of Tournai, 156
Strata, 166
Stutz, Ulrich, 118, 252, 253
Sugrominio, 94
Syracuse, 232

Tellenbach, Gerd, 127
Temporal tithes, 5, 237; *see also* Dominical tithe
Tercesium, 147
Terra decimalis, 217
Terrage, 227

Terraticum, 210, 211, 220, 223, 227, 238, 239, 240
Theodicius, duke of Spoleto, 34
Theodore of Tarsus, 32
Third Lateran Council, 143; *see also* Lateran councils
Three Books Against the Simoniacs, 109; see also *Adversus Simoniacos*
Tithe, *see* Ecclesiastical tithe
Tithe of the dead, 194, 199, 209
Tithe of the regalia, 234-237
Tithe of the sea, 197-198, 209
Tithes, *see* Ancient tithes, *Decima*, Dominical tithe, Ecclesiastical tithe, Episcopal tithes, Lay tithe, Noval tithes, Personal tithes, Predial tithes, *Quartese*, Sacramental tithe, Spiritual tithe, Temporal tithes
Tituli, 51, 53
Todeschini, G., 150, 151, 248
Toletan system, 125
Tolls, 3, 4, 244
Torelli, Pietro, 215
Tortona, 185, 203, 212
Toulouse, council of, 116
Tours: council of (813), 43; synod of (567), 28; synod of (1060), 116
Trasimundo, duke of Spoleto, 34
Trebenciolo, 148, 224
Treviso, 149, 161
Trieste, 22
Trent, council of, 161, 163
Tribur, council of, 144
Tripartition, 76, 79, 231, 232, 233, 234
Troina, 232
Tunis, 197
Turin, 125, 137, 154, 172-176, 185, 199, 200, 201, 212, 262
Tuscia, 229
Tuscany, 7, 34, 60, 83, 229, 246; *see also* Arezzo, Florence, Lucca, Pisa, Pistoia

Uberto Bobio, 181
Ulric-Manfred, count of Turin, 104, 125

Umbria, 223; *see also* Gubbio, Spoleto
Urban II, Pope, 265
Urban parishes, 53, 148, 200

Vaccoli, lords of, 97
Vaison, council of, 52, 61
Val del Po, 137
Val di Castro, 110
Valvassini, 100
Valvassores maiores, 102
Valvassors, 100, 115
Varia, 203
Venetia, region of, 8, 9, 11, 147, 229, 250, 251; jurisprudence of, in regard to tithes, 15, 16-17, 19-25, 250, 251; *quartese* in, 4, 19, 147, 151; *see also* Padua, Treviso, Venice, Verona, Vicenza
Venetian Republic, 3, 4, 6, 194
Veneto, 15; *see* Venetia
Venice, 2, 3, 20, 22, 198-199, 209
Vercelli, 137, 169, 175
Verdeto, 158
Verona, 86, 148, 158, 167, 219, 224, 266
Viard, Paul, 2, 143, 226, 227
Vicarage system, 162, 201
Vicenza, 150, 151, 186, 188, 219, 220, 223, 248
Vici, 49
Vicini, 194
Vigesimo, 94
Vignati, Cesare, 215
Vignolio, 176
Vigonzone, 201, 203
Villa, Tommaso, 9
Villeinage, 221
Vimercate, 201, 202
Visigothic law, 4
Voghera, 213
Volta, 201

William II, king of Sicily, 236

Zacharias, Pope, 36
Zanardelli, Giuseppe, 9, 10